JUNKPOLITICS

THE TRASHING OF THE
AMERICAN MIND

Books by Benjamin DeMott
The Body's Cage
Hells & Benefits
You Don't Say
A Married Man
Supergrow
Surviving The Seventies
The Imperial Middle
The Trouble with Friendship
Killer Woman Blues
Junk Politics

Books edited by Benjamin DeMott
Scholarship for Society
America in Literature
Close Imagining
Created Equal

JUNKPOLITICS

THE TRASHING OF THE
AMERICAN MIND

Reports and Essays
by
Benjamin DeMott

NATION BOOKS
NEW YORK

JUNK POLITICS:
THE TRASHING OF THE AMERICAN MIND

Copyright © 2003 by Benjamin DeMott

Published by
Nation Books
An Imprint of Avalon Publishing Group Inc.
245 West 17th Street
New York, NY 10011

Nation Books is a co-publishing venture of the Nation Institute and Avalon Publishing Group Incorporated.

Library of Congress Cataloging-in-Publication Data is available.

ISBN: 1-56025-565-X

Printed in the United States of America
Interior design by Paul Paddock
Distributed by Publishers Group West

The essays in this book appeared originally, in some cases in different form, in the *Atlantic Monthly, Harper's, First of the Month, The Nation,* the *New York Times Book Review,* the *New York Review of Books,* and the *Washington Post.*

To the memory of my dear friend
Eric McKitrick

171 3. Tomorrow: The Only Winning Ticket

The least well-understood influence on the rise of no-politics politics is the contemporary war on the past—the insistence that whatever mattered yesterday (politics, for instance) shouldn't detain us now.

237 PART THREE
Beyond the Politics of "Heart"

The first step toward solving the problem of apoliticality is recognizing it as a problem--facing up to its social and psychosocial costs, seeing it as the unraveling of democracy rather than as a triumph of manners. The next steps involve working toward two ends: bringing to life the human insides of "social deficits," and putting beyond public doubt the difference between sympathy for the oppressed and political action to end oppression.

239 1. The Weight of Self-Scorn

247 2. Sympathetic Horror v. Political Action

Preface

The goal of this book is to strengthen resistance to the forces which, for well-masked partisan purposes, are promoting apoliticality as a national ideal—forces pressing for an "end to fractiousness," denouncing political passion, working to erase consciousness of difference from the public mind. My subjects range from the themes that won a place in George W. Bush's Inaugural Address (civility, compassion and character) to the war on terror, from the celebrity and consumer cultures to the assault on the past (and gross ballooning of ego) that commenced with the half-century old sexual revolution. My belief is that broader understanding of the background and consequences of this politics—no-politics politics, *junk politics*—will hasten its demise.

What exactly is junk politics? It's a politics that personalizes and moralizes issues and interests instead of clarifying them. It's a politics that maximizes threats from abroad while miniaturizing large, complex problems at home. It's a politics that, guided by guesses about its own profits and losses, abruptly reverses public stances without explanation, often spectacularly bloating problems previously miniaturized (e. g.: Iraq will be over in days or weeks; Iraq is a project for generations). It's a politics that takes changelessness as its fundamental cause—changelessness meaning zero interruption in the processes and practices that, decade after decade, strengthen existing, interlocking American systems of socioeconomic advantage. And it's a politics marked not only by impatience (feigned or otherwise) with articulated conflict and by frequent panegyrics on the American citizen's optimistic spirit and exemplary character, but by mawkish fondness for feel-your-pain gestures and idioms.

In theory the shortcomings of feel-your-pain chatter—touchy-feely personal testimony—are well known; the usual charge is that it's gimmick-ridden and money-driven. But the more significant defect is its implicit claim that leadership's main concern should be with setting an upbeat tone and demonstrating sensitive response to hardship, rather than with identifying injustice, spelling out practical correctives, arguing for the correctives in public forums, working for their ultimate enactment.

Let me tell you my story, said speaker after speaker at the quadrennial party conventions in the year 2000 and on the campaign trail thereafter, recounting learning experiences or tales of privation endured and overcome. For years my church had few members, could not get a loan . . . I was a foreigner, the child of immigrants, had no standing—yet here I am on this platform . . . I was a welfare mother but now I take home $200,000 a year . . . As a child I played on a toxic waste dump but now. . . .

Hadassah Lieberman spoke affectingly about her parents tortured in concentration camps. The departing President mentioned his humiliation but reported he was now "at peace." President-to-be Bush remembered his visit to a juvenile jail in Texas during which he talked with "angry, wary" young inmates who had committed grown-up crimes. (When he looked in their eyes, Bush told audiences, "I realized some of them were still little boys.")

The new President also remembered an activist minister in Minneapolis who labored tirelessly for the homeless:

> I think of Mary Jo Copeland, whose ministry called "Sharing and Caring Hands" serves 1,000 meals a week in Minneapolis, Minnesota. Each day, Mary washes the feet of the homeless, then sends them off with new socks and shoes. "Look after your feet," she tells them, "They must carry you a long way in this world, and then all the way to God."

In speech after speech in the 2000-01 campaign, by candidate after candidate, experiential reminiscence pushed one-on-one goodness, positive thinking, prayer and character forward into the spotlight. And the 2003-04 cycle brings more of the same. The media as always abets the personalizing (George Stephanopolous inquiring as to whether Joe Lieberman is "just too nice" to be president). But Kerry, Edwards, Gebhardt —and the Liebermans—all deal extensively in personal history, personal pain. Hundreds of audiences learned that Gebhardt's mother ("she gave me everything I have") died in the summer of 2003. They also learned that Gebhardt's father suffered a back injury ending his days as a milk truck driver, that Gebhardt's 26-year-old daughter is an underpaid schoolteacher, that his 30-year-old-daughter lately endured coming-out-gay anxiety, that his son, at age two, was diagnosed with terminal cancer ("a tumor the size of a volleyball"), and that Gebhardt and his wife "went home that night [of the diagnosis], knelt down by the bed and prayed that we could find an answer to our horrible problem." Happily a doctor called in the morning and advised them about a new experimental therapy and today the toddler, named Matt, is a 32-year-old married resident of Atlanta, Georgia. ("I get warm all over when I see this young man," Gebhardt reports. "He's a gift from God.")

The use of personal testimony in political oratory shapes an experience of intimacy, sincere and authentic; the feelings and thoughts aren't easily dismissed as abstract, predictable, partisan mouthings. *Let me tell you about my sister's fatal illness. Let me share with you a jailed boy's haunting question. Let me reveal to you in passing that I am a man of prayer* . . . .Quiet accents of candor bring a sense of closeness between speaker and audience, Republican, Democrat, whatever. The impression strengthens that character—character alone, not positions on issues, not argued-for priorities, not expressive, persuasive talents—character must be the electorate's pivotal concern. At the 2003 NAACP convention in Miami, Julian Bond excoriated no-show would-be presidential candidates, declaring that it was "as much by their presence as by their words" that the missing would be judged. Supporting that view, Kweisi Mfume, the NAACP president, gestured at a crippled woman in a wheelchair, claiming that the candidates' failure to appear "was an affront to people like her who came to the convention to see the presidential candidates." (Lieberman and Kucinich raced to Florida to apologize for their absence, the former saying "I was wrong, I regret it and I apologize for it," and the latter announcing: "I'm very sorry I wasn't able to be here. Amazing grace, how sweet it is, once was lost, now I'm found.")

Leaders need prove only that they can feel . . . a child's or parent's or stranger's pain. Problems aren't as difficult as Phi Bete wonks claim; they have one simple cause: human selfishness, negativism, failure to show. By shedding a moral defect and following the example of a caring leader patient enough to hear out a young convict—by attending to the example of a concerned activist willing to wash the feet of the homeless—by being the buoyantly admirable, minority-sensitive, elder-

and-cripple-cherishing people that we necessarily are—Americans can make problems disappear.

But can Americans thereby reach basic terms of injustice—fundamental discontinuities between affirmed democratic values and standards and officially approved rules, practices, laws?

The revered English historian R. H. Tawney warned almost a century ago against addresses to "humanitarians whose feelings are more easily stirred by hardship than their consciences are by injustice." He contended that the voices rousing American colonists against the Crown and American abolitionists against slavery had staying power less because they talked hardship than because they clarified rights and wrongs. This is even truer of the noble voices of the civil rights struggle. Great causes—they still exist—nourish themselves on firm, sharp awareness of the substance of injustice. Blunting that awareness is a central project of junk politics.

And touchy-feely personal reminiscence is by no means the only or chief resource available to projectors. Anatomizing junk politics calls for attention to the striking multiplication, in recent days, of methods of bypassing great causes (and doing dirt on the political arena)—styles, gestures, strategies that trivialize basic issues, diminish the visibility of pertinent social and moral choices, and instill suspicion that, in the phrase *political differences*, the word political signifies either *faked* or *pointless*. Pundits and columnists deprecate the political calling by obsessively reminding readers, in overimpressed tones, that this or that officeholder—Senate Majority Leader Frist or Governor Howard Dean—isn't "just" a career politician but a *professional*. (David Yepsen, *Des Moines Register* columnist on Dean: "He is presidential . . . Unlike the Gephardts and the Kerrys of the race, Dean's not a career politician. He's a doctor who got into politics.") Highly political persons in mid-political career voice scorn for politics. Hillary Clinton refuses to answer reporters' intelligently prepared questions about the "political content" of her *Living History* (2003).

Large corporate campaign donors dismiss, as jokes, differences between themselves and their employees regarding the positions of candidates whom the donors support. (The countercultural millionaire who invented Urban Outfitters, Inc., a major contributor to Senator Rick Santorum's gaybaiting campaigns, first denies then acknowledges the contributions, later tells the columnist Joe Conason—who broke the story—that his workers hold "all kinds of political views," and finally adds that he and his employees "joke about our political differences.") Officeholders of power and authority undermine—by unexplained reversals of position—belief in the coherence and depth of the thinking on which their fateful opinions rest. The President vigorously denounces on television in January 2003 the University of Michigan's affirmative action admissions policies; a few months later the White House submits a brief to the Supreme Court against those policies; in July 2003 the Supreme Court upholds the policies; at once the President praises the court, hails its recognition of "the value of diversity on our nation's campuses," and declares that, "like the court," he "look[s] forward to the day when America will be a truly color-blind society."

No mention, as the *New York Times*'s Linda Greenhouse observes, "of the fact that the administration had asked the court to invalidate both Michigan programs as thinly disguised quota systems that violated the holding of the Bakke decision." No allusion, as the advocacy group People for the American Way notes, to the brief submitted not long before the decision came down that mockingly "derided the law school's goal of having a critical mass of underrepresented students in each class."

Issue-vaporizing in this mode is regularly accompanied by pseudo-heroic posturing by incumbents or aspirants, whether the subject is state budget crises or chicken-hearted competitors in election races or terrorists. Echoes of gospel hymns ("Stand up, Stand up, for Jesus!") abound. "Somebody has to stand up [against Gray Davis's budget] and say enough is enough!"—California State Senate Republican leader James Brulte. "Let us stand up [against the Dixie Chicks and other foreign threats] and let us be the human shields of prayer . . . for the President!"—Alabama's State Auditor, Beth Chapman, at the "Stand Up for America" rally that put her on the Deep South political map. "The only hope Democrats have . . . is to behave like Democrats and stand up [against wishy-washy candidates for the nomination]!"—Vermont's Howard Dean.

A major effect of junk politics—its ceaseless flood of patriotic, religious, macho and therapeutic fustian—is to pull position after position loose from reasoned foundations. Oil drilling in the Alaska Wildlife Refuge is linked with nursing and doctoring. (Interior Secretary Gale Norton says her Department aims to "heal our landscapes and restore health to our national forests.") The Glorious Fourth somehow inserts itself into "debate" on increases in low-income child tax credit. "You've got 12 million children this year that will be celebrating the Fourth of July," says Senator Blanche Lincoln, Democrat of Arkansas, "that will be left out of the advantages of additional tax relief that could go for getting them ready for school, or other things their parents need. It's sad that the president didn't think this was important enough to do something about." Pundits of various stripes seize on misconduct by a young black reporter for the *New York Times* to redefine affirmative action complexities as a simple—and banal—family conflict between a spoiled child and a softheaded (i. e., liberal), executive editor/parent.

As the ground noise and clutter swells and thickens, miniaturists shuttle gleefully from medium to medium—reductive apothegems, arresting redefinitions, poll questions, photo-ops, most unforgettable character sketches, choose your genre. Large-size long-range public causes shrink to impulsive individual New Year's resolutions (vice-president Dick Cheney: Energy conservation is simply "a sign of personal virtue"). The often monumental, often selfless labor that produces enactable legislation is likened to psychotic sexual assault (Grover Norquist, head of Americans for Tax Reform: "Bipartisanship is another name for date rape"). Pollster miniaturists drop issues in favor of "mood and attitude" love-me/love-me-not non-questions (Does President Bush care about problems of people like yourself? A lot? Not much? How much?). Damage control miniaturists cut an entire section from an EPA report detailing scientists' estimates of harm caused by rising global temperatures. Promotion for tax cuts is silent on huge gifts to the rich, windy and teary about checks—minuscule checks—for "folks." Signing the tax bill in the East Room the President introduces not millionaires pleased by their booty—starting at $10,000-plus a month—but an Air Force sergeant's wife, Jenny Tyson of Omaha, mother of two. (The Tysons, says Bush, modestly proud, "will keep an extra $1,300 a year of their own money.")

From the hospitable Miniaturizing Party big tent, nobody is excluded. Republicans invented the most notable figure of speech in miniaturist jargon—"points of light." Republicans were also responsible for inventing the boldest attempt yet made—the Faith-Based Initiative—to persuade people that their neighborhood church or mosque can solve national crime, poverty and education problems. But John F. Kennedy was miniaturizing when he proposed to cure Africa with a Peace Corps, and so was estimable Jimmy Carter when he lent his weight to the volunteer Habitat for Humanity project (solving the national housing problem one sawhorse at a time)—and the first head of the White House's Faith Based Initiative Office was himself a Democrat.

And neither party dares to forswear personalizing rubbish during controversey. Republicans battling to pass a bill capping malpractice jury awards reduce the complicated issues to a choice of whether to reward or refuse to reward cynical opportunists. (Mort Zuckerman repeats in *U.S. News and World Report* a long-ago discredited myth about a "woman [who] throws a soft drink at her boyfriend at a restaurant, then slips on the floor she wet and breaks her tailbone. She sues. Bingo—a jury says the restaurant owes her $100,000.") Democrats counter with heartbreak—the poignant facts about 17-year-old Jesica Santillan, killed by doctors who gave her a heart and lung of the wrong blood type.

It follows that the difficult questions about junk politics don't center on relative party guilt. They concern how to draw fair lines between melodramatic arias and responsible effort at animating real life consequences, for the majority, of political choices and decisions. Yet more urgently, the questions that matter concern the why and how of the current junk political insurgency—the unexamined factors operating in its background—and about the best means of confronting it. All who know 19th century campaign biographies—Nathaniel Hawthorne's *Franklin Pierce* for one—know that the American hogwash tradition didn't begin yesterday. But they also know that today's idioms are vastly different from yesterday's, and so too are the sources, the channels of expression, the impact. Effective resistance depends, in part, on clarity about those differences.

Achieving clarity is impossible without weighing broad cultural influences—signals passed within separate generations, by and within millions of households, about the place of political affairs in human life, and about right relations between self and society. But more directly palpable influences also demand reckoning, none in our day as consequential as the needs and longings arising from the Twin Towers and Pentagon disasters. In their immediate aftermath, sustainedly coherent policy debate could hardly have been expected. The national need was for reassurance—proof of solidarity and goodness, proof that the suicide bombers and their backers were mad to believe anything in this country's nature deserved such monstrous loathing.

Who will forget that time! At first the need for reassurance was met creditably, with respect for the gap separating the fearful suffering of the victims and the bereaved from the anxieties of the unwounded. Reassurance came in the form of guarded hope that the extraordinary sacrifices of rescue workers and the moving demonstrations by public leaders of unfaked grief at the ghastly slaughter of innocent thousands could be read—reasonably—as evidence of the moral worth lying at the American core.

A worn, unflinching, hitherto coldeyed mayor traveled ceaselessly through the boroughs to the funerals of the humble, a model of responsive leadership that was valued in towns and cities across the nation. The President spent hours in Manhattan with the bereaved, hugging and praising firemen, police, rescue workers ("Can you hear me? I can hear you!"), shedding tears that drew us close, ruler and ruled. Newspaper editorialists and columnists found themselves catching intimations of a new considerateness—even tenderness—in public manners on the streets, in the grateful embrace of sectors of the "service population" formerly taken for granted or harshly viewed. The humanity of the unsung—bottom level secretaries, sales people, custodians—

the heroism of the uncelebrated aboard American 93 who saved the U.S. Capitol—was honored without extravagance. Brief, gripping lives of the dead ran daily in the *New York Times*, offering readers opportunities to confirm their capacity to care about the suffering of the survivors and to imagine the terrible last moments of those torn and mangled in the collapse. Grown men and women of many ranks and stations were stirred by the discovered strength of their sympathy—and the discovery helped in itself to shore up belief both in personal decency and in the existence ("we are all in this together") of a country-wide community of the good.

Much in that early post-9/11 period possessed dignity: the forthright advocacy, in pulpits and elsewhere, of a reassessment of values, the many restrained but deeply felt expressions of belief in the feasibility of recovering the national best self. Nor is it the case that, as terror and grief subsided, the memory of the promise of solidarity and mutuality quickly withered. To the contrary, the memory still breathes—actually figures, by a paradox, in the resurgent politics of no-politics.

But realizing the promise turned out, to nobody's huge surprise, to be a project easily coarsened. Outrage and despair that initially stimulated thought and awakened consciousness of forgotten meanings of fraternity came quickly to be treated as clinical conditions. The authority-preferred nostrums included an escalating politics of the heart, ever more beamish salutes to American unity, character and sympathy, ever more hostility to argument, difference, skepticism. And ever more piety as well. Prayer was proclaimed a significant element in the deliberations about attacking Iraq. Asked at a press conference "How's your faith guiding you?" the President, eyes moistening, replied that he "pray[s] daily that war can be averted." Self-questioning metamorphosed into self-cosseting. Public discourse began edging back into the mishmash-making currents of moralizing reductivism I've sampled here. The thread holding together, in the party in power, sentimentalities, contradictions, passionate overnight embrace and rejection of this or that policy, was, as I say, commitment to the abolition of awareness of difference. The audible summons wasn't to political sobriety and democratic asceticism; the summons was to enthusiasm for wish-fulfilling fantasies of unity.

Nothing more bolstering to the fantasies than a wartime call for the shedding of "partisan differences" (Support Our Troops) and the anointing of America—a nation inferior in public control of private rapacity to more than one country labeled corrupt—as international moral arbiter. For a moment the post-9/11 psychology had seemed in process of begetting a politics aware at least in some measure that optimistic faith in the goodness of our kind would be stronger if founded not on delusory self-celebration but on fair public policy and thoroughgoing debate about substantial public issues.

But myths of holy war overmatched the nascent psychology, pitting homeland courage and righteousness against pusillanimous evil, simultaneously flattering and medicating the electorate out of its shortlived leaning toward self-critique. The chief junk-political themes predating 9/11 were rescored—more brass, fewer strings—the better to harmonize with martial projects. In the context of combat the voice of upbeat became not a mere mood-enhancer but a weapon. Donald Rumsfeld led the charge against negativism in his daily Pentagon briefings; media managers tuned to his note. "After September 11," said the official who runs MSNBC, "the country wants more optimism . . . It's about being positive as opposed to being negative." Placed high on the list of officialdom's patriotic duties was the duty of recharging citizen self-esteem (the President delivered paean after paean on our shared, difference-banishing moral excellence—"the goodness of the American people," America as "a nation of kind hearts").

Placed nowhere on the list of officialdom's patriotic duties was that of reenergizing citizen wariness of extravagant fear of instant, any-second-now destruction by foreign enemies. At the United Nations, Secretary of State Powell simultaneously miniaturized doubt and maximized threats with hot rhetoric about imminent peril, comically overplayed "readings" of photographic images (see this tractor trailer, look at this hole in the ground), and paraphrases of translated passages of intercepted conversations that expunged their dense ambiguities. (The Secretary re-translated an Iraqi headquarters command to "inspect for ammunition" as an order to "clear out all of the areas, the scrap areas, the abandoned areas . . . Make sure there is nothing there.")*

---

*An aspect of junk politics worthy of separate, extended study is the readiness of the American press to treat its spokespersons solemnly, rarely training skeptical light on their messages. A starting point for such a study would be the response to Powell's UN address—a response brilliantly surveyed and analyzed in a *Washington Post* editorial column by Gilbert Cranberg, who wrote as follows: "An examination of a mix of some 40 papers from all parts of the country, shows that while some were less convinced than others by Powell's attempt to link Hussein to terrorism, there was unanimity as to Iraq's possession of weapons of mass destruction: "a massive array of evidence," "a detailed and persuasive case," "a powerful case," "a sober factual case," "an overwhelming case," "a compelling case," "the strong, credible and persuasive case," "a persuasive, detailed accumulation of information," "the core of his argument was unassailable," "a smoking fusillade . . . a persuasive case for anyone who is still persuadable," "an accumulation of painstakingly gathered and analyzed evidence," "only the most gullible and wishful thinking souls can now deny that Iraq is harboring and hiding weapons of mass destruction," "the skeptics asked for proof; they now have it," "a much more detailed and convincing argument than any that has previously been told," "Powell's evidence . . . was overwhelming," "an ironclad case . . . incontrovertible evidence," "succinct and damning evidence . . . the case is closed," "Colin Powell delivered the goods on Sadam Hussein," "masterful," "If there was any doubt that Hussein needs to be . . . stripped of his chemical and biological capabilities, Powell put it to rest."

The war itself was shortly serving as the setting for fresh campaigns against difference. War correspondents traditionally maintained space between themselves, their bestarred briefers, and ground forces, preserving the possibility of objective criticism; the command decision embedding them with combat units eliminated the space ("we're all in this together"). Personalizing flacks bent themselves to the work of putting a likable human face—symbol of American togetherness—on combat defeats and horror. A quarter of a million troops were on the ground in Iraq; one gutsy, attractive casualty named Jessica Lynch became a universal feel-good emblem of the massive invasion—a single charmingly candid, humbly born West Virginian and a (possibly staged) rescue mission displacing issues of lost lives, lost treasure, lost international standing. Positive thinkers commanded the talk shows. No need to fret about finding or not finding weapons of mass destruction, in the opinion of Frank Luntz, a Republican pollster. What counts is that licking Saddam made *all* Americans "feel good about themselves."

Questioned about giant, world-wide, anti-war protests, the President downsized them—"Size of protests, it's like deciding, well, I'm going to decide policy based on a focus group." When protests moved from the streets to prestigious editorial pages, miniaturists practiced at shredding EPA reports and poverty surveys turned to downsizing the President's own exaggerations and falsehoods about the Iraqi threat; the Leader's "mistake" wasn't a matter of a dozen speeches over months but of a "tiny" (Paul Wolfowitz), "insignificant" (Condoleeza Rice) "one sentence" or "sixteen words."

The adjunct on the domestic front was an increase in the number of national problems represented as small and local, in the badmouthing of federal government solutions as wasteful, and in the jettisoning of economic fact. The Administration argued for solving the (negligible) poverty/literacy problem by allowing the states to run Head Start and shrink it. The Administration held that American wage workers would be better off if fewer had a shot at overtime pay and more were recategorized as "managers"; accordingly Congress was asked to approve new rules that reduced by hundreds of thousands the number of workers eligible for overtime pay benefits. Seemingly convinced everybody would be better off if they heard no upsetting economic news, the Administration killed the Mass Layoff Statistics program—a Bureau of Labor Statistics report that kept track of and publicized factory closings (the month the report was killed it listed 2,150 mass layoffs in the previous 30 days). The Administration moved ahead, through executive order, with its faith-based enterprise, finding solutions in the story lines of selected, contemporary, urban saints' lives for socioeconomic trouble spots.

There was, indeed, no sector that remained untouched by reductive, wish-fulfilling, unity-dictating junk politics. Phenomena as mysterious as the difference between planned per capita expenditure for Homeland Security in Wyoming and in New York—seven times more per capita there than here—disappeared into no-comment reductive silence. Homeland Security resources were spent in an attempt to shut down dispute in the Texas State Legislature. Junk togetherness even infected Congressional argument about deficits and tax policy—discussion which for a time had seemed capable of casting clearer light than previously available on relations between trickle-down capital formation (and expenditure) and economic justice for all. Floor debate dwindled into close harmony cheering for equality, both parties joining in denunciations of "the class warfare crowd," both parties competing for a title only extreme dimness could covet (Top Proselyter for Classless America).

To repeat, terror attacks, the Iraq War and their aftermath

had intensified the public need—heartless to mock it but wrong to pander to it—for compelling images evoking the promise of democratic happiness: companionship, solidarity, expectation, street fairs (not wrangling) in the public square. The refashioned, reenergized politics of self-esteem and unity met the need— defused fear and bewilderment with a winning grin, mirroring American content in less troubled times. We like ourselves, said this politics. We trust our neighbors— lessers, betters, kids, whitetops, bleacher folk, skyboxers, leaders, followers, the lot. *You couldn't tell them apart, the Commander in Chief and those kids*— not, that is, in the restorative footage shot on the carrier flight deck that led the news shows. Leader and followers fanning and laughing together as equals, at ease, down to earth, same suits, same helmets, no side. Taking in such images slaked the hunger for signs that divinity hadn't chosen to shine its grace permanently elsewhere. Taking in the images could also be counted as a political action, because the images appeared to validate the quasi-political assumption that this nation is built less on its commitments to articulation and debate—to the brokering off and negotiation of differences over time—than on fine-hearted good guys *of all ranks* hitting it off the minute they meet.

In the ideal world the buried issue of the hour—national infantilization: the babying of the electorate, spoiling of voter-age "children" with year-round upbeat Christmas tales, the creation of a swelled head citizenry, morally vain and irremediably sentimental—would have made its way in time out of the shadows into public discourse. Candidates battling for nomination and a chance to mount an effective challenge to the sponsors of infantilization wouldn't have allowed the issue to become inexpressible. In the ideal world commentators on the right, left or middle would be fully conversant with the mix of elements—mucker-pose manners, bitty legislative initiatives, phony underdog empathy, Celebrities-R-Us equality—which, in their managed coalescence, were once again marginalizing substantial issues. But in the post-9/11 world most candidates were intimidated and the commentariat lacked the requisite conversancy. The result was that even the Administration's unrelenting critics rarely brought junk politics into full steady focus. Alert to the showbiz and heroicizing dimensions of the politics, they were inattentive to aspects yet worthier of notice: the junk politico's unremitting campaign to erase difference from the public mind, the link in this politics between scaling down and dumbing down.

The inattentiveness in question showed in coverage of the President's photo-op descent onto the deck of the Abraham Lincoln. Much hostility in newspapers to the repositioning of the ship, the risky landing, the swaggering progress across the deck, the cued cheers—objections that this was a staged, made for TV event, lacking authenticity. (At the journalistic high end, Norman Mailer stepped forth as lecturer on modesty to complain that Bush's donning the flight suit ranked as a cowardly act by a poseur who, having bought out of combat in youth, shamelessly claimed an exalted hero's stature in middle age.) But the theme of the flight deck drama was sameness not heroic difference, palship not leadership, and the contribution that truly counted was to the broad cause of issue erosion. The staged event—flight suit, shore-slighting carrier, the rest—were (like nukular, "Bring 'em on," the ranch, the Rangers, etc.) elements of an act of identification with "folks" that produced intimacy and erased distance and difference. No difference and distance ("they're all in this together out there"), no issues. No issues, no change.

The useful lesson to be drawn is that traditional frames of reference—complaints about staged as opposed to "real" events, anger at unearned appropriation of the heroic mode—

don't help much to clarify the feeling-content and implication of moments of junk political self-dramatization. And obliviousness of the needs that junk politics addresses—failure to grasp the psychological bearings of the politics—sharply decreases the chances of successfully competing against it. The old rule applies: Know Your Enemy.

Not easy work, to be sure. The chief characteristics of the language of junk politics can be brought across in quick phrases—miniaturizing, moralizing, etc. But mapping the fronts on which the language has currency, coming to terms with its intricacies and contradictions, is another matter. What's required is familiarity with and understanding of the conventions and background of the language—knowledge that reaches beyond even the immediate post-9/11 war-on-terror context to subtler but not less potent influences on its ascendancy. It's this kind of knowledge that the book in your hand aspires to provide.

I begin with scrutiny of the particular matrix that stamped the apolitical style of those currently in power. The first six essays focus on some defining features of recent anti-politics rhetoric and action: leveling instincts and tones, the manners of moderacy, unargued assumptions (e. g., poverty is a moral problem), character puffery, the vision of "leadership" as first of all an emollient. Later sections dig in the cultural soil that nourished the foundational attitudes and behavior and that probably will insure they outlive the present regime. At the end I examine some alternative ways of thinking and feeling that conceivably could build a resistance to junk political attitudes and behavior.

A word or two about bias and original intentions:

I believe that current successes in encouraging impatience with political conflict owe much to President George W. Bush's gift for for presenting himself as morally earnest yet genial, commonsensical, scornful of supersubtle bookish arguefying, given to hunches and seat-of-the-pants navigation, devoted to folk recreations, hostile to curbs on self-expression in the private realm, and a staunch backer of the proposition that the United States in its present form rates as "probably the best society that now exists or has ever existed" (fanfare by D'nesh DiSouza). *Junk Politics* is in part a protest against the cynicism, anti-intellectualism, and slick duplicity that I believe figure— together with some less objectionable elements—in this self-presentation. The book has another bias as well: in favor of choice and possibility. I regard current arrangements of power and place as the results not of immutable law but of human decisions still worth debating, still highly revocable. (Equally subject to change are standard contemporary beliefs about success, failure, property, labor, and the nature of human fulfillment.)

My chief concern throughout, however, is the process by which a relatively new ideology made its way in individual minds—the development of no-politics politics from odd seedtimes to remarkable bloom. The essayist in me regularly yields to the polemicist, who's angered by the sly buffing of mean, jagged-edge opinions—views once expressible only by rabid zealots and talk show crazies—into forms pleasing to "refined" tastes. A recurring target in the pieces is the ambition, common among precursors and exemplars of junk politics, of being perceived as at once hardnosed and warmhearted: the dream of having everything both ways.

But my central fascination remains the stages of growth— and the multifariousness—of apoliticality: its striking reach as an influence on opinion and behavior. In former days apoliticality surfaced chiefly in academic discourse—the debates of "consensus historians" and their opponents regarding the

American past, the "end of ideology," the "end of history," and the like. Now the signs of its influence are everywhere. They begin with low voter turnout, include the reduction of the citizen to mere consumer, fan, ethnic representative, jim-dandy friend of tolerance, or singular sexual self—and extend well beyond. Contending against no-politics politics requires above all awareness of the dimensions of the phenomenon— its impact on every sector of contemporary thought and action. *Junk Politics* will succeed if it broadens this awareness.

As for the origins of these essays: they were conceived as reports on particular moments—renderings (or imaginings) of events or movements of mind and feeling in myself or others occuring over a period of thirty years, give or take. The commentary linking the pieces, pointing up the bearing of each on the book's large subject, sometimes strikes the irritating note that I (probably others, too) associate with brazen hindsight.

But the reports themselves are what count. For me they animate symptomatic events, bringing back at least some of the flavor of the recent past, and recalling separate stages of the "progress" toward Now: the world, that is, wherein the young— often the very talented young—announce to each other with absolute conviction that politics has ceased to matter. They alone—bits of history on the fly—serve as the experiential basis for the suggestions, at the end of the book, on how to turn the no-politics politics world around.

August 2003
Worthington, MA

JUNKPOLITICS

THE TRASHING OF THE
AMERICAN MIND

PART ONE

Bush Era Apoliticality: Moves, Styles, Tutors

In the George W. Bush regime explicit hardselling of no-politics politics began with the repetition, in the Inaugural Address, of a three-C mantra: Civility, Compassion, Character. In succeeding weeks the cause of civility was trumpeted by Congressional leaders, party chairmen, and pundits. The elevation of this cause on the right marked the end of a strain of overt public harshness that had been erupting intermittently for decades in conservative campaigns and rhetoric. (At an extreme of virulence in the language of Barry Goldwater, the strain was far from expunged either by the brilliantly successful—and goodhumored—Ronald Reagan or by the miserably unlucky—and suppressed—Bob Dole.)

What made civility fly? Endless criticism of the incivility of the Sixties kept the cause green, as did lessons learned by both parties from wins and losses in national elections. Personal traits of the country's new Chief Executive—including distaste for implacable stances and over-earnestness—also were a factor. As Governor of Texas, Bush displayed a stunning absence of vengefulness vis a vis political opponents—a seeming determination to greet every rupture with a grin. Once, when the Democratic Lieutenant Governor, Bob Bullock, announced in a meeting that he would have to oppose a Bush proposal ("I'm sorry, Governor, but I'm going to have to fuck you on this one"), Bush responded—in front of staff—by standing up, grabbing Bullock by the shoulders, pulling him forward, and kissing him. "If you're going to fuck me," Bush said, "you'll have to kiss me first."

But the role played by personal tastes and post-millennial events can easily be exaggerated. As the report just ahead confirms, intense marketing of Civility, upscale and downscale, had begun years before George W. Bush took over at the White House. Other more recondite factors deserve mention: the founding and surprising expansion of a bipartisan "communitarian party" by the Washington-based sociologist Amitai Etzioni, the appearance of a widely read, statistics-laden essay documenting declines in civic participation (the piece, Robert Putnam's "Bowling Alone," was much editorialized upon in major metropolitan dailies), a nationally publicized conference on Civility held at Yale Law School and addressed by a cluster of stellar intellectuals whose talks filled the Op-Ed pages.)

But, absent the ongoing transformation of the conservative image—the makeover of all manner of spokespersons from elected officials to pundits to tycoons—the civility banner could probably not have flown on the right. Humane incarnations were needed—friendly conservatives (not Bill Buckley condescenders), characters whose enthusiasm for the American entrepreneurial system coexisted with civil fondness for and close familiarity with the people's pleasures (baseball, for example), models utterly clean of the bad temper surfacing in the line from Westbrook Pegler to James J. Kilpatrick to Robert Novak. The hard-driving business hero long associated with big money Republicanism needed to lose his incivil, skinflint, screw-you past and wear a kinder and gentler face—an expression communicating happiness over the imminent closing of the gap between owners and owned.

The late twentieth century ascent, on the right, of the cause of civility owes much, in short, not only to the plainspoken down-to-earth style of "Dutch" Reagan, but to the "character" of the columnist George Will (his civil progeny now includes Paul Gigot, Bill Kristol and Tucker Carlson among others), and to the appearance— in bestsellers by Tom Peters and other writers—of business heroes as men of tender feeling. The essays in Part 1 deal first with the broad outlines of the civility boom that was in place a half-decade before the 2000 election, and, second, with the new models of courtesy that, two decades earlier, began redefining the conservative image. A recurring subject in the pieces is the ambition, common among the various precursors and exemplars of Tory Niceness and shortly to be standard among the powerful, of being perceived simultaneously as hardnosed and warmhearted: the dream, in short, of having everything both ways. My tone toward this aspect of no-issue politics is harsh.

Seduced by Civility

What is the real American malaise? Why is this country in trouble?

Lately the leader classes have been floating a fresh answer to these queries, talking up a new "root cause" of national woes. Not race, not class, not dirty lyrics or cheap scag or toe-sucking consultants, not under- or over-taxation. The true malaise or disorder, says today's enlightenment, is subtler. The republic is suffering from rampant intemperateness on the one hand (loss of the inner check on which social intercourse depends) and distaste for associated living on the other. Citizens are shouting too much, as on *Geraldo* and talk-radio. They've forgotten how to listen and respect and defer. Furthermore, the once-vaunted native genius for collaborative, not-for-profit, git-go, volunteer problem-solving is disappearing down the drain, and people feel the disappearance. Putting the country back on track requires a rediscovery, by ordinary folk, of mutuality as a value. Our not-so-secret malaise is, in a pet leader-class phrase, the *decline of civility*.

Judged for seductiveness, the emerging orthodoxy on civility ranks high. It has a radiant vocabulary—*common good, civic trust, communal participation, social capital.* . . . It shrewdly selects, as representative villains, characters with jumbo negatives —not just the uncivil prick in the pickup who gives you the finger as he cuts you off but rabble-rousing Buchanan with his pitch-forks, Farrakhan with his demon whites, Robbie Alomar with his wad and (from the past) the demonstrators who chanted "L.B.J., L.B.J., How Many Kids Did You Kill Today?"

What's more, civility orthodoxy's models of behavior are beyond anybody's faulting. If you've lived awhile in a place where, when sickness and other troubles hit home, the neighbors volunteer to feed and bathe your baby, plow out your car, plant your garden, carry you for months, you're bound to listen hard to bigfoots who deplore Americans' increasing reluctance to lend a hand to neighborhood projects and local improvement organizations.

But seductiveness isn't substance. Incivility now is best understood as a protest, by Americans outside the ranks of the publicly articulate against the conduct of their presumed betters. The current orthodoxy on volunteerism and immoderacy shuts its ears to this protest, simultaneously beatifying the undeserving and sapping democratic energy and will. Sold as diagnosis or nostrum, civility is in fact a theater of operations—the classless society's new class war zone.

Background notes: Robert Putnam's "Bowling Alone: America's Declining Social Capital" is the decade's sacred civility text. The piece, by a Kennedy School of Government prof, studies communal association, and views membership drops in P.T.A.s, fraternal organizations, church-related groups and the like as signs of an allegedly "mysterious disengagement" by the citizenry from civic life and social trust. Published almost two years ago in the *Journal of Democracy*, "Bowling Alone" went gold overnight among the elites and is still heavily cited by high-profile opinionizers —from editorial board members of the *New York Times* to PBS "essayists." The link between the decline of volunteerism and the demise of civility was forged more explicitly by Putnam's well-placed fans than by the prof himself. David Broder, who ranked "Bowling Alone" as last year's most important magazine article, writes columns recommending the "strengthening of civic life and the return of civility in our public discourse"; the idea is to connect—somehow, anyhow—the upsurge of political nastiness with dwindling enrollment in service groups. And the notion of a commutative relationship between volunteerism and good civic manners is widely endorsed.

The sitting President is among the endorsers. Before the election and after, in speech after speech, Clinton developed civility and common-ground themes (seven such speeches in one pre-campaign strech of eleven days, according to Amitai Etzioni's count) and at the same time plumps for a proposed $10 million program to reward high school student volunteers. The President has huddled frequently enough with Putnam to turn him into a guru. Clinton inspired his alma mater, Yale, to devote an alumni weekend to a symposium on civility. A Yale Law teacher Clinton admires, Stephen Carter, is finishing a book-length treatise on civility. And the various ripples widen. New York's Ethical Culture Society runs an assembly on civility and the media. Columnists, talk-show hosts, editor-spinners, spinner-editors—Ellen Goodman, Paul Samuelson, Hendrik Hertzberg, Ken Bode, Charles Krauthammer, Mary Matalin, Bill Kristol, Rush Limbaugh, many more—hold forth on civility. The *Chronicle of Higher Education* looks saucer-eyed at growing incivility in academe—professors calling each other assholes and cunts at department meetings and elsewhere, administrators struggling to establish rules of "collegiality." *U.S. News & World Report* devotes eight pages to "The American Uncivil Wars." Paeans to civility fill the Congressional Record. Colin Powell and Tipper Gore salute civility at their political conventions. So, too, do Al

Gore and Jack Kemp during their debate. Post-debate, post-Alomar rumination garnished with "civil" and "civility" resounds on the networks and crams editorial pages from the *Houston Chronicle* to *The Wall Street Journal*. A week after Election Day, Miss Manners, speaking at the Woman's National Democratic Club in Washington, describes the election itself as a "pro-civility landslide." ("We had a national referendum on whether we want a civil society," says Miss M., aka Judith Martin, and the results establish that "the American romance with rudeness is over.") Days later, Supreme Court Justice Anthony Kennedy reveals he is preparing a speech on civility for the American Bar Association, and Bill Bennett and Sam Nunn announce the formation of their new "Forum on Civility."

In a word, a miniboom in progress.

Two ghastly and unforgettable terrorist acts—the murder of Planned Parenthood clinic workers in Brookline and the Oklahoma City bombing—surface often (seldom relevantly) in discussions of "lost civility" and restraint. The budget wars are also mentioned: Congress and the White House hammering each other daily last winter, with partisan denials of space sending legislators outside the Capitol to discuss Medicare in the rain.

Most leader-class discussion is preoccupied with causation—with the question, Why has civility declined? In answering, the discussants analyze others, never themselves, and invariably the perspective is *de haut en bas*. Self-scrutiny doesn't exist.

In the dearth of it lies the great disgrace. For some time now, a knowledge explosion has been delivering into your hands and mine, hour by hour, day after day, unprecedented quantities of source-checked data regarding top-dog patterns of conduct, top-dog feelings and attitudes toward personal privilege, top-dog understandings of good/bad, right/wrong. Partly because it meshes with mid-twentieth-century eruptions against the patriarchy and racism and class privilege, the information in question has different clout from that achieved by yesteryear's muckrakers. The material lays down a blunt, useful challenge both to national mythologies (one nation indivisible) and to popular attitudes and feelings that, broadly positive and hopeful, once granted those mythologies an automatic pass. At one level the challenge is general—aimed at the vast self-satisfaction of I've-got-mine whites, males, "liberally educated" corporate management teams, local and national authorities—and, at another level, the challenge is particularized, directed at individual deeds of officals reported on, more or less responsibly, in striking detail.

Non-mainstream figures joke about the challenge, even as they exploit it. I think for instance of Pat Buchanan grinning at the idea of Buchanan heading up a pitchfork brigade against the selfish rich. But mainstream voices, especially editorial voices, tend to adopt graver tones, counseling officialdom against taking the challenge lightly, and advising against cover-ups: *You only make it worse; everything is bound to come out.*

And come out it does—masses of documentation flowing from sunshine law disclosures, survey research, advances in computing and duplicating, better-financed investigative reporting in scandal sheets and elsewhere. Numbers: how much money is made how quickly and cunningly (as "welfare mothers" are nickeled and dimed and worse) by the can't-lose "investments" of senators or wives of governors or majority leaders—or by corporation executives whose huge, self-immunizing "deferred compensation" schemes screw fellow workers by the thousand or by whichever celebrities are sinning their way to fortunes this month (a call girl reports that a presidential consultant is a client, whereupon the consultant's publisher renegotiates his book contract upward into the millions). Paper trail documentation of official lies: executive oaths that nicotine isn't

addictive, that our firm would never dump poisons into suburban canals, that survival concerns alone dictate downsizing, that the U.S. government absolutely would not allow
one of its agencies to wink at drug trading that enslaves
African–Americans and others by the tens of thousands, that
U.S. top brass absolutely would not hide the facts about soldiers' exposure to chemical weapons, that the White House
absolutely would not conceal from the people that it was
escalating a foreign war.

More: details filling out elite attitudinal profiles—evidence
that the well-placed admire successful stonewalling, rate "reputation for integrity" above integrity, disbelieve that persons of
modest means or inferior coiffure can attain distinction or
escape shame, believe that it's acceptable for university presidents to keep trustees in their pockets by buying them $200
bottles of Cheval Blanc with dinner at one's club. Videotaped
proof of police brutality by ranking officers. Strong evidence
that a heroicized Chief Executive welcomed prostitutes into
his White House bedroom at a time when he was acceding to
the proposition that taxpaying blacks deserved physical abuse
for seeking the vote. Proof that the U.S. officer class engaged in
mass murder on foreign soil. Proof that the Vietnam draft
policy—a policy that, by exempting the well-off from service,
contravened the national value of shared sacrifice in
wartime—was actually conceived as a means of gulling the
educated into ignoring the war. Proof that, under pressure
from the corporate health megalith, thousands of doctors
have broken their oaths of personal responsibility for the care
of their patients. Proof that racism is rife among top oil-
company executives. Data disclosing that the reduction of the
U.S. producer class to the status of hamburger flippers or unem-
ployables is looked upon with equanimity not only by the
managers in place but by significant numbers of their someday

replacements: subfreshmen ticketed for training in gatekeeper institutions of higher learning. And so forth.

Material of this sort is often accompanied, in the media, by low-key coaching on how to shrug off corruption (yesterday was worse, nobody's perfect, etc.). But the coaching seems not to have taken. The University of Michigan's Center for Political Studies polls voters biannually on their views of the leader class. Decades ago when the center first asked, "Are government officials crooked?" 24 percent answered, "Quite a lot." Two years ago 51 percent gave that response. The center also asks: "Would you say the government is pretty much run by a few big interests looking out for themselves or that it is run for the benefit of all people?" Thirty years ago 64 percent of the respondents answered, "For the benefit of all." In 1994 that figure had dropped to 19 percent.

Mistrust of the authorities runs in the native grain, as everybody knows. But quantitative changes in levels of mistrust are capable of producing qualitative differences—witness the current dismissal by an apparent majority of "character" as a requirement for high public office.

Returning to civility: While the citizen disengagement from public life that civility promoters term "mysterious" is clearly a complex phenomenon, some influences on it aren't arcane. Rude, abusive speech and action reflects, in one of its dimensions, belief in the need for an attitude—some kind of protection against sly, sincerity-marketing politicos and boss-class crooks. "Uncivil" refusal by ordinary citizens to labor unpaid in the cause of points-of-light good works reflects, in one of its dimensions, the daily exposure of ordinary citizens to powerful anti-mutuality instruction from above—oblique but persuasive lessons on how to pull your oar ceaselessly for the benefit of Number One; how not to fret about hungry children in the street; how to feel good when, in the age of homelessness, a corporate bright boy spends $45 million on his own one-family dwelling; how to avoid being suckered into caringness. The "new incivility" needs to be recognized, in short, for what it is: a flat-out, justified rejection of leader-class claims to respect, a demand that leader-class types start looking hard at themselves.

Which, as I said, is exactly where civility discourse encourages them not to look. Unsurprisingly, leader-class talk about civility and incivility deals neither with justified withdrawals of respect nor with impotent fury at corroded leader-class values and standards. And it avoids basic elements of civility such as considerateness, modesty, faith in the rough rightness of democratic values—items readily comprehensible and well suited to plain speech. Talkers sift trends that social science or Tory whimsy finds relevant to the "decline of civility," measuring the degree of their influence. Putnam's "Bowling Alone," the sacred text, is set up as a whodunit. The "crime" is the murder of citizen solidarity, mutual concern, volunteerism. The author casts himself as a detective bent on solving the crime; the "suspects" include longer working hours, women in the labor market, rising racism, mobility (geographical and social), several others. Introduced and assessed with an array of stats and graphs, the suspects are at length dismissed, Poirot–style, one by one. At the conclusion comes the unveiling. "The culprit is TV." Volunteering is declining and civic trust is withering, Putnam explains, because Everyman and Everywoman are bemused by the tube.

Similar etiological dabblings occur at Friends of Civility parleys, public and private. (Bids to civilitarian parleys go out to the right, left and muddled; civilitarianism is vain of its inclusiveness.) And here, as in Putnam's pages, there's zero self-scrutiny.

Consider the symposium on civility at the Yale Law School meeting mentioned earlier. The group assembled to ruminate for the edification of law school alumni included accomplished men and women. Arthur Schlesinger Jr. delivered the keynote, and a panel of editors, authors and teachers (Gertrude Himmelfarb, Hilton Kramer, Victor Navasky, Randall Kennedy, Martin Peretz) spoke for the world of ideas; Representatives Barney Frank, David Garth and Peggy Noonan spoke for practical politics.

Kramer threw off in familiar vein on scum demonstrators, quoting old anti-L.B.J. chants; he also slammed "vulgarity and ignorance based on the precipitous decline in public discourse." But he found his central example of bottom-dog dimness and unsophistication in the press. Kramer recounted how he learned—during a "long Paris lunch" with Flora Lewis—the secret of mounting stupidity among reporters. (He personified reporters as "some young man" from the provinces who knew no better than to get close to "the trenches.") The secret, according to Lewis, was that:

> The *New York Times* had had to send, in effect, relays of mostly young men, although there were one or two women, to cover the [Vietnam] war . . . Most of these young reporters had little if any experience of the world outside the United States. And what they discovered, or believed they discovered in Vietnam, was that the world was divided into two parties: the evil party, which was the United States, and the rest of the world, which was the good party. . . . Those reporters had to be rewarded with more glamorous assignments. And wherever they were sent out into the world, they were still reporting the Vietnam War, where America was to blame for whatever was wrong with the world, and the locals—the natives, whether they were in Moscow or wherever—were to be given the benefit of the doubt.

Himmelfarb's bottom-dog targets were ill-educated black teachers unwisely allowed to participate in public forums. "Civility, like conversation," she opined, "assumes a commonality—a commonality of purpose, of beliefs, of manners and morals, a common human nature"—but minority multiculturalists have destroyed the commonalities. "I am told," said Himmelfarb, that

> in speaking of shared values, I evoke memories of exploited black sharecroppers. Now these are not off the cuff remarks thrown out in the heat of debate or at a private dinner table. They come from very reputable professors in public forums, generally speaking from a prepared text . . . We are in a culture war. And one of the first casualties of war is civility.

Arthur Schlesinger Jr. had still different targets: bottom-dog boorishness and inability to follow arguments. He wittily reviewed lowbrow griping at White House high style, and went on to claim that the chief difference worth mentioning between yesterday and today is that in the past "the tradition of scurrility" had "a real offset"—namely, a "countertradition of gravitas" (political argument and oratory published full-length in newspapers and elsewhere). Today, said Schlesinger, "our attention-span-challenged audiences" have abolished the countertradition.

Had this been another kind of meeting, each of these Friends of Civility—several others at the parley as well—might have been set straight. Kramer might have been told that a sector of the public has lately awakened to the truth that the American imperium is something different from the selfless light of the world shown in the approved portrait, and that the agents of

13

this awakening over the decades have been the few American reporters who, by giving the benefit of the doubt to natives rather than official briefers, produced the only reliable reporting from a long string of places—Mexico, Chile, the Dominican Republic, El Salvador, a dozen more.

Himmelfarb might have been told that many blacks are aware that their exclusion for centuries from schooling and power continues to have appalling caste consequences for most brothers and sisters, and that privileged whites who harp on "shared values" and commonalities are implicitly and infuriatingly asserting that nothing separates black history from white history. Schlesinger might have been reminded that entertainment conglomerates shape tastes as well as reflect them, and that blaming TV viewers for dumbed-down politics oversimplifies a number of highly knotty matters. All three might have been chastised for coupling intellectually and morally irresponsible oversimplifications with the kind of supercilious insult characteristic of—so Matthew Arnold thought—barbarian-aristos.

This, though, was a civility fete, hence Kramer, Himmelfarb, Schlesinger *et al.* heard little or no direct critique. Behaving decorously, respondents turned away from fatuity, greed and obliviousness near at hand to the fairly distant past or else engaged in explicating paradoxes (civility as incivility and vice versa). Randall Kennedy emphasized that nineteenth-century civility promoters had indicted abolitionists for incivility: "The people who marched under the banner of civility, the people who were the compromisers, the people who were being afraid of being labeled as radicals and extremists, were the people who were willing to allow slavery to continue."

Venturing close to the present, Victor Navasky, publisher and editorial director of *The Nation*, addressed himself directly to Kramer and Himmelfarb, averring that the sit-ins gave him his example of a "supremely civil and civilized act." No sooner had Navasky spoken than civilitarian whistles commenced shrieking. Kramer cried that the speaker "violated the standards of civility." Himmelfarb rapped the blackboard, warning that "we seem to be not only discussing incivility, we seem to be on the verge of practicing incivility." Angered, Kennedy told the room that "if you're in an argument with a thug, there are things much more important than civility." For a minute it seemed possible that the inhibiting, intimidating power of civility discourse might not be absolute.

But they who define the issues win the debate. The subject at Yale was the decline of civility, not of fairness, justice or decency among the privileged. And that definition of the subject certified that the problem under consideration had to do with inferiors, not superiors; no tie was made between it and disrespect for the leader classes stemming from thuggish leader-class beliefs and behavior. Kennedy didn't press on with his case. The vision of the "civility problem" as, at its core, one of bottom-dog manners rather than top-dog morals underwent no sustained examination.

The current civility boom is, of course, only one of several indicators of rising establishment impatience with the notion that, on these shores, class interests stand in ever sharper conflict. The most obvious indicator was the 1996 campaign itself, which saw Dole and Clinton vying with each other for the title of politician most angered by allusions to U.S. classlessness as a "myth." (Clinton noodled on "common ground" through every whistle stop; Dole shouted, "We're not a class society; we're a classless society," to audiences from Russell to Hartford.) Other indicators include establishment refusal to accord courtesy to any insider critique of the mega-rich, and establishment eagerness to bash those who dare to murmur moral objections to the moeurs of the stylish professional classes.

Item: Ted Turner recently let fall that the *Forbes* Four Hundred Richest list is "destroying our country." He argued that the "skinflints" and "Scrooges" on the list "won't loosen up [as philanthropists] because they're afraid they'll reduce their net worth and go down the list." He added: "They're fighting every year to be the richest man in the world. Why don't they sign a joint pact to each give away a billion and then move down the Forbes list equally?"

In her *New York Times* column on Turner, "Ted's Excellent Idea," Maureen Dowd veered between nervous giggles and hints that the man is a kook. She had some of Turner's comments set in caps ("THEY [multibillionaires] SHOULD DO IT [namely, curb their greed and part with serious money for urgent public needs] NO-O-W!"), communicating that he's a loudmouth. She referred to Turner variously as a "Rhett Butler romantic," "America's flashiest extrovert," "Captain Outrageous" and "the Mouth of the South." The impression her column left wasn't that a member of the megarich had offered sane counsel to his fellows (in an idiom updated from Andrew Carnegie's essay on "Philanthropy") but rather that Turner is one more self-aggrandizing know-it-all, shooting off his mouth for publicity purposes.

Item: Yesterday the moneyed classes heeded the prudent rule of silence against responding to those who make noise about greed, obliviousness or fatuity—but not now. Evidently convinced that the populace as a whole shares their repugnance for those who refer unashamedly to moral standards, they greet such critics not with silence but with explosions of hatred and countercharges of hypocrisy and sanctimony.

During a recent interview with the *New York Observer*, Jonathan Kozol spoke slightingly of frequenters of the city's luxo restaurants. He said he was "far more scared in Manhattan [than in the South Bronx, setting of his most recent book], because that's when I feel my soul is in peril, when I have to go to the Four Seasons." The simple message was that a culture that treats hundreds of thousands of children as garbage while consecrating three-star lunches and $45 million hideaways probably ought to look to its soul, and that complicity with such a culture for the length of a meal betrays whatever knowledge one possesses of suffering.

Pow. *The New Republic* fired in fury, jeeringly quoting Kozol's fears for his soul, accusing him of having "made a career of his immunity to transgression," and slaughtering him for moral pride: "He dined for our sins."

It doesn't matter, in sum, whether the critical whisper comes from an ascetic or a billionaire. The leader classes sense that their weapons in hand (civility discourse isn't the least of them) suffice to still any insurgence in an instant.

Idealizers of the civilitarian impulse aren't found exclusively on the right. The religious left, once admirably clear-headed about the difference between substantive and marginal political questions, today evinces a desire to fold a wide range of concerns, moral, political and economic, into the issue of civility. The September/October *Sojourners* has an article by the editor, the Rev. Jim Wallis—a decent man with strong left-activist credentials—titled "A Crisis of Civility." The piece says barely a word about incivility as a response to an unendurable surfeit of corruption. It begins with the usual animadversions on abusive campaigning and concludes that "honesty, respect, principle, openness, fairness, accessibility, and involvement are all issues of civility."

The sentence sounds the theme that tightly binds old myths of classlessness to new scams of civility—that inequity is verbal; flows from tone, not structure; bears no relation to power differentials. Sanitizing and miniaturizing the worst of the past and present, this theme—the language of civility and incivility as a whole—sweeps away human meaning from slavery, the civil rights struggle, one episode after another of murderous cruelty and greed. It has similar effect on differences of opportunity and education: drains them of meaning, persuades the privileged that insulting the weak keeps up standards, encourages those who surmount "disadvantage" to forget that they didn't rise unaided, hence owe others help, not insult. In this cloud of abstraction nothing survives except pieties of the airheaded: faith that no talk on earth is more exalted than talk about talk.

In theory it should be easy to counter such faith—but try it. Criticize a civility promoter, and you hear that you're a fan of rap lyrics about cop-killing, or that you're the sort of nutcake who tries to silence by boos any idea you happen to disagree with, or that you believe differences of opinion on large matters preclude collaborative work toward limited objectives, or that you lack feeling for the glories of civil discourse in the public square to which Hannah Arendt sang her lyric in "On Revolution". In short, civility boosters can't be defeated, they can only be held out against, with arguments built on patient repetition of truisms about the nature of our kind of polity, *viz.*:

Democracy continues to oblige citizens to resist—as Richard Hoggart once put it—"the constant pressure to undervalue others, especially those who do not inhabit 'our own' publicly articulate world."

Democracy continues to oblige citizens to render serious, right-valued judgments on others as well as upon themselves.

Democracy can coexist with the belief that all humans are sinners but not with the belief that all sins are equal.

Democracy has within each of its camps, not excluding the civilitarian camp, thugs in number. And *when you're in an argument with a thug, there are things much more important than civility.*

The aim of no-politics politics is to limit (if not end) criticism of institutions and public policies that are founded on socio-economic advantage. The basic tools employed to that end—diversion and deflection—are the same from one regime to the next, but techniques and mediums vary. At one hour effort to eliminate political intensity focuses on process and tone (lectures on civility and incivility). At the next it concentrates on fabricating mini- or fringe-issues attractive by reason of novelty and relative innocuousness (the Dick Morris school uniform initiative). At the next it backs confusion-sowing proposals that induce intra-party quarrels—disputes within the right or left or both that lead all sides away from equity concerns (the Bush Administration Faith-Based Initiative).

The FBI proposal was perfectly tuned to no-issue politics because of its emphasis on "changing hearts" and "changing lives," and its insistence that social problems arise from failings that counselors with religious convictions are best placed to meet—individual moral failings separable from group interest or past suffering. Poverty as a character problem has roots in the most widely read conservative texts of the last generation as well as in social policies reaching back as far as post-Civil War federal pension policy. The virtue-vice issue developed by the Bush regime out of its mix of character, civility and faith-based themes belongs not to parliamentary bodies but to houses of worship; because it neatly displaced, in public discourse, the subject of the moral obligations of—and moral claims against—the state, the FBI represents no-politics politics at or near its most ingenious.

Tweaking Poverty:
Inside the F.B.I.

Early in 2001 George W. Bush announced his determination to end federal "discrimination" against religious organizations that seek federal support for their literacy, anti-addiction, and other social service projects. Civil wars broke out swiftly thereafter. More than 850 clergy signed a petition declaring they opposed the President because they wanted "to keep government out of the churches, temples, synagogues and mosques." Close to 400 other-minded clergy turned up at a conference, held in the marble banquet hall of the Library of Congress, promoting religious-based charities. (Congressional Republicans sponsored the conference.) White ministers were slated, in print and elsewhere, by individual whites and blacks, for obliviousness to social needs that black ministers can't evade. *The Nation* published a lengthy attack by a leftist critic, Ellen Willis, on "faith-based politics"; pro-church leftists filled the magazine's letters columns with protests. In angry op-ed pieces and talk show appearances Pat Robertson, Garry Wills, Al Sharpton, Jerry Falwell, Eugene Rivers and others added further heat.

Given the noise, the Faith-Based Initiative looked—at first glance—totally at variance with the project of increasing civility and diminishing political conflict. But on closer view another reading seemed possible, one that assessed the Initiative as a near-triumph for Bush advisors and strategists.

Consider the challenges on the welfare front facing those advisors and strategists. How to keep the discourse of "reform" on the moral track. How to police the nuisance few who saw budget surpluses as an incitement not to cut taxes but to explore fresh, publicly financed steps toward fair social provision. How to bring off the policing while continuing to wear the face of compassion. How to insure that, if discussion of social provision arose, the Administration would appear passionately activist in heart but hamstrung by " politics" and "hypocrisy." How to situate "traditional" Democrats in any such discussion so that they would be obliged to shed their old-timey image of unbuttoned openhandedness and take on the pinched features of the stereotypically ungiving right.

The White House Office of Faith-Based Initiatives has dealt successfully with these challenges. It's evoking war on the appearance of indifference to poverty as identical with war on poverty itself, and, in the process, it's redrawing the entire map of American moral politics. Whatever the ultimate fate of the Office—George W. Bush reiterated often that he absolutely would not give up on the idea—Faith-Based Initiatives already qualifies as a win-win venture. The controversies it has generated have brought liberal-left spokespersons for justice in social provision under repeated attack for *in*humanity and abstraction. In some instances the attack has been voiced with truly remarkable levels of *saeva indignatio*—apparently unfeigned fury at alleged liberal coldheartedness and abstraction. And the deep problem demanding serious political address—how to overcome poverty—has all but vanished from general view.

These successes resulted from certain modifications of

earlier American definitions of poverty as a problem of moral character, from the choice of a new face and persona for conservative messages regarding the "underclass," and, as I say, from nurturing discussion focussed elsewhere than on the commensurateness of Administration proposals with basic social needs. The particular methods and strategies employed have received far less notice than they deserve.

As early as the 1890s the prevailing elite ideology identified the fundamental division in American society as that " between industrious and idle, virtuous and vicious, community-minded and selfish," not as that between rich and poor. This notion of difference helped to shape the first functional equivalent, in America, of an old age and disability pension system—the benefits that were paid to a million and a half Civil War veterans and their survivors. According to one sociologist, writing on "The Political Origins of America's Belated Welfare State," Civil War pension benefits flowed "primarily to members of the middle class and the upper strata of the working class, rather than to the neediest Americans." From the time of those first pensions to the present, when, as Theda Skocpol among others notes, social security for "deserving workers" is still set apart from welfare for "barely deserving poor people," the distinction between the decent and indecent, virtuous and vile, church-going and wayward, has dogged American social provision.

No news in this. The political power of the moralizing language of character has been well understood for generations, and present day character education, leadership education, and faith-based initiatives had precursors well before the politics of no-politics achieved its present ascendancy. But the accidents of George W. Bush's life as an alcoholic and born-again Christian mean that such initiatives stand beyond, for him, academic/ministerial causes or devices for concealing a do-nothing disposition. Presidential passions are engaged; the beliefs in question have behind them the convert's conviction, bulwarked not only by Republican hostility to big government but by Jesus the Lord.

The advisors who direct these passions, Christian believers themselves, acknowledge the influence, on their views, of the major conservative texts of the 1970s and 1980s: works by theorists of dark forces who grew increasingly bold in their own day in attributing program failures to moral corruption, and in dismissing the notion that improved public policy could succeed at the task of moderating inequity. The theorists in question deployed an array of weapons, including pseudo-science, in arguing for the existence of what was termed the "pathology of poverty." Purporting to provide objective, penetrating, social-scientific accounts of things as they humanly are, they adopted a candid and unflinching manner, suggesting readiness to face the worst. What they had to say induced feelings of despair—a sense that the crises of the age were biologically foreordained and that utopians alone dreamed of abating them. Which bureaucracy on earth has ever known the answer to Evil?

The leading promoter of the pathological fallacy, Edward C. Banfield, a government professor at Harvard and head of Nixon's Task Force on Cities, presented himself as "a social scientist [thinking] about the problems of cities in the light of scholarly findings." ("Facts are facts, however unpleasant.") He claimed that American cities were in ruins because the underclass individual wasn't normal—was mentally ill, pathologically sick: "[He] lives from moment to moment . . . Impulse governs his behavior, either because he cannot discipline himself to sacrifice a present for a future satisfaction or because he has no sense of the future . . . Much of [his] violence is probably more an expression of mental illness than of class culture."

A famous white paper of the period had "discovered" that the unanticipated consequence of welfare programs was the destruction of the black family; dark force theorists developed the point into a fullscale indictment of government itself, with emphasis on bureaucrats' moral blindness. Charles Murray, the Reagan era welfare theorist, claimed in 1983 that the "liberal ascendancy" failed to grasp that the real cause of anguish in Harlem and comparable communities was the moral collapse of the poor, attributable to the new welfare programs; all such programs should go. Let politicos be mindful of the consequences of ignoring the ineluctable individuality of each of its citizens. Let them ponder the costs of deleting the moral substance from "conditions" and pretending that life is a social problem soluble by technical means. Let the whole country remember the truth of original sin.

The summa version of these themes appeared in 1996, under the title *Body Count*. The book argued that the nation was coming into the grip of "superpredators"—a new generation of street criminals, "the youngest, biggest, and baddest generation any society has ever known . . . radically impulsive, brutally remorseless youngsters, including ever more preteenage boys, who murder, assault, rape, rob, burglarize, deal deadly drugs, join gun-toting gangs and create serious communal disorders." According to *Body Count*, the reason this was happening was essentially quite simple: recent, politics-ridden public policy ignored moral reality, which meant that "most inner-city children grow up surrounded by teenagers and adults who are themselves deviant, delinquent, or criminal."

Filled with echoes of Banfield and Murray, *Body Count* was the result of a collaboration of three authors, two of whom (William J. Bennett and John P. Walters) credited the third, John J. DiIulio, professor of criminology, as the main theorist of the work. John DiIulio was to become chief of the White House Office of Faith-Based Initiatives.

From the perspective of the new Republican strategists—figures often burned by Clinton-style empathetics—one large weakness of the Banfield-Murray-D'Souza body of writing lay in its taunting tone. *I will leave no child behind*: these words reverberated throughout Campaign 2000 and thereafter. "Everyone knows," the new Chief Executive has repeatedly averred, that "there are still deep needs and real suffering in the shadow of America's affluence, problems like addiction and abandonment and gang violence, domestic violence, mental illness and homelessness. We are called by conscience to respond." Tens of millions without health insurance, one in six children growing up in poverty (one in three black children) . . .

Banfield-Murray *et al.*, on the other hand, sounded undisturbed about leaving the mentally ill behind, even pleased by the defects and afflictions they exposed—certainly not moved by determination to improve the lot of those suffering the deficits of conscience they anatomized. Echoes of their stoniness were heard in the elected officials—Giuliani types—who undertook to build back the missing "discipline." Their tone had become part of the welfare problem. Public enthusiasm for banishing the squeegee man and the homeless from the street and for stripping the welfare queens of the Cadillacs that Reaganites saw them driving mingled with faint awareness that these and similar measures were essentially negative—might not reach below the surface. The unrelenting focus on morality and character—on the *badness* of the poor—moderated but didn't cancel the qualms stirred by the sternly negative direction of conservative urban policy. The expression worn by country club Republicanism when it glanced toward the poor was, in a word, too harsh; the points of light talk of kindness and gentleness introduced by Bush *pere* softened it, as did the invention of compassionate conservatism.

But could the frequent deployment of the latter phrase assure every doubter that actual effort would be spent seeing that no child was left behind?

Re-enter John DiIulio. Soon after publication of *Body Count*, during the period of his anguish about the emergence of the "superpredators," DiIulio had a conversion experience of a sort—a rebirth in Christian teaching—while praying at Mass. He answered the call by adding another dimension to his labor as a professional criminologist who dealt mainly with statistical reports and trends. Becoming a social activist, he worked with Philadelphia ghetto youngsters, attempting to change hearts one by one. And the essays he published describing this work earned him in a few years a reputation for commitment that no theorist of similar views before him had possessed. DiIulio's pessimism about governmental intervention would have had George W. Bush's approval, but it was DiIulio the anti-bureaucrat, anti-government man who understood rebirth from within and acted on that understanding—who *believed in changing individual hearts*—who was chosen to head the White House Office of Faith Based Initiatives.

As Director of the Office DiIulio has adhered firmly, from the outset, to the cornerstone themes of dark force theorists and their historical predecessors: 1) the basic problem is moral (and in DiIulio's words, "a moral problem—a deficit of conscience, of values, of connectedness—requires a moral solution and only a moral solution"); 2) for the last quarter century all broad-gauged efforts to help the poor have been a bust. "The real history, whether it's come from the Democrats or the Republicans, of social policy," DiIulio declares, is that it hasn't "lift[ed] up the children, youth and family of any community [and] it's not really going to achieve very much in the end."

The case is, of course, that some broad-gauged secular

efforts have taught invaluable lessons about the scope of the problem and the nature of the changes in national priorities (and in tax, school financing and health care policy) necessary to contend successfully against it. For twenty years the several dozen "social development" public schools, in communities from New Haven, Connecticut to Lee County, Arkansas, have been building groups of teachers, parents, job trainers, employers, and community leaders—collaborators seeking to cope simultaneously with problems ranging from job ceilings to drugs to parental alienation from teachers and schools. And the founder of these schools, James S. Comer, knowledgeable about the difficulties arising from unrealistic assumptions regarding possible rates of progress, the uses of testing, and prospects for one on one mentoring in religious settings, argues that "three generations of continuous access [to the development school experience] are necessary if a family is to gain the type of education that will allow its members to function successfully in the postindustrial economy."

Implicit in Comer's argument—namely that the basic problem is the "profound, ongoing failure to educate poor Americans"—are several assumptions regarding expectations and scale.

- Sanity understands that welfare programs are bound to fail if they miniaturize the problems and indulge in fantasies about the true size and nature of the obstacles and about the resources necessary to overcome them.

- A society that funds two dozen or so social development schools for a maximum of ten years when the need is for several hundred such schools in full operation for longer than a half century should expect to wait several generations for the transformation of its underclass.

- Ending fantasies requires political resolve—articulated challenges to existing values, criticism and debate from bully pulpits and elsewhere, soundly conceived attempts to define and dramatize the practical, publicly financed steps that alone can transform leaving no child behind from feel-good sloganizing to the beginnings of a serious address to issues of social justice.

But broadening public understanding of the good sense of these assumptions was hardly the project of the new White House Office. Its project is, as I said, to begin the work of reducing and at length eliminating doubts about the efficacy of moralizing stances toward the poor. The Office has moved in a variety of ways on this front. Old-style moral/religious preceptors spoke *de haut en bas*, and derived their authority as chastizers of the errant from high professional and socio-economic rank. Faith-based moral/religious preceptors are conversant with the 'hoods and possess moral authority by virtue of good works. Old-style moral/religious preceptors were flinty, impersonal and objective character types, relatively disinclined to self-dramatization and self-mythologizing. The Office is led by a moral/religious preceptor who mixes purity and intensity in a quasi-messianic persona, sounding now like Dostoyevsky's Alyosha and now like Swift's modest proposer, and claiming the aura of authenticity that contemporary culture tends to reserve for self-ironists.

More important, the Office is developing a version of the enemy different from any plotted on the the crude black and white map of good conduct and bad, diligence, idleness, etc. that old-style preceptors followed. Still partly committed to the traditional view that poverty and allied crimes result —in DiIulio's phrase—from "a correctable moral defect of individuals," the new preceptor presents himself as a warrior for humane wholeness and against abstraction—the kind of abstraction that breeds frivolous litigiousness, anxiety about phony "constitutional crises," coldheartedness which, rather than feeling the suffering of the poor and acting to ease it, shuts itself in the law library and hunts reasons and precedents for uncaringness.

These and related changes of emphasis and tone, persona and strategy, are pivotal elements in the diversionary power of the church-state dispute orchestrated by the Faith-Based Office. Taunting has vanished from versions of poverty as a character problem; it's replaced by sorrow and sympathy. Attention is shifted from the beleaguerment of the poor to that of workers under fire by strict constitutionalists for excessive longing to aid the poor. And as the church-state dispute has modulated into a conflict between the caring and the uncaring, spokespersons for the liberal left have been forced to adopt postures hitherto associated with the hardnosed right.

New in some dimensions but continuous with the longrunning American evasion of issues of social justice, the church-state dispute will survive only if the Faith-Based Office survives. But no matter: it has already edged issues of social justice out of the welfare and poverty debate, and, at a moment when trillions at hand seemed a potential resource for social transformation, it has rendered hopes for social transformation inexpressible.

The first Faith-Based briefing at the National Press Club sketched out the pertinent pattern of reversals and contradictions. The arrangements at the briefing, which defined the church-state debate as critical, insured that the matter of the commensurateness of the Initiatives with the problems addressed would figure marginally if at all. And DiIulio's self-presentation simultaneously placed that debate as a necessity and turned it into an object of fiercely ironic derision—proof that, when it comes to taking real steps to help real people, both the right and the left are composed of spoiled, nitpicking, overeducated hypocrites.

An Ivy graduate and professor, DiIulio often mentions his humble past in his writing—growing up in "rough-edged, white-ethnic, working class Philadelphia neighborhoods," "stay[ing] close to home" after college, "hang[ing] out with the same working class relatives and friends I've known all my life . . . liv[ing] a few minutes by car from some of Philadelphia's worst black neighborhoods." A man of the folk, in a word, not of the folks on the hill. And his introducers, whether of exalted or moderate station themselves, regularly salute him as a down to earth person of character with a proven record of moral generosity ("Nobody I know," said Dionne, this day's introducer, "is more dedicated to the cause of poor people or racial justice. John brings the passion of a committed person to this work").

DiIulio's talk at the briefing began with extended praise of a selfless doer—a former cop named Tom Lewis, founder of a community safe haven in the nation's capital. "I just rushed back," DiIulio told the audience, from an event at Lewis's Fishing School, and he explained that:

> The Fishing School is a small community-serving ministry in Southeast Washington, DC run by Tom Lewis. Tom is a former DC police officer who spent two decades on the force, was in the Officer Friendly program, and then after his two decades of service, having seen so many children and so many young people in such distress, promised that if he could get through his service in the police department, he would mortgage his home, and he did that, and borrow money, and he did that, and

just open the door on that street in a little structure, and call it the Fishing School, and invite children in. First, just as a community safe haven, and then over time one thing led to another, an after school program, a computer-assisted literacy and learning program . . . I had the honor introducing Tom Lewis before he introduced President Bush . . . But stand[ing] there next to Tom Lewis [I felt] like he was truly the most important man in the room. I really believe at that moment, and I believe in his life, he is.

With this for openers, DiIulio proceeded to the work of his Office, naming three goals: increased charitable giving, leveling the playing field "so that community-based groups, whether they're religious or secular, that are not now part of the government funding loop in the area of social services, can get a better shake," and "finding effective models of public-private partnership and cooperation where you can have institutions, both sacred and secular, working across the usual racial and denominational lines, the usual urban-suburban divides, on particular civic purposes."

The invited opponents of Faith-Based Initiatives (they included the legislative director of the American Jewish Committee and a Virginia Congressman versed in church-state issues) were immediately called on and they set forth at length their constitutional fears. DiIulio responded that the government would not be put in the position of of favoring one religion over another because projects would be evaluated on their effectiveness at serving stipulated needs, that careful surveys in selected cities proved existing faith-based aid projects rarely engaged in proselytizing activities, and that the fear of a "horror story" as regards proselytizing should not be allowed to prevent the search for non-proselytizing religious-secular collaboration from going forward. Dionne, the moderator, mounded up more questions, from antis, and within minutes DiIulio was being pelted from all sides:

You have Branch Davidians, Wiccans, or Nation of Islam, are they going to get money?

If a Christian is seriously obeying the command of Jesus to make disciples of all nations, to baptize and teach, wouldn't some consider that proselytizing?

What role can government play in trying to figure out whether an organization is being religiously coercive and stepping over some line? How do you mediate? How do you find that line?

How within your office are you going to evaluate which religious institution is a genuine religious institution?

A performance now began. DiIulio rose to his beleaguerment with a goodnatured joke expressing nostalgia for the sheltered life of scholarship: "I'm taking a leave and writing a book," he said, "it will be out in eighteen months, that will answer all your questions." But quickly thereafter he transformed the briefing into a stage on which he performed as mocker of "white policy elites," a caring, can-do walker of the walk (no paleface talker of the talk obsessing over lawbook technicalities while children die in the street).

As a man with a sacred mission, equally remote from the overprivileged, overtheoretical left and from rich habitues of Republican country clubs, he professed to have been beaten down by the church-state debate in progress. ("We can have this debate and we're having it and believe me I'm dizzy from having it . . . ") Yes, he said, "there's a lot to fight about," but, unlike his harassing questioners—"you'll have a good time fighting about it"—this fight didn't make *his* day. He again linked himself with Tom Lewis and little people utterly distant from high-powered administrators with their luxo funding, staffs, chauffeurs and the rest. "We don't have any money. I go home on the Metro. I have no money. We've got no money, please don't send your cards and letters." Comically dramatizing his isolation, he told of seeking support, on a public occasion, from his "fellow New Democrat," Senator Lieberman ("I embraced [him] and held onto [him] and told him I am now surrounded by Republicans"). He lectured the room on the futility of church state "philosophical disagreements," insisting that we could "spend all our time disagreeing, and it will not put bread on anybody's table. It's not going to put a mentor in any child's life." He warned that:

> You get all this survey data on levels of people mistrusting the government, people mistrusting each other, people are bowling alone even though they may be praying together, and if that is the case, if that's what we're dealing with, then we're going to [have to] stop on the philosophical disagreements. . . .

At the end, shifting into Swiftian gear, he insisted not only that the church-state debate be allowed to continue but that it should not be allowed to end until all who participated in it were beaten into exhaustion. He, John DiIulio, aware of the tragic costs of legalistic quibbling that could one day cast the little ones at the Fishing School back onto the streets, nevertheless upheld the right of those on the other side of the issue to drive the church-state issue to the highest court in the land. "We ought to sue each other," DiIulio cried bitterly, "because when Americans are serious about something, they will sue each other. So we ought to sue each other until we drop."

A striking performance, closed off abruptly with an allusion to a higher summons ("And I must go, because my person is not my own"). Given the speaker's repeated returns to the argument about church-state separation, the central placing of that argument in the structure of the briefing, and above all the self-presentation (a virtuous man who has been there, who has seen and suffered with the sufferers and means by God to succor them), there wasn't space, time or will for discussion in his presence of issues beyond church and state. No issues, indeed, existed beyond church and state. The poverty problem, essentially traceable to "a correctable moral defect of individuals," demands an address to individual hearts and souls that no government can undertake: an address that calls for lovingly intense labor by those selflessly prepared to mortgage their house and their own children's future to help poor kids one by one. You are with us or against us and our "us" has no connection whatever with the cruelly oblivious taunters whose reign ended with the promulgation of compassionate conservativism.

The church-state debate continued for a time after DiIulio's departure from the briefing, and before the session ended, a minister-social activist—Jim Wallis, editor of the liberal magazine *Sojourners*—took the floor and raised the missing questions: whether "faith-based organizations [should] replace government responsibilities [and] become the cleanup crew for bad social policy, [fixing] what good social policy needs to help take care of." Wallis made all the pertinent points: faith-based organizations "can't provide healthcare for forty million Americans," "can't provide all the low income housing, the affordable housing necessary for working families," "can't provide supplemental income for senior citizens," can't end the "moral scandal" that we "have one of six childen poor in the most prosperous time in the richest nation in history." He urged that those organizations need to "weigh in with this administration about things like the tax cut proposal, which if it is as large as is being anticipated, has profound implications for people who are poor;" that they need also to "be very vigilant that we not just be service providers, but prophetic interrogators of why so many people are poor, and that we talk . . . about national agenda and national direction."

In thanking and saluting Wallis as a "cardcarrying moderate," the moderator used—smilingly—a dismissive codeword that recalled an age when anyone who linked government with fairness in social provision was a "Red sympathizer." But neither the dismissal nor Wallis's attempt to return the outlawed subject—"how to overcome poverty"—to the room counted for much. The argument about church and state had marginalized the matter.

And set the stage for the no-politics diversions that followed. It was barely a month after the birth announcement of Faith-Based Initiatives that *The Nation* ran the Ellen Willis attack on religious absolutism and "the earnest centrists and liberals who are doing [the] dirty work" of Bush and the Christian right. And, as already indicated, the piece launched a series of quarrels about relations between religion and democracy, and the arguments raged through the pages of subsequent issues—liberal leftists berating each other. Wallis himself was drawn into the scrap; his response to Willis raised none of the concerns that animated his words at the briefing; it concentrated solely on "the way that 'secular fundamentalists' like Willis continue to caricature and belittle religion and people of faith." (Willis answered that Wallis had "ignored what I actually said.")

The quarrels thus launched—Wallis against Willis, DiIulio against the world—were just beginning their run. Soon the opinionizing talk shows were chockablock with Pat Robertson and others fretting about government grants to Scientologists and the Nation of Islam; *Crossfire* featured the Rev. Al Sharpton going head to head with the Rev. Lou Sheldon of the Traditional Values Coalition about whether Faith-Based Initiatives" is or isn't, as Sharpton called it, "a trick"; C-Span broadcast forums in which Republican and Democratic legislators wrangled about the risks of "prosleytizing"; DiIulio and Jerry Falwell exchanged harsh words about each other (Falwell: "Obviously [John] doesn't know what he's talking about"); a group of black ministers announced themselves "impressed" after their White House meeting, on the Initiative, with Bush; much more lay ahead.

When the run ends, the country will emerge with tweaked millennial definitions of poverty as a character problem (a "correctable moral defect of individuals") to be measured against those found acceptable in the nineteenth and twentieth centuries. A victory will have been chalked up in the war on the appearance of indifference to poverty (the substitute, to repeat, for war on poverty itself). The Bush administration will have established itself as a pinned-down Gulliver, bursting with longing for the freedom that would allow it to serve the poor, but shackled by a mob of legalistic twits on the right and left. As for the trillions in "people's money" which, had the notion of fomenting a church-state debate not occurred to somebody shrewd, might have surfaced more prominently as a resource for social provision (underwriting, say, an expansion of the social development schools): that money will be on its way back to people many of whom might have been persuaded, by a sane political debate, not to begrudge its use for the benefit of the social whole.

Miniaturize. Personalize. Moralize. As the civility campaign and faith-based initative indicate, these are core precepts of no-politics politics in its most recent incarnation. The governing fantasy is that, in contemporary America, all forms of right and wrong flow from the good and bad behavior of neighbor to neighbor. Sustaining the fantasy calls for an undeviating focus on individual character—one reason the mantra of the Inaugural Address of 2001 specifically stressed character together with civility, compassion and courage. George W. Bush asserted that "Our public interest depends on private character"; he declared, further, that "If we do not turn the hearts of children toward knowledge and character, we will lose their gifts and undermine their idealism"; pursuing the point in his Budget Address, he noted that, because "Values are important . . . we have tripled funding for character education to teach our children not only reading and writing, but right from wrong."

To many in the immediate audiences for these first two speeches the phrase "character education" was unfamiliar—but within primary and secondary educational circles it's a name brand. Character Education became high fashion in the Nineties, featured in numberless conferences and summer seminars, rising to the status of a special field of graduate study, and becoming, at the apex, the central pledge made by Miss America 2001, a schoolteacher in Hawaii, in her drive toward the crown:

> *"First, I will urge every educational institution [promised Miss Hawaii] to adopt or create a formal, high-quality initiative that infuses character development into its daily school culture and curriculum.*

> *"Second, I will encourage schools to investigate the various character education options that exist and then choose or develop one that meets the unique needs of its students."*

An important link between civility promotion and character education is the shared emphasis on curbing criticism—ending "negativism" and fault finding, representing objections to things as they are as, necessarily, proof of a nagging uncooperative nature. Many public high schools with character ed curricula observe a regular "24-Hour Challenge" ("All school members are challenged for 24 hours to 'Resist the Urge to Criticize,' 'Make No Complaints,' etc.")

The following report on a Character Education gathering in Washington, DC dates from the mid-Nineties; it contains reminders of Clinton-era language on the "politics of personal meaning," as well as some detail regarding police roles in the character curriculum, in Texas, during the tenure of Governor Bush.

Morality Plays:
Inventing Character Education

ate last July 1994, when people of high principle gathered here in Washington for a White House conference on "Character Building for a Democratic, Civil Society," stories about Bill Clinton's character were dominating the news, along with speculation about how many millions in lawyers' fees Whitewater and meeting Ms. Jones might wind up costing the First Family. The conclave, however, wasn't about the "character problem" of the person in the White House. This was a White House conference about building character in us.

The host was the President's deputy assistant for domestic affairs: a political-science professor named William A. Galston. The conference organizer was The Communitarian Network, founded in 1991 by the sociologist Amitai Etzioni. The well over 200 character-building attendees were foot soldiers in America's mighty army of worriers about our declining moral fiber. The army's commanders were, of course, household names: Dan Quayle, of the mantra "Dan Quayle Was Right"; William Bennett, of *The Book of Virtues*; the First Lady herself, concerned about the "politics of personal meaning"; Peggy Noonan, announcing that "the New Frontier of the Nineties is an inner one."

The White House conferees consisted of foundation executives, school superintendents, "activist mothers," social scientists, church leaders, youth leaders, air force colonels, congressional aides, high school teachers, and front persons and lobbyists for such outfits as the Character Counts Coalition, the Character Education Partnership, the Center for Civic Education, and the Association for Supervision and Curriculum Development. Unlike their leaders, they were not celebrities; but like their leaders, they were wicked worrywarts—handwringers united by absolute certitude regarding the existence of a "crisis of values," an "erosion of culture," "a hole in the moral ozone [that's] getting bigger," and so on. (I was there by invitation.)

The announced purpose of the meeting was to "deliberate" on various character-education proposals, some of which were before Congress—a bill, for instance, appropriating $6 million to finance "the design and implementation of character education programs." The conference schedule called for morning and afternoon small group sessions at the National Press Club, with speeches afterward, at the Old Executive Office Building, by cabinet members, senators, and a possible mystery guest. (A pre-conference mailing pointedly emphasized that Deputy Assistant Galston was well regarded by the First Lady: "Hillary Clinton . . . acknowledges that she has been most influenced by the writing of Vaclav Havel and William Galston.")

Arriving early at the Press Club building on Fourteenth Street, I was directed to a top floor. Big lobbies and banquet rooms done up in mannish mahogany and high-gloss dark leather—an early-twentieth-century boardroom look suitable for magnates, not beat reporters. The corridors were filling with dressy, middle-aged, mainly WASP-featured types; the air was Class of '59 college reunion prior to serious drinking. "Oh, really," said a double-breasted blazer to a silk floral print as I edged past toward Registration. "I'm over in Scotland myself next year, doing moral education."

My badge checked out (no misspellings), and the glossy conference guide was chockablock with study material, copies of legislation—even a slick little lapel pin advertising the Character Counts Coalition (six pillars of virtue against a sky-blue background). Half a jammed corridor was given over to literature-handout tables piled with books, offprints, and paper from every organization present (there were scores) on institutional goals and pedigrees and "teaching strategies." I was stuffing my backpack when the summons came for a "briefing."

"There's a deep cultural and moral crisis," said Amitai Etzioni, the briefer—a small sixtyish man with wiry gray hair and mischievous eyes. The auditorium was overcrowded, dark, and windowless. "We must attend to the moral infrastructure. Values don't fly in on wings. . . . Children are little animals. . . . Members [of humanity] have been increasingly nonfunctional . . . "

Warm applause and we were bundled off to our groups—three dinky, airless rooms where the facilitator and rapporteur sat at one end with sixty or so conferees packed around them two and three deep on bridge chairs. People sorted themselves out slowly. There were the usual self-advertisers and hobbyhorse riders. Sixties bashers. A Sixties retread. An Anglophile extolled the English gift for doing religious education calmly in the schools. An Anglophobe explained that the English are atheists.

The emerging issue concerned whether the values to be taught in schools should be supplied from above or generated "from the community." Nathel Burtley, Flint, Michigan's superintendent of schools, inveighed against nitpicking, assuring the room that matters would go well as long as "the community, the community's values, were involved in the process." Larry Nucci, an Illinois educator, argued to the contrary that community values can't be trusted. "We'll begin to have problems," said Nucci, "if we take the values from the neighborhood, okay? If we say we'll get the values out of the community, we'll be sunk."

Discreetly my hand slid south, rummaging in my backpack. I inserted the history of the Character Counts Coalition into the Conference Guide and browsed as I listened.

The talk around me sounded tense, embattled; there was much use of the word "politics." A pertinacious, diminutive social scientist named Myriam Miedzian complained that "there's nothing here about entertainment. . . . These kids are wired from morning to night." A lady from Dayton dwelled an the completeness of the indoctrination provided by her city's character-education program (the local "value-word of the week" is inscribed everywhere, including school cafeteria place mats). Charles Haynes of Vanderbilt University's Freedom Forum complained that "what's missing for me is . . . civic virtue, the public square, rights, citizenship. If we begin there, it's easier to carve out the role for schools." An urgent-voiced elderly party complained that "there are no students here" and praised the private school he ran in Bath, Maine—an institution in which "students discover the purpose of societal values for themselves." "The way you really teach values," said this gentleman truculently, is by giving students "a chance to explore their own nature."

"Don't give me paradigms," I heard somebody say behind me, not quite claiming the floor. "I'm sick of paradigms. Let's do it."

No anger, no raised voices—but an undertone of edgy imminent militancy, as though it went without saying that enemies close by were spoiling for a firefight. What enemies? The conferees were against kiddie porn, broken homes, getting stoned, rudeness, laziness, murder in the schoolyard. Who exactly was for these things? Even the wildly left-leaning, far-out

New York Times doesn't advocate divorce or schoolyard slaughter.

The thought came that the politics of personal character or personal meaning might amount merely to a politics of no politics. Nothing in it but longing to transform all public issues into simple matters of good personal conduct versus bad—together, perhaps, with fear of dealing with the demands of fairness in social policy.

Sixties bashing had resumed among my fellow deliberators. Pulling a fresh sheaf of documents from my backpack, I was aware of a new restlessness in the rows—a reaction, maybe, to the dismal, shut-in cell. The facilitator began pushing harder for consensus. First Lady quips commenced. "I thought," said a front-row wit, "I thought we were just going to hand all this along to Hillary."

It was time for lunch.

Everybody from Prince Philip to Ken Burns has lectured in the National Press Club's storied mile-high banquet room, but the place serves a lousy meal. Wisely, the conference managers had extracted payment for lunch ($25) weeks before. Chicken-like pork or pork-like chicken, gallons of iced tea, circular tables seating ten. The university dean on my left told me he connected "character buffs" with New-Ageism—a movement that interested him. The young, pretty, elegantly dressed utilities rep on my right was uncommunicative.

A U.S. congressman who had authored many character-education bills was the main speaker; he quoted the wisdom of "the English poet Wadsworth." There was a panegyric on Sir John Marks Templeton, "the dean of global investing" and himself a character-education guru. Sir John's "Laws of Life Essay Contest" claims to provide "a unique opportunity to positively impact core values of a school"; his book *Discovering the Laws of Life*—free copies for all conferees—contains forty weeks of one-per-school-day moral lessons. (Week Twenty-Four, Law E: "Kindness comes back, like a boomerang, to those who are kind.")

No mystery guest showed. Relaxing in the Press Club library after coffee, I admired sunshiny Washington spread wide below. Outside in the lobby two Air Force character builders were discussing their uniforms. One was testing a new Defense Department model. The other felt the material approvingly, and the two had a laugh about the expense of the redesign. On a sequestered leather bench I settled into quiet time with my backpack.

Research report: the current character-education boom reflects not only the increasing popularity of doomsday chatter among the educated middle classes but the furious activity of the organization called the Character Counts Coalition. The hot doomsday topic of the moment is, naturally, schoolyard mayhem. "Why character education?" asks a Character Counts Coalition handout, and it answers in caps with "A FEW FACTS": a daily average of 16,000 crimes are committed on school property, a fifth of high school students say they're scared to use the lavatories, 135,000 students carry firearms to school, and so on. Kids screw up, so goes the concept, because they haven't been taught not to.

But the watershed moment in the recent history of character mongering seems not to have been some particular eruption of school violence or children killing children. The moment—described at length in another CC handout—occurred two years ago, during school vacation, in Aspen, Colorado, and involved the Twenty-Nine Character Counts "Declaration Signatories"—citizens who climbed the mount to frame a new covenant.

Moses at Horeb this occasion was not, one gathered. Instead of a single prophet there were a couple of rooms full—values education coordinators," "character education specialists," members of state education boards, psychologists in number, businesspeople (including the presidents of Good Idea Kids, Inc., and Sports Learning Systems, Inc.), and the angel of the entire enterprise—one "Michael Josephson, Esq.: President and CEO, Joseph and Edna Josephson Institute of Ethics, Marina del Ray, CA." Turned off by the wordiness of Old Testament commandments, the Twenty-Nine signatories chose People talk (their six "pillars"—respect, responsibility, trustworthiness, caring, fairness, and citizenship—were all one-word jobs). And instead of the sound of the voice of God on the mountain speaking out of the midst of the fire, the printed transcripts were filled with foxy grandpa manipulativeness and standard-brand mulishness—people digging in for "religious reverence" as opposed to "reverence," for "persistence" as opposed to "perseverance."

MICHAEL JOSEPHSON: I would just like to propose instead of "honesty" the word "trustworthiness." It involves a more subtle area, sometimes a lack of candor. You know, people think they're being honest sometimes as long as they don't lie, but sometimes not saying can be a betrayal of trust. We can embody some other things, like loyalty, etc.

DIANE BERRETH (facilitator): Okay, now are you guys going to discuss this? All right. Great. So the conversation right now is on honesty versus trustworthiness as to the best descriptor of this value.

KEVIN RYAN: You've got down here "work ethic." And I'd just mention a value that I think is really missing in American life, and certainly American schools, is persistence.

SYLVIA PETERS: Perseverance.

RYAN: As I look at my own children, one of the things I want them to do is be persistent. Learn how to stay with a task.

BERRETH: Okay. That's a new value you want on the list?

RYAN: Yeah. You might put it as an alternative to the work ethic.

BERRETH: Okay. Are there any others?

MIKE CAROTTA: It was on one of these lists. I think it was called something about "spiritual reverence" or something to that effect. I would like to propose it and see where it goes.

BERRETH: Okay. Do you want it to read "reverence" or "spiritual reverence.?

CAROTTA: "Spiritual reverence."

Roughly the same level of talk as in my small group.

In addition to a nascent apostolate (the Designated Signatories of the Aspen Declaration), Character Counts has Magnum P.I.—Tom Selleck—for its "national spokesman." It has more than fifty member organizations, from the American Federation of Teachers to Little League Baseball. Operating on an annual budget of $300,000, it produces an array of "Six Pillars" logo products, including not just lapel pins but patches, posters, "ethical thought bombs" (wallet cards bearing messages: "Ethics is not for wimps"), T-shirts, sweatshirts, hats—the works.

And because the signatories were first on the ground with selected virtues, the coalition has a head start in testing character-education materials—an advantage they've eagerly exploited in schools all across the country, from Brooklyn to Tyler, Texas. Lone Star enthusiasm is especially high, said a Wall Street Journal report included in the CC package. "Many schools declare a value of the month, which businesses advertise with signs in store windows or on billboards along the highway. Police officers hand out baseball-style cards featuring their pictures on the front and their favorite value on the back.... Sometimes, officers riding in squad cars will turn on their sirens and stop children for doing a good deed, giving them a certificate that allows them to enter a school raffle." Most important, the coalition has power in its pocket. Sixteen senators and representatives were primary sponsors of a Character Counts Week resolution approved by Congress. When President Clinton proclaimed National Character Counts Week in October, he said: "I call on the people of the United Stares and interested groups to embrace these Six Core Elements of Character [he named the CC pillars, one by one and to observe the week with appropriate ceremonies and activities ... integrat[ing] these Six Core Elements of Character into programs serving students and children." Character Counts has clout.

For the afternoon session our group had a new facilitator and a new rapporteur, but no large change of subject or improvement in the air. Colonel David Wagie, director of the Air Force Academy's Center for Character Development, spoke of military successes in addressing, via "the character perspective" and "the character approach," undefined "cases." Differences of viewpoint among the character builders grew clearer. Sitting with us was the head of the Character Education Partnership, a former school superintendent named A. John Martin. The partnership helps communities build consensus within themselves about character education; it doesn't come bearing precooked virtues like Character Counts. Neither does the other powerhouse in character politics, the Center for Civic

Education, also represented in the room. Like the Freedom Forum man who talked in the morning session, the center seeks to revitalize civics education—the public square, etc.

The morning notes of beleaguerment. and pugnacity lingered despite the clarification of differences. An argument started over what to call teen pregnancies, one conferee lobbying at length for "replac[ing] the word 'illegitimacy' with 'abrogation of parental responsibility.' " Others disagreed.

Your mom asked you not to play with your bat inside, but you did and accidentally hit the leg of a table. It is only a small chip off the table and she might not notice it. What do you do?

I was mired in a Character Counts folder of curricular materials. "Activities Preschool 1-6" stressed moral problems suitable for toddler cogitation. Illustrated ethical sayings for grade-schoolers carried echoes of Sir John Marks Templeton ("Respect is like a boomerang. If you respect others then in return they will respect you"). An exhibit of "personal dilemma" writing showed high-schoolers honing their casuistical aptitude and talent for self-laceration. Tuning out the group, I read about Fred, who dropped a fly ball in a championship game; life was a torment of options for the student author of this piece. *I could tease [Fred] like all the other kids, I could walk away from the situation, or I could stand up for Fred. If I joined in and started to ridicule him, I would hurt his feelings and I probably wouldn't feel good about myself. If I walked away from the situation I would be ignoring the whole thing and approving of what the other kids were doing. If I stood up for Fred I could stop the other kids from teasing him. I had a tough decision to make and I couldn't decide what to do.*

Sample diary entries showed American youth struggling day by day—possibly with devilment in its eye but obedient to Teacher's Assignment—to heed "at least one core ethical pillar/value."

Day #1: Today I was patient most of the time with my family and other people. Although I was patient, I insulted my brother about ten times. This makes me realize that I will have to try very hard to achieve my goals.

Day #2: Today I wasn't very patient with anybody. This could be due to lack of sleep considering I only got about six hours of it. Even though I was sleepy, my courtesy improved. I only insulted my brother six times, and I even apologized a couple of times.

Day #3: Today I did good in both categories, courtesy and patience. This might be because it is Friday and it is the last day of school before the weekend. I was very patient with everybody and I only insulted my brother four times.

Day #4: Today I did real good in both categories. I was very patient with everybody and I only insulted my brother twice. I feel good about myself because I was kind to other people.

"We just need to spell out the universal basic values." Feisty Dr. Myriam, the diminutive social scientist, was speaking again. "Spell them out very, very clearly. Explain that this is all about lying and cheating, nothing else. The basics. That allays parental fears."

"We don't have a consensus," said a loud, male, back-row voice.

"Suppose your student's father is in advertising," said Professor Edward Wynne of Illinois University's College of Education. "What will you tell him about lying?"

I felt a flicker of anger. Among the conferees there were differences, yes, but none of consequence. They all knew themselves to be, seemingly, morally superb. And the hilarious but scary student writing samples suggested that they could easily have 10 million schoolkids mouthing the same jargon tomorrow. Was there no limit to the zeal of the right-minded for battling phantoms? Did the Authorities really believe that their own absurd moral pretensions—their own self-serving public policies—bore no responsibility for offensive social behavior?

People of principle lament the collapse of decorum and simultaneously vote themselves annual pension subsidies and tax exemptions in the tens of billions of dollars—funds that build terraced perches, in country clubs and elsewhere, from which to observe and discuss the decline of values. They read with approval attacks on mindless mass reveling in TV freak shows and thwart every approach to levels of equity in public-school financing capable of moderating the mindlessness. In the space of three years, the total compensation of the average American CEO rises, in the midst of the age of downsizing, from forty times to ninety-three times that of the average factory worker—with no sign of an executive performance leap (or drop in worker productivity) to match the raise.

But here were the "goodies"—Emerson's name for the self-congratulatingly high-minded—"deliberating" as though these and related social realities were marginal and unworthy of remark. The Association for Moral Education, the Points of Light Foundation, the Giraffe Project, the "Enough Is Enough" Campaign, the Institute on Religion and Democracy, the Resolving Conflict Creatively Program, Critical Linkages Consulting, Cities in Schools, Inc., Christianity Today, Students Taking a Right Stand, Children Now, the United Church of Christ, the American Bar Association, and scores more—all battening on the same obliviousness. Each giving assent, direct or indirect, to the proposition that the national decline of respect and discipline, having nothing to do with the mounting greed and egomania of the privileged, can be reversed by supplying cops with value cards and teaching upcoming generations how to Hamletize about pop flies.

"You have a choice." Somebody official was talking at the front of the room. "You can walk the two blocks or there are buses around the comer on Pennsylvania. We have to ask you to move right along.

Small group was over. The conferees had made it almost to plenary.

Today looked better outside in the blazing muggy light. Packed tight in double-decker buses, dutifully waiting on the EOB steps to clear security, people sparked up cheerfully. "Just amazing," said a Character Counts rep a couple of steps above me to a fellow conferee, pointing his chin at the White House next door. The man was talking about White House reaction to a recent drop-in from Tom Selleck, CC spokesman. "Everybody fell all over themselves when they heard he was in, wanting to meet Tom, shaking his hand. He's so real. They all came down—Dave Gergen, McClarty . . . "

I had been looking forward to plenary—to the featured speaker, that is. William Galston's *Liberal Purposes* (1991) wrestles shrewdly with major political theorists of fairness from Oakeshott to Rawls and beyond. The book probes the link between the collapse of values and the collapse of fairness. It attempts to conjoin the truths of "traditionalists [who] charge liberals with ignoring or undermining self-discipline and self-restraint" with the truths of "liberals [who] charge traditionalists with ignoring or undermining the demands of fairness, particularly with regard to the least fortunate members of society." I sought my invitation to the conference partly out of curiosity about the author.

Galston showed up promptly—a short, small-boned, late-fortyish, euphonious-voiced man with big Clintonian hair (white). Affectionately, if slyly, introduced by Etzioni as a "philosopher-king," he described himself as someone "trying to tell truth to power." He told the conferees they were "an extraordinary assemblage" and added that when, at that morning's senior staff meeting, he had been asked to do a briefing for the President about the conference, everyone was fascinated—asked copies of the agenda and process, and so. "People came up to me and said, 'Wow.' "

The man's formal talk was a bust—further evidence that the price of "inside access" for intellectuals remains readiness to tell half-truth to power. Galston said not a word about fairness. He declared we are "somehow failing to transmit appropriate moral convictions, habits, and traits of character to the next generation," and treated character education in the schools as a promising solution He dismissed the notion that government can speak or act effectively against greed ("laws and regulations cannot adequately protect us against selfishness . . .") and saluted the Clinton Administration for its concern with "seedbeds of virtue" like the family, and for "respect[ing] and support[ing] the efforts of the bipartisan 'Character Counts' Coalition . . . "

"Seedbeds of virtue"—a true soul-darkener of a phrase—roused the troops of rectitude to an ovation. A long line of congrulators subsequently formed. "I love what you're doing," said one fan to Galston. "Love it, love it, love it." The euphoria lasted straight through adjournment to the famous Indian Treaty Room, where corporate sponsors were kindly pouring nice drinks.

For a while it was comedy and chaos that came to mind when I reflected on "Character Building for a Democratic, Civil Society." I thought of the kid diarist struggling to cut down on brotherly insults and remembered myself suppressing a giggle, mid-session, when I happened upon his screed. But this past fall as the big-gun character builders took their turn toward brazenness, humor faded fast. Quayle preening his moral plumage, Clinton sermonizing to the Baptists in New Orleans and Harlem. Natural enemies jointly bad-mouthing freedom instead of sensibly vilifying one another. Al Gore laying it down that he expects freedom to be exercised "with decent restraint," Bill Bennett laying it down that "Christianity does not endorse unfettered freedom." There seemed to be new relish in Charles Murray's voice as he pitched for lowering the boom on helpless pregnant teenagers. Dan Yankelovich was all nostalgia for the yesteryear when you could be ruined for life if you had a baby out of wedlock. Everywhere rampant punitiveness kept escalating—cop sweeps in housing projects, youth curfews, massive prison-building programs, caning proposals, three strikes and you're out, two years and you're off, kill the deadbeat dads, hang smokers, teach by-the-numbers necking, lockboxes on TV sets, jail cells for rappers.

What this country needs, I've had to conclude, is a good counter to the pillar virtues. For openers, try this: Never take a value card from a man in uniform with a blaring siren.

Several principles of no-politics politics are rooted in the myth that affirms the momentousness of one-on-one relationships—the faith already mentioned that all forms of right and wrong in contemporary life flow from good and bad behavior by neighbor to neighbor. Equal in importance to the principle that personal character is all is the principle that true leadership is essentially emollient in aspiration and function. True leadership doesn't, that is, frame or pursue agendas that reach beyond neighborhood comity or point a direction for public policy or alter distribution of resources. True leadership is a skill facilitating the harmonious interaction of upright neighbors. It not only avoids taking sides but implicitly holds that the ideal polity is side-less.

Disingenuousness, always and everywhere an element of no-politics politics, is a shade more visible here in the leadership principle than elsewhere. The reason is that, while leadership presents itself as a kind of abstract, contentless techne, no axes to grind, no overt platform, it has a cause, of course: the cause of changelessness —which is to say, the continuing strengthening of existing socio-economic advantage.

George Bush Senior was the first President to sign into law legislation authorizing federal funding of projects in "leadership education." There's ground for believing (see below) that at the time he signed the bill (1992) he didn't know what leadership education was, and he certainly could not have been aware, then, of how the theme of leadership as emollient would figure in his son's version of no-politics politics. It bears noting that leadership education wasn't singled out for attention in the 2001 Budget Address. On the other hand, it was praised repeatedly by Candidate Bush during Campaign 2000, and did earn mention in the 2001 package of education proposals. More significant, the chief qualification George W. Bush claimed for himself as Candidate was that he brought Texas Democrats and Republicans together. Developing precisely that ability—bringing together warring factions—is the avowed mission of leadership educators.

As for the connection between Character Education and Leadership Education: both are, in their main dimension, enterprises in miniaturization. Conflict is needless, says the Character Educator; it results from insufficient appreciation of one's neighbor, ignorance of the rules of right and wrong in personal relations, uncorrected habits of negativism, incivility. Conflict is needless, says the Leadership Educator; it results from ineptitude at techniques of one-on-one reconciliation, failures of Authority to dramatize harmony as the ultimate socio-political ideal, poor self-discipline, incivility.

The present writer learned by intention about Character Education; as the upcoming piece discloses, accident introduced him to Leadership Ed.

Leadership Cults and Coolants

One steam-broiled August morning in 1993 I found myself in a hotel conference room at 16th and M Streets in Washington, D.C., receiving instruction in how to judge grant proposals for something called the Dwight D. Eisenhower Leadership Development Program, a modest new slice of federal pork purveyed to the country's academic gentry courtesy of Senator Arlen Specter and Representative William Goodling, both of Pennsylvania.

I'm not, as it happens, a leadership scholar—wasn't even aware, in fact, that the genus "leadership scholar" existed. (I've been an English professor for forty years.) A government computer looking to assemble a panel of "peer readers" simply coughed me up. Academic jury duty is the name of this game—it pays stingily ($100 a day) but is otherwise painless; I'd been snagged for it a half-dozen times before.

This time, however, was different. Peer reading for the Eisenhower program emerged first as a fiasco, then as an education. I learned many new details about the ways of government waste, of which the Eisenhower program stands as a small, perfectly formed specimen. More important, I was introduced to the leadership-studies cult, a no-less-perfect specimen of late-twentieth-century academic avarice and a precise depth gauge of some recent professorial descents into pap, cant, and jargon.

The leadership cult, I discovered, embraces both public and private entities: governmental bureaucracies, nonsectarian youth agencies, academic institutions, the corporate complex. Its reach stretches from the Kennedy School's Leadership Education Project, at Harvard, and Penn's elite Wharton School and the Kettering Foundation (a major sponsor of specialized leadership research and publication) to the U.S. Military Academy (which requires cadets to study leadership in formal courses) and the YMCA, which conducts summer-camp-style "leaders' schools" for teenagers throughout the nation. As this suggests, the cult has many grassroots presences: state education departments and university extension services that support 4-H and other "leadership-training initiatives"; new, business-backed "leadership institutes" springing up at on-the-make private universities; a cluster of Eastern liberal-arts colleges pursuing images as leadership specialists; "centers for creative leadership" like the one at the University of North Carolina at Greensboro.

In some respects the leadership cult resembles a real culture. It possesses a distinct language. It honors heroes and texts comparatively unknown to the general public. It consistently defines past and present reality on its own terms. And it displays a strong determination to enlarge the spheres of its influence.

Thus far, the most visible sign of that influence is the enactment of the Eisenhower program—the show for which I was dragooned and a contender, arguably, for the title of worst-conceived taxpayer-financed program in the history of the republic. The program was enacted in 1992, part of that year's education amendments—the array of new, old, and restructured Education Department programs financed by annual congressional appropriations. By summer 1993 bureaucratic wheels were churning. A call for proposals ran in the Federal Register, producing 135 bids. The summons to read arrived in mid-July and included the text of the legislation—Part D of Title X of the Higher Education Act as Amended.

Congress hereby authorizes, said the text, $10 million for a program, "to be known as 'the Dwight D. Eisenhower Leadership Development Program,'" the purpose of which is to develop "new generations of leaders in the areas of national and international affairs." The program's primary "function" was defined as "stimulat[ing] and support[ing] the development of leadership skills among new generations of American college students." Other "functions" include "direct[ing] a national program that identifies, recruits, inspires, and educates outstanding young men and women regarding leadership roles," "develop[ing] curriculum for secondary and postsecondary education," and "stimulat[ing] the theoretical and practical study of leadership and leadership development. . . . "

Seemingly aware that the Eisenhower program was a turkey, the government managers in charge of the eighteen readers summoned to move the ball down the field evinced little relish for their responsibilities. On previous juries I'd been supplied with regulations interpreting the pertinent law. Not this time. The feds' letter of notification commented that "it was too late to go through that procedure." The same letter urged, in frantic capitals, that readers "BE SURE TO READ THE LEGISLATION." And, further, the letter listed substantive questions to be dealt with presumably at the opening briefing: "What is the definition of leadership? How does one teach leadership? and why! To whom should leadership be taught? When and where?"

You tell us.

At the initial briefing the program director, an earnest, harried, but somehow still-humorous thirty-year Education Department vet named Donald N. Bigelow, told us that a large number of American colleges and universities—close to six hundred—"now do something formal about . . . education for leadership." He added his personal view that teaching leadership "was like teaching sex—you can go just so far. . . . " Another, higher-ranking bureaucrat said that he himself had always thought leadership "was a trait," not an academic subject. With this guidance we were divided into two-person teams and dispatched to our rooms for a one-hour "training exercise." Pick a couple of applications, skim them, make notes, come back with your questions, and we'll help. We returned minus conventional questions but noisy and irritable.

Picture the usual economy-class-hotel meeting room, managers up front at the usual baize-covered table, readers seated in rows of folding chairs, the usual coffee, ice water, pens and pads available in the rear, traffic sounds just penetrating the windows. The managers said little, pointing to one raised hand after another as long as the meeting remained orderly, obliged to hear out the protests, powerless to alter the basic situation.

A gray-haired Californian in front of me asked acidly, "Is there any philosophy behind this thing? Should we talk about it?" From the rear: "This one I read claims they've been teaching leadership for fifty years. So why are we giving money to colleges to teach what they've been teaching for fifty years?" A professor from Arkansas raised the issue of fairness: the Federal Register said the grants would average around $175,000 but the pitch she was reading asked for a million. With a million you can do a lot you can't do with a fifth of a million. "Shouldn't this be thrown out?" Another voice from the rear: "This is bullshit, really. Nobody can teach this stuff. You can't have a curriculum. All you can do is some hands-on out in the community. Identify people and go out and do something, for Christ's sake."

A late-arriving, short, trim, fiftyish gent on the aisle—a teacher of "Quality Management" at a midwestern state university who turned out to be my own teammate—defended the enterprise. "Look," said he in a reasoning tone. "You're going to get some repetition of words. Commitment, empowerment . . . What you do is look beyond, at the conceptualization. Is it logical? Has it got the overlay of science? Remember," he told us, "nothing is as practical as good theory. There has to be a science overlay."

Suddenly, all eighteen readers were talking at once and the director at the front of the room was shouting to make himself heard. He could have assembled a group of eighteen specialists in "the field," he said, but the present route was better. "We have a number of specialists who write on leadership, but most of you haven't even thought about it." Struggling, sweating, the man shook his head: "This is the first time I've had a panel many of whom don't know a damned thing about what they're judging. . . . Usually people have a glimmer."

The room erupted once more. "It's messy," the director cried out into the din. "I know it's fuzzy. . . . But we're not going to get our oar in. You have to be the judge."

End of briefing.

A bit of genealogy: The current leadership boom has at least one root in an early 1980s pop phenomenon—best-selling business manuals such as *Management Secrets of Attila the Hun*, *The One-Minute Manager*, and *A Passion for Excellence* by Tom Peters and Nancy K. Austin. Leadership theory then trickled down (or up) into the universities and the public sector; the Eisenhower program heralds its arrival. As leadership scholars snuggle to the new public teat, a new industry and special interest are born.

I learned during Eisenhower peer reading week that the leadership cult's quasi-official language is a blend not only of

Tom Peters and John Naisbitt but of Thomas Kuhn, Zen, Pentagonese, and traditional psychobabble as well. Keywords and phrases include "megaskill," "capstone experience," "futures-creative," "program design matrices," and "diversity training." Key proverbs and sayings are pretentiously gnomic. ("Your self is your paradigm." "Your paradigm is that part of you which your enemy wants to know.") Literary tastes within the leadership alliance are erratic—the works of Ayn Rand are canonical and read in full; Tolstoy is read in snippets.

Further new knowledge: The U.S. Military Academy has a Department of Behavioral Studies and Leadership. One of the nation's first schools of leadership studies is at the University of Richmond, in Virginia, and it appears to be heavily endowed—financially. The school's basic course, taught by a Dr. J. Thomas Wren and entitled Foundations of Leadership Studies, includes as required reading Aristotle, Plato, Machiavelli, Tolstoy, and Marshall Sashkin, author of "Visionary Leadership: The Perspective from Education." (Five pages of *War and Peace*, eleven pages of *The Republic*, seven pages of Aristotle, four pages of Machiavelli, a quantity of Marshall Sashkin.)

Yet more learning: tenured academicians belonging to the leadership cult have delivered papers at "administrative leadership" conferences on the following topics:

"Robert Browning's "My Last Duchess": A Contrast in Management Styles."
"Lessons for Leadership in T. S. Eliot's *Murder in the Cathedral*."
"Group Dynamics and Crisis Management in *For Whom the Bell Tolls*."
"Christopher Marlowe and the Crash of 1987: Literary Lessons for the Contemporary 'Overreacher.' "

The Eisenhower applications ranged in length from fifty to one hundred pages, and the level of discourse was by no means uniform. A few proposals were ambitious and displayed the theoretical sophistication my teammate desiderated. (The most ambitious, from the Wharton School, proposed "a cross-cultural study of leadership to be conducted in approximately forty nations.") But despite institutional differences in location and presumed academic distinction, sameness ruled overall.

Time and again applicants recited the views of Max DePree, former CEO of the Herman Miller furniture company and author of *Leadership Is an Art* (1989), concerning leadership and bicycles. ("We have placed a restriction on the use of our bicycles [in the manufacturing plant]. No supervisor may ride one. . . . You can't have a conversation or ask a question from a bicycle.") Endlessly the grantsfolk warned in italics that "the definition of leadership skills cannot be static, but must incorporate traditional, current and evolving knowledge of what leadership is."

The same allegedly seminal leadership theorists (John Gardner and James MacGregor Burns) were quoted by one applicant after another; one after another the proposals cited the same allegedly revelatory business-press articles. A 1988 *Fortune* piece, "What Makes for Magic Leadership?" was accorded reverence befitting Paul's second letter to the Corinthians.

Grammar sucked ("There is a major difference in today's world than in the world of yesterday's great leaders": Arizona). Spelling was relaxed ("DeGaulle and Miterand [sic] are examples": the Wharton School).

The following is a sampling of the initiatives proposed:

- The University of Richmond wants to publish a humanities skim-creaming anthology of snippets of Tolstoy,

Plato, Sashkin, and others on leadership. ("Only such a reader—carefully organized and annotated—can provide the student with this kind of depth and texture in the study of leadership.")

- West Texas A & M will bring one hundred "at-risk fifth graders to campus for a leadership workshop," will "present sixteen 'Rap and Eat' programs to campus and four programs to public schools" (the group to be hired is called Chillin' Time), and will conduct "peer education" in fields such as "You Booze You Lose."

- The University of Arizona wants to spend tax money redesigning an existing course called The Spirit of Inquiry into a new course called The Spirit of Leadership. The old course was a variety show meeting once a week on topics ranging from extraterrestrial intelligence to Mexican folklore to "It Ain't Over 'Til the Fat Lady Sings'—a discussion, so titled, of Verdi's *Don Carlo*. ("The intrigue of a royal triangle is played out against the fiery background of the Inquisition and Spain's lust for conquest.") The new course will keep the sparky magazine format.

- Wayne State bets on "leadership development seminars" to develop new habits in "a cadre of young leaders." (The new habits are those "proferred [sic] by Stephen Covey in his 1989 book *The Seven Habits of Highly Effective People* . . . [The young leaders] will focus on Covey's 'Paradigm of We.' ")

Tax dollars will also underwrite a "Washington International Walkabout"—six days of visits "to the State Department, Congress, the Department of Education, and the Smithsonian Institute [sic]. (At each site visit, students will be asked to think about and respond to the following questions: 1) What do you think the agency does?

2) What is the agency's role in foreign policy? 3) Where does the agency get its operating money?)"

- Clemson plans its own federally financed Walkabout, but Clemson walkers will spend twice as long in South Carolina (ten days) as in Washington, and "will gain actually diverse experiences as well as enrichment through interaction with leaders who have overcome physical disabilities." The university will broadcast its leadership vision. ("A five-meter FU band satellite uplink-downlink mounted atop the Communications Center facility . . . a separate C/KU downlink and portable C-bandlink are available," etc.)

On the face of things, a gap yawns between West Texas A & M ("You Booze You Lose") and the Wharton School ("cross-cultural study" of forty nations); the class factor was everywhere evident in bids for leadership money. But much of the poignancy of the leadership cult—and much of its power to disturb—arises from the truth that it appears to have succeeded in binding its socially varied sectors into a unity. Leadership-cult top dogs have managed, in short, to convince bottom dogs as well as themselves that the country's problems stem not from evaded issues of injustice or inequality but from technically faulty administration.

A query: Whatever prompted elected officialdom to guide this beast to the public trough? Signs indicate that the Pennsylvania Republican sponsors—Specter and Goodling—had in mind nothing more than diverting a tiny rivulet of the mighty federal cash cascade to an upright local institution by the name of Gettysburg College. On the Senate floor, as he "put in" the Eisenhower program, Senator Specter quoted Ike telling a Gettysburg College convocation that "the future of our country depends upon enlightened leadership"; he also commended Gettysburg College for "helping ensure that Eisenhower's legacy of leadership will continue to exercise a beneficial influence on the nation he loved."

There was, of course, no House or Senate debate on the program; like hundreds of other "minor" bits of federal largesse in the past, the thing was simply folded into a quiet corner of a major bill by prior arrangement with the bill's managers. According to an Education Department worker I talked to, Gettysburg administrators assumed that most of the money appropriated would go directly to Gettysburg College because the school was an Eisenhower neighbor and a leadership-cult leader. (Gettysburg has a Department of Management led by a "Professor of Eisenhower Leadership Studies.") But that dog didn't hunt: the department's bureaucracy insisted on a competition.

George Bush signed the 1992 education amendments, including the Eisenhower program, at a Virginia community college jollyup, and he waxed inspirational at the close of his remarks. "We are toiling upward in the night," he declared, "and today we climb a little bit higher. And when we've reached our plateau, we will look out upon a new generation of American schools and a stronger foundation for our nation."

Most of what Bush said—to the amusement of all—dealt with the likelihood that the contents of the legislation he was signing were unknown. "After this is over, we're going to pass these [amendments] out to everybody, and then tonight we will have a quiz [laughter] on the ingredients therein."

But although the grand unifying assumptions of the leadership culture surfaced nowhere in the paper trail, they were fully visible in the Eisenhower applications themselves. The grantswriters' first assumption, frequently repeated, was that scorn of leaders is a major destabilizing force in American society, and that "leadership training" can solve this problem. The grantswriters' second assumption, also often repeated, was that the American people are as one in their desire for change (referred to invariably as "positive change," specifics undefined) but are frustrated because they are unschooled in the arts and skills of effecting change.

Old ghosts walk in both assumptions. One ghost is terror of a self-aware, politicized proletariat—the age-old mugwumpish fear that the mob may organize to destroy the last fragile vestiges of civilized life. Social-scientese natter about paradigms differs in tone and level of literacy from yesteryear's self-pity as voiced by Henry Adams, William Graham Sumner, or the Charles Eliot Norton who laid it down that *"The Nation* and Harvard Yale College" stand alone as "barriers against the invasion of modern barbarism and vulgarity." Its accent seems distant, too, from that of Richard Hofstadter in a more recent celebration of leadership—*Anti–Intellectualism in American Life* (1963). But the importance of these tonal differences can be exaggerated; fear of the mob lies deep in the American grain, and the leadership culture reflects its continuing pervasiveness.

The other ghost in leadership cant is that of America as the land of happy consensus. Beamish jingoes in the history trade have long worked at instilling belief that seemingly profound and fiercely articulated social conflicts in this country actually are figments, that all good Americans share a feeling for the Universal Unwritten Understanding in the Sky, and that if people of intelligence will but consent to work together, no so-called serious political or cultural issue need ever be joined.

One reason for this vision's current vitality is the arrival of neoliberalism—the Clintonian gospel slyly proclaiming that Harvard/Rhodes slickness can negotiate any domestic-or foreign-policy issue into nothingness. (Labor Secretary Robert Reich edited a leadership tome in 1990; it contained, among other pieces, an essay called "Political Leadership: Managing the Public's Problem Solving," by the director of Harvard's Leadership

Education Project.) The two operative political fantasies here, which are shared by "enlightened" corporate types, hold that: (1) there are no major differences of interest in American society demanding fair settlement; (2) ways of evading the responsibilities and entailments of a democratic political system can always be found. The new key to successful evasion lies in teaching upcoming generations, from fifth grade onward, how to pretend—as more than one Eisenhower application pretended—that the key explanation for urban disasters such as Camden, New Jersey, is that the residents were never properly trained in conflict management and team building.

Leadership non-believers among the readers—we took to calling ourselves antis—didn't go quietly. We pressed for low scores, wrote hundreds of critical words on evaluation sheets explaining why this or that project shouldn't fly, and pushed unsuccessfully (not enough time, said the bureaucrats) for a plenary session at which general reservations could be aired. At lunch and dinner and in the bar we told one another that "this leadership racket" was only the latest stage in the depressing struggle for the American soul waged by elitism and populism, twin killers of democratic hope—only another sign of Establishment enthusiasm for replacing politics with social science, open argument with manipulated consent.

Ceaselessly we harped on the themes of governmental, academic, and corporate waste and corruption. Bitterness mounted on getaway eve when final reports about grades—proof of the nonexistence of a standard by which to judge a leadership project—began circulating. It emerged that one team gave more than twice as many "A" grades as were given by the eight other teams combined. No problem, our Ed Department handlers told us: computers would "normalize" the scores and the appropriated funds would be spent.

At this news our table of antis fell silent. Later, over coffee, someone said in a taking-it-in voice, "I don't believe this. I mean, I find it disgusting." The Californian who had asked a question about philosophy at our first briefing nodded gravely; the table went on to another subject.

Our resistance to leadership cant originated, doubtless, in a vestigial memory of husbandry—some notion of careful-ness and frugality as values in themselves. Implicit in the dutiful, wordy critiques we broke our wrists writing was the conviction that good and bad—norms and structures—exist and that only the foolish pretend otherwise. Wasters of tax revenues (from Star Warriors to mohair subsidizers) and even their self-proclaimed enemies (Clinton-Gore government reinventors) have moved some distance, to be sure, from what are now called "values issues." Questions about moral impact—how waste works, the processes of corruption and enervation it sets in train—aren't asked. Might a Washington Walkabout introducing sophomores to the craft of junketry inspire cynicism, not leadership? Who knows or cares? Obvi-ously someone should know and care.

But in the story of the leadership cult, as in many others resembling it, the emptying of a bag of millions to the winds is in truth only a sidebar. The substantial meanings reside else-where, in the rationale behind the waste—the purposes the waste is meant to serve. It is, finally, a mere incidental that the leader-ship cult squanders tax dollars; what matters is that the cult appears eager to squander the democratic essence as well.

A corollary of the no-politics rule holding that leadership should abolish sides is that leadership should also banish "side" (the old-timey New England sense of the word). Leadership should seek our views, in short—should wear a vulnerable face and look pained when obliged to behave in accord with hierarchy's dictates. It should celebrate the mystique of participation—because participation fosters unanimity. Among the outward signs of commitment to anti-side leadership: informality of manner, absence of cultural pretension, readiness to tease one's own ignorance and laziness.

Partly the anti-side project is simple garnish on traditional American hostility to elites, powered by anti-intellectualism and democratic patriotism. But more specific and surprising factors are at stake, not least of them the developing wars of management theory from the mid-Sixties onward. The texture of contemporary apoliticality reflects a consensus about leadership style hammered out in that period.

Courses in "Leadership" are taught, today, in several graduate schools at Harvard University, including the John F. Kennedy School of Government. But in George W. Bush's Cambridge such instruction had only one home: the Graduate School of Business. The Biz School in Bush's period of residence was a rather less sleepy place than hitherto. Japan had emerged as a presumed pinnacle of illumination as regards management skills. Countercultural visions of the good society had unsettled settled opinion about power and its ways. Bestsellers in the works—by futurologists and others—were framing new visions of corporate possibility and new standards of distinguished executive performance.

Discussion of George W. Bush's conversancy with management theory has tended to concentrate either on externals—team structures, patterns of delegation inside the White House, management by objective, and the like—or on the preoccupation with voice and tone. Insufficiently heeded are the tensions and conflicts that can be traced back to yesteryear's countercultural rows. Interest was mounting, during Bush's time at Harvard, in changing the image and behavior of chief executive officers. Quality circles in Japan stressed intimacy between supers and underlings—equality as a stimulant to productivity. The counterculture had insisted on the primacy of feeling, rejecting stereotypes of toughness, honoring tears, aligning itself (when not demonstrating) with the party of playful tenderness. And these themes infiltrated the larger society. Futurologists and business writers put them in play in corporate America and its favored institutions of higher business learning, arguing that the business hero needed to be reconceived—softened, humanized. Naturally their line of argument was mocked by traditionalists who despised the new dogmas as sentimentality. Battles raged in business papers and in the "quality" monthlies. But nobody who tried to run a business in the Eighties—oil business, baseball business, whatever—could easily avoid exposure to the battles, whether or not he or she turned the pages of Toffler or Tom Peters or Business Week. *High fashion recommended an end to kneejerk bottom line harshness, and the beginning of displays of intense concern for underlings. Critics of high fashion took aim at the new cults of feel-their-pain management, thundering that Authority must keep its strong hand on the tiller.*

Toward the close of the 20th century cultural historians began to focus on the remarkable ways in which countercultural influence as channeled by business—particularly advertising—affected popular beliefs and tastes. (See for example Thomas Frank's stimulating and thorough The Conquest of Cool, *1997.) But by then time had eroded memory of the resistance to that influence. And the resistance matters.*

The decades-old conflict between business traditionalists and innovators can be felt in current White House compromises: in the having-it-both-ways strategy that promotes the Chief Executive as easygoing, relaxed, and democratic while demanding strict staff adherence to chain-of-command rules and decorum. The essay ahead reports on the bookish quarrel in progress a quarter-century ago—between business theorists and futurologists, and their critics—about whether the time had come to replace the CEO as old-style, remote, hardnosed Top Dog with the CEO as gemutlich, sideless, self-teasing true pal. That quarrel is among the odder corners of site preparation for the edifice of "soft," compassionate, no-politics politics to come.

The Weeping CEO: Anatomy of a New Business Hero

Iacocca . . . *A Passion for Excellence* . . . *In Search of Excellence* . . . *Reinventing the Corporation* . . . Business books were hot tickets in the Eighties, and in theory this was good news for the political right. In benighted earlier times muckrakers made the bestseller lists; negative business images proliferated; abuse of corporation hands as greedy, dull, stiff, cold, timid, abstract, arrogant, conformist, bureaucratic and hierarchical was a convention. The new celebrations of entrepreneurism seemed to confirm a new disposition in embryo. The place of business in national life was growing less embattled, more comfortable; irreversible cultural change was under way.

As it happened, though, there was nothing like agreement on what the new business leader should look like or about standards for evaluating business conduct in a new cultural climate. The business P. R. picture was, in a word, problematic. Practical works such as Mark McCormack's *What They Don't Teach You at Harvard Business School* were innocuous—plainspoken guidebooks providing advice to fledglings about "how to read people," how to "take the edge," when to order Perrier, when to order Scotch, other business skills. But business books with grand, image–transforming ambitions were selling even better than McCormack's guide, and they occasioned concern. Both social critics and academicians within the business establishment fretted publicly about them. No casual browser could miss the conflict ripening in their pages.

The trouble sprang mainly from incompatible versions of the business hero—the newly reconceptualized, refurbished business hero. Bestselling business writers shared a belief that business leaders were attractive people and that conceptions of corporations as faceless and colorless were wrongheaded. But they shared little else. Some were committed to the notion that sensitivity was the virtue that deserved emphasis in tributes to new entrepreneurs. Others were keener on roughhewn individualism. And many were muddled about both values. In some books the new Sensitives resembled mawkish wimps; elsewhere roughhewn individualism was indistinguishable form knee–jerk macho; business organizations themselves were frequently mistaken for religious assemblages or theaters of epic adventure and combat. Impressionable young entrepreneurs in need of models were badly served by all this—could, indeed, have been split down the middle, impaled in executive maturity on contradictory ideals.

Two books by futurologists—*The Third Wave* (1980) by Alvin Toffler, and *Megatrends* (1982) by John Naisbitt–figured in the background. Neither possessed intellectual distinction; Toffler's was rambling, self-indulgently repetitive, often vexingly cute ("the new indust–reality"); Naisbitt's was dense with cliches. What counted for the actual as opposed to the fantasized future was that each was sanguine about the prospects for tomorrow's business civilization. Each hailed a revolution in progress in the American work world— a revolution on behalf of human scale, humane work–places, management–work force unity, joy through information and innovation. And each was vastly popular (*Megatrends* and *The Third Wave* sold, respectively, six million and four million copies.)

The popularity can be variously explained. Throughout the previous half-century, wolf-criers had regularly threatened audiences with nightmares—death by managerial revolution, hidden persuaders, media hype, computers, The Bomb, energy crisis, inflation, unemployment. Yet the majority still found itself awakening in the morning, getting children to the bus and itself to work . . . A we–have–come–through psychology was nascent, bringing with it an appetite for non–doomsday–syndrome versions of the high tech future—an appetite further whetted, in the Eighties, by the entrancing optimism of the winning presidential candidate. Toffler (cautiously) and Naisbitt (less cautiously) fed the appetite, borrowing freely from upbeat predictions about technology put into print, much earlier, by Marshall McLuhan, celebrator of the Global Village.

There was one other factor—subtle, surprising, consequential—behind enthusiasm for the Toffler and Naisbitt gospel, namely its hospitality to certain themes and motifs of the countercultures of the Sixties and Seventies: Small is beautiful, back to the land, unisex, feminism, openness, participation, simplicity, do–your–own–thing. The futurologist found "second wave" offices and plants to be places haunted by facelessness and powerlessness; nobody felt happy in them, nobody was capable of charting an individualistic course unintimidated by hidebound carpers, nervous Nellies, moldy figs, "squares." Toffler and Naisbitt also found second-wave places to be haunted by insensitivity—the specter of brutal money–obsession, blindness to the existence, in coworkers and underlings, of human feelings.

And they imagined a future in which qualities dear to folks concerned about feelings became norms. Tomorrow's ideal work world (for Toffler) would be bare of bureaucratic plodders and stuffy authorities; workers and managers would collaborate like jazz musicians picking up cues from each other—like people who, because they're "complex, individualistic, proud of the ways in which they differ from other people," always behave "sensitively." Naisbitt's metaphors pictured the coming workplace as a learning community (he and his collaborators predicted an imminent exchange of identities between corporations and universities). Both writers were speaking about work not play, about jobs not flower-power demonstrations or communal rituals. But the work world they envisaged was nevertheless decentralized and sunny—filled with kindly people who, as they briskly cope with new "information/mass ratios," rejoice in the clean comfort of the "electronic cottage," and utter no autocratic or other exasperating word. No need, in this easy-to-love future, to turn truant in order to breathe free.

The business utopians weren't the only progenitors of the new friendliness toward business. (Another important voice was that of George Gilder, who presented capitalism as love in *Wealth and Poverty*.) The good feeling needed, furthermore, a pro-business sitting President to fan it, and probably couldn't have survived a lengthy economic downturn. But sustained cheer of any kind requires more than a merely political or economic shelter. To those craving poetry and hope, a dream to replace the nightmares, Toffler and Naisbitt offered the boon of a direction, a detailed pointer. Go, they said, go where Americans have always gone for fresh nourishment of the dream. Not to religion or art or scholarship or controlled substances, but to where the action is, and the rich resources. Go to the can-do world of business; this is the place where vital new values will be found.

Conscious mythmakers following in the wake of such a vision couldn't have missed their marching orders. The task was to fashion business heroes in whom individualistic potency and resolution are combined with nonauthoritarian, flower-power compassion and playfulness—figures of broad emotional range who meet payrolls and marketing targets on schedule yet remain delicately in touch with their feelings and their humanity. Probably there were no conscious mythmakers, there almost never are—but there were, seemingly all at once, numerous best-selling business books describing real-life business leaders who were, to a man (no women here), vulnerable apostles of love.

The most famous of these works, *In Search of Excellence* by Thomas J. Peters and Robert H. Waterman Jr. and *A Passion for*

Excellence by Tom Peters (Thomas J. Peters using a chummier version of his name) and Nancy Austin, were books intended as definitions and descriptive catalogues of first-class corporate performance. The introduction to *A Passion for Excellence* declared that "the best bosses . . . are neither exclusively tough nor exclusively tender," but in the body of the work sympathy and tenderness were the authors' constant preoccupation. Their chapter titles and subtitles—"Emotion and Feel: Being Human," "Empathy," ". . . and Love"—sent a clear message. So, too, did their slogans ("Love translates into joy"), their emphasis on intimate, sharing corporate communities and their management "musts": "You gotta love . . . you gotta care." The authors quoted with approval a Xerox executive's claim that "the most commonly practiced crime in industry today is a fundamental insensitivity toward personal dignity." They were ecstatic over a bill of rights for employees of the Herman Miller furniture company, that included "the right to be needed." And, most striking, they were ceaselessly on the alert for the special quickness to tears that, for them, was the talisman of managerial goodness.

A retiring Delta Air Lines chairman showed emotion as he recalled the generosity of his employees ("There was wonder in his voice. His eyes misted over"); Peters and Austin were moved. Hearing a speech by an Army lieutenant general on the subject of a leader's fast attachment to his followers, Peters "listened and wept." *A Passion for Excellence* did not contend that managers alone are capable of the requisite demonstrativeness. On occasion its pages reported on line employees, who, because they were well-treated, themselves passionately cared: "When the steelworkers saw the problem their defects were causing, they were 'practically in tears.' "

But it was management–level vulnerability that truly excited the authors. The model to whom they repeatedly returned was Tom Melohn, chairman of North American Tool & Die. At one moment in the book Mr. Melohn is asked what he looks for in a prospective employee:

"Melohn scribbles something on a table napkin, hides it momentarily, and asks Elli Parrnelli, the office manager who makes the hiring decisions along with Melohn, what she looks for. She answers without hesitation: 'Someone who's a caring person.' . . . As Melohn looks at Parrnelli and nods his agreement, his eyes are filled with tears."

At another moment Mr. Melohn is honored because "talking about his people, [he] broke down in front of television cameras during the filming of our January 1985 PBS special."

Portraits of the Sensitive as CEO were not enough, in themselves, to fill out the myth of the new business hero. A redirected how–to literature was needed (how to become sensitive, that is), as were uncompromising declarations, by recognized authorities, that companionability not profit is the true name of the business game. These arrived swiftly. Whole chapters in business books following Peters's and Austin's were devoted to instructing corporate managers in techniques of demonstrativeness, vulnerability–incitement, tear–production and the like. In *The Making of the Achiever: How to Win Distinction in Your Company*, a work dense with paeans to warmth and vulnerability at the top, Allan Cox observed that "warmth is not only the province of the do–gooders and naive, but also of those top executives who thrive in their jobs." A management consultant, Mr. Cox provided tests enabling top dogs to rate their softer sides: "My Warmth Index," "My Vulnerability Index." (Sample question: "Do visitors and subordinates feel uncomfortable in your office?") And he offered step-by-step counsel on how to loosen up and become "your most innocent, childlike, and audacious self."

As for uncompromising pro-companionability declarations: one of the strongest appeared in yet another business bestseller—*Re-inventing the Corporation* (1985) by John Naisbitt and Patricia Aburdene. This work opened with kudos for a company that rated the objective of "having fun" on a par

77

with that of making money, and it moved on to praise the sporting style as glimpsed in another, real-life, medium-sized corporate headquarters: "The CEO's office was so nice, with such a great view, that the CEO moved out and it is now used by everyone." Soon thereafter the authors bite the bullet, voting up a guideline requiring customers to be sensitive, and proposing that, in judgments of business success, the quality of social intercourse take priority over profit. One executive revered by the authors announced his fundamental rule: "We only do business with people who are pleasant." Make love, not deals.

Traditional, hardboiled, hardheaded business personalities didn't instantly vanish from the business press, of course. They not only remained highly visible but were in some contemporary representations—perhaps in reaction to the teary competition— rather corkier than in the past. Business statesmen loyal to this older model tended to begin discussions with brusque denials that the business hero's personality was worth wasting any words over. Business literature is "full of stories of the 'entrepreneurial personality,' " said Peter Drucker in *Innovation and Entrepreneurship*, but "in the light of our experience—and it is considerable—these discussions are pointless." The essentials for achievement are sound strategies and proper "policies and practices." People who preach otherwise, crying up emotion and fun, and downplaying discipline, are on a dangerous course. Drucker defined sound strategies in military lingo, drawing on "battle-winning Confederate" commanders in the Civil War. The key strategies are: "1. Being 'Fastest With the Mostest'; 2. 'Hitting Them Where They Ain't.' " There was continual reference to "dominating the market" and "dominating the industry" and to management techniques summarized as "entrepreneurial judo." There was no talk whatever of companionability, love or whimper-competency tests. Implicit on nearly every page was a vision of the business hero not as an amalgam of St. Francis and Woody Allen but as a general officer in supreme command during a shooting war.

Which is to say, as Lee Iacocca. In his 1984 autobiography, Iacocca, the often-embattled Ford executive who switched to Chrysler, presented himself as a scrappy, straight-talkin' hombre prepared to lay it on the line, any day, to top brass, "working guys," whomever. "If a guy's giving me a lot of baloney," said Iacocca, "I tell him to buzz off." "Your timing stinks," he told his employer, Henry Ford Second. "You don't know how . . . we made [the money] in the first place." The author sometimes compared himself to an Army surgeon in combat, but more often his favored self-characterization was as on-the-line field commander:

"I like to be in the trenches. I was never one of those guys who could just sit around and strategize endlessly." "I flourish where the action is." "I was the general in the war . . . I had to go into the pits."

In *Re-inventing the Corporation* Ms. Aburdene and Mr. Naisbitt commented favorably on a new corporate institution called the "quiet room"—a sanctuary from "day-to-day stress" to which playful, fun-loving, tender-hearted executives could repair at will for renewal. Obviously General Iacocca would have shut this place down.

Even harder-edged than the portrait of General Iacocca was that of Tom West, hero of *The Soul of a New Machine* (1981), Tracy Kidder's account of the building, by Data General, under competitive pressure, of a super mini-computer. A Data General business development executive, West is introduced in an opening chapter that takes place on a small sloop bound for New York from Casco Bay, Maine. Foul weather strikes and instantly the executive, who isn't the sloop's captain, takes charge ("his face is lifted, his lips pursed"). West, the businessman "at the helm," "the person in command," shames the rest of the crew—a doctor, a professor, a psychologist. They get sick, he doesn't. They become exhausted, he's indefatiguable. (" 'He didn't sleep for four nights!' ") When the captain frets, West laughs ("a low and even noise"). When others try to engage West in small talk, he's pure Ahab, imperious, remote.

"All leadership is show business," Peters and Austin declared; in Tracy Kidder's account, Tom West's leadership style is authentic showbiz—but again, *sans* misty eyes. From start to finish this is a new-age image of macho sublime—a hell-for-leather skipper racing to cut off the competition upwind, a toughie who'll deck anybody dim enough to chide him about his low Vulnerability index. Impossible to imagine Admiral West gently sharing with a confidant. Impossible to imagine General Iacocca as a love-in softie melting at the phrase "caring person." And, given the evident discontinuity between these figures and the flower-power bosses desiderated by Peters and Austin, impossible to miss the image gap that had opened in business leters. The academic business establishment was especially concerned about the situation, as I said. In *The New Competitors*, D. Quinn Mills, a Harvard Business School professor, condemned promoters of "buzzwords" and "current fads of management" who claimed that corporate America should be considering a momentous choice of leadership style. In successive chapters he treated a series of standard business problems—coping with management-level deadwood, waiting out losses incurred by a division experimenting with nonhierarchical work systems—as case studies proving the senselessness of strict adherence to either a hardline or soft-line approach. "Top performers succeed," Mills wrote, "by a judicious combination of old principles and new ways of applying them." Trust eclecticism, in a word. Forget about reinventing the corporation. Back off from these new dogmas of total democracy and passionate love.

But not too far back—not so far that you miss the benefits that can accrue from wary, limited submission to their dictates. Just here, in the fine-tuning of adjustments to themes hyped in the new buzzwords, lay the problem for the business mentality—and really for all officialdom as well. Essentially the problem was one of moral confusion, and it centered on ambiguities, in American culture, in relations between moral distinction and the bitch-goddess, Success.

Trivializations of moral distinction in business best-sellers went back at least as far as Bruce Barton's book *The Man Nobody Knows* (1925), which reduced Jesus Christ to a profit-hustling, team-building go-getter. And moral confusion was everywhere manifest in eighties discussions of leadership style. In the School of Sensitivity the confusion appeared in sly suggestions that, by conjoining "love" and manipulativeness, "vulnerability" and trickery, managers can seize a competitive edge. "If we can learn," said Allan Cox in *The Making of the Achiever*, "to recognize those occasions when we should combine a babe-in-the-woods vulnerability with the right people on the right matters at the right time, we can bring a creative management process to bear on the challenges of business."

A matter, in sum, of learning when as well as how to have things both ways.

But there was a time—this bears remembering—a time when corporate managers couldn't imagine, even in wild fantasy, successfully passing themselves off as figures of tender-hearted humanity. Once Tom Peters and his ilk brought that possibility to birth, a whole new continent of imagemaking opened up, and an altogether unprecedented language of corporate public service began to be spoken. It would take a while for the right to grasp the scope—the richness—of the gift bestowed thereby upon it. The learning of that lesson set in place the corporate base of compassionate conservatism.

Touchy-feely management theory functions as a handmaid to apoliticality by implicitly treating conflicts between labor and management, the propertied and unpropertied, as pointless. But those conflicts don't instantly wither when so treated. Promoters of worker-boss solidarity come under suspicion as New Age costcutters. Why are the owning classes sloughing off the stern mien and detached or contemptuous manner once seen as essential to maintaining discipline among the help? Not, says suspicion, because they have discovered the delights of fraternity and mutuality, but because they have at last grasped that discipline maintained in mean terms legitimizes resentment and cuts productivity.

In fact, of course, the project of dismantling old structures of antipathy is no short-term venture—nothing do-able, by management theorists or anyone else, overnight. It requires action on the shop floor and in the board room, and it also requires long-term, expansive, imaginative measures: effort at fashioning personnae that body forth, in a new key with fresh lyrics, the ancient American theme of the essential sameness of every human creature on these shores.

Denials of difference conceived in these terms are larger and bolder propositions than those sampled earlier in this book. We're no longer dealing with denials of the existence of divergent positions on issues, nor with denials of the gulf separating the propertied and unpropertied. What is now on the table is the claim that, take us one by one, single American citizen by single American citizen, we are ineluctably the same. Setting forth that claim and making it stick: this is the ultimate challenge of no-politics politics.

Many performers on many fronts have taken up the challenge, and among the more interesting are those who became, in the last quarter of the twentieth century, the new spokespersons for conservatism in the world of mass communications. Gradually they came to speak with one voice, shedding the condescension that stamped William Buckley and his clones; gradually conservatism reinvented itself as a friendly, easy character whose enthusiasm for the American entrepreneurial system coexisted with civil fondness for and close familiarity with the people's pleasures (baseball, for instance); gradually the new model made its way in living rooms and showrooms. It was utterly clean of the bad temper surfacing in the line from Westbrook Pegler to James J. Kilpatrick to Robert Novak. It announced to the country that cheerful good humor and basic Toryism weren't mutually repellent, that the irascible, abrasive note stamping (say) Roman Catholic anti-Communism in the Joe McCarthy era marked an individual not a group neurosis, that a pro-business outlook could coexist with general likableness. Most important, it preached at every opportunity not on conservatism proper but on our basic sameness: the ultimate cornerstone of no-politics "thought." Few commentators were more winning on this theme than George Will.

At the Tory Charm School:
George Will & Co.

Public enthusiasm for George F. Will, the conservative columnist and talk show star, built fast from his debut onward. Appetite for new faces and new manners was partly responsible. Suited up in a vested navy pin-stripe—specs, bow tie, youthful shock of straight hair—Will offered the not-then-stale look of the professorial-comer, and his air of patient courtesy contrasted nicely, on *Agronsky & Co.*, with the impression of fuming bad temper left, on the same show, by James J. Kilpatrick. Will's ability to speak in complete sentences unassisted by Teleprompter, also stimulated awe. (Both on the page and in person Will fancies balance, antithesis and alliteration, as in his declaration, regarding a federal decision to loan money to Poland, that the Reagan Administration loves commerce more than it loathes communism. And some WASPs praised Will in terms that suggested eagerness to show the ecumenical flag (Will is a Roman Catholic).

But approval of this self-proclaimed Tory came from other, less easily discounted sources as well. Several sound journalists admired Will in print. The readership of his newspaper column and semimonthly pages in *Newsweek* included swarms of left-leaners and independents. The newspaper column won a

Pulitzer prize in 1977. Dan Rather quoted his sayings to President Reagan. Norman Podhoretz quoted his sayings to MacNeill and Lehrer. The Reagans came to his house for dinner. The President called him his friend. David Brinkley added him to the cast of his Sunday ABC show. The man hung on.

A considerable media success. More than a hundred of Will's columns were collected in *The Pursuit of Virtue and Other Tory Notions*, organized under such headings as "Conservatism, Rightly Understood," " 'Rights' and Wrongs, and Life and Death," "The War Against the Totalitarian, 1939—" and "Lives, Private and Public," a series that juxtaposes commentaries on Sir Thomas More and John Wayne, Pope John Paul II and Ray Kroc, Alger Hiss and Strom Thurmond, among others. Few positions taken in these pieces seemed remarkable to readers acquainted with rightist tunes of glory of the last half-century. The government is too intrusive; today's youth—except in Salt Lake City and the military academies—behaves badly; parents are taking child-rearing too lightly; subsidized abortions encourage promiscuity; get tough with Russia; Joe Louis over Muhammed Ali any day. Early in the work a certain predictability in the material awakened suspicion that the extraordinary response to this writer might testify only to the deepening dishevelment of the country's political and cultural life.

Still: *The Pursuit of Virtue* warrants the close attention of cultural historians. The book lights up a mental landscape that in time became that of our policymakers, and in the process shows how the uglier, old-line Tory sounds—from hauteur to hardheartedness—were dubbed out of contemporary advocacy of old-line Tory causes (defense of privilege, denial of class dispute, idealization of *noblesse oblige*). The book also writes an instructive new chapter on "image," as that concept eats its way farther into our woodwork, burrowing from star system politics into star system punditry. And, most important,

Will's obliviousness of substantive social reality dramatizes an undernoticed cultural problem: the increasing readiness of media heroes to replace grainy knowledge of what's Out There with "charming" self-display. An initially striking item in *The Pursuit of Virtue* is the author's indulgence in a limited mimicry of left critics of capitalism. In the introduction and in several early pieces, Will comments disdainfully on entrepreneurial dynamism: "Karl Marx . . . got one thing right: capitalism undermines traditional social structures and values; it is a relentless engine of change, a revolutionary inflamer of appetites, enlarger of expectations, diminisher of patience." Similar talk surfaces at intervals elsewhere. There's a warning about "an economy increasingly geared to the manufacture of frivolous appetites ('How many Calvin Kleins in your closet, America?')." There's praise of Pope John Paul II for his effort to call "the affluent societies" to a life "less partial and distorting than the pursuit of pleasure."

Solzhenitsyhn's commencement speech at Harvard is quoted and understood, and there's approval for that writer's doubts that "a society founded on lightly regulated selfishness can summon the vision and sacrifice necessary for combating deter-mined enemies." Two charities—Saint Jude's Ranch for Chil-dren in the Mojave Desert and the Little Brothers of the Poor in Chicago—come in for notice. And there's an assertion that "the world's . . . Most Serious Shortage . . . is imagination. (I mean imagination of a particular kind: the kind that produces social sympathy—the ability to comprehend, however dimly, how other people live.)"

Observations and admonitions of this sort became conven-tional, to be sure, among essayists on the right—conservative chic. In *Two Cheers for Capitalism*, for example, Irving Kristol asked: "Can men live in a free society if they have no reason to believe it is a just society?" (He answered: "I do not think so . . .

They cannot for long accept a society in which power, privilege, and property are not distributed according to some morally meaningful criteria.") Moreover, it seemed conceivable that down the road such admonitions could attain more than ritual significance. There's no reason, certainly, why a writer whose form is the short newspaper or magazine column can't make that form serve a serious critical purpose.

Pithy firsthand reporting on neglected sectors of experience helps to clarify the moral uses of the sympathetic imagination. Case studies of commercial rapacity, whether in a pharmaceutical house or a law factory, help to dramatize the destructiveness of laissez-faire dynamism. Will's book includes pieces about advertising, the environment, the porn industry, luxo shopping (Rodeo Drive in Beverly Hills), McDonald's and West Point; plenty of opportunities here, if wanted, for fleshing out the indictment of "lightly regulated selfishness."

But, unsurprisingly, the opportunities aren't seized. Will's approval of traditional values, social sympathy and Marx's lucky shot as regards capitalism leads away from anatomies of greed or accounts of the constructive imagination in action. Strokes of self-display rather than foundations of argument, they function as softening agents, means of easing the outlines of the rightist personality. The conservative who speaks from the start as a person offended by hustler-style tycoonery separates himself from high rollers, Yahoos, unbuttoned Nofzigerians and others whose coarse manners and obsession with profit and fortune give the right a bad name. And the conservative who, like Will, presents himself as a student who's read Marx through on his own, sifting and winnowing mounds of junk in hope of gleaning whatever concept may yet be worth preserving, establishes thoughtful curiosity and lack of prejudice as identifying marks of his kind.

And Will's New Right is to be appreciated primarily on this

level, as a style and posture, not as a source of ponderable ideas and correctives, as a winning personality rather than as a summons to a certain height. In the past, smart conservatives have been exceptionally skillful summoners, bracing people to the wall. Their feeling for history is close-grained. Their faith in the primacy of individual human relationships and in the need for high standards of individual conduct freshens the conscience. They invent memorable intellectual commands (clear your mind of cant). And they insist on explicitness—the spelling out, in sentences, of the underexamined moral foundations of political views, and of the reasons for maintaining continuity with the past. Like other people, they're not proof against extravagance; on bad days they confuse being hard-nosed with being intelligent and behave as though they alone converse with reality.

But their strength on good days—the impersonal strength of Michael Oakeshott reproaching Utopians or Burke shaming "sophisters, economists, and calculators," or F. R. Leavis in *Scrutiny* excoriating British Marxists—is inestimable.

But this kind of strength isn't sought by George Will. His voice is purely personal and his major interest is self-presentation.

The key characteristic of the self that's presented is agree-ableness, and it's brought into view in a variety of ways—by a portrait of the writer as fundamentally unrestive in a society that's one-dimensionally middle class, by a treatment of our ills that stresses the healing possibilities of lightly ironic humor, and by a steady insistence that causes and tastes necessarily repellent to each other can be neatly harmonized within a single, likably relaxed mind.

Following the opening salute to the sympathetic imagination, source of knowledge about "how other people live," Will moves swiftly toward skepticism that genuinely different "other" people can be found out there in any number. The country is all of a piece; everybody belongs to the well-off middle; actually there are no "others." The Pope and Solzhenitsyn have held, each in his special way, that Americans are universally affluent and fun-seeking, rich and pleasure-soaked, and they're roughly right. It's middle America that will be paying for the Reagan economic program; the President "is asking Congress to pull a bit of padding from the 'padded society' which means in large measure from the middle class." If low-income men and women aren't a mere legend, they surely constitute so tiny and exotic a group that it would take a Mr. Kean, finder of lost persons, to locate them. Who among us knows a working person? Coal miners, says Will, belong to a working class that's "as foreign as Mongolia." So do subway riders: "In New York subways I am told (I am not crazy enough to venture down to check) . . . it would be an improvement if many would just stand around loitering and spitting." If more working-class people existed, we'd profit, because, as it happens, they're superb critics of sentimental liberalism. (Will is taken with the workers depicted in the film *The Deer Hunter*, trashers of peacenik fatuity.)

But the case is that few if any exist. Naturally we, the pleasure-soaked masses, stand prepared to extend sympathy to the halt and the orphaned through our favorite charities. Naturally the pleasure-soaked masses remain alert to the possibility of encountering unfamiliar forms of social life. But good sense tells us that the most reasonable thought we can have about the other side is that the life we'd find there is probably exactly the same as our own. "How many Calvin Kleins in your closet, America?"

The faint ideological thrust of this attitudinizing is that no constituency in the United States could benefit from radical solutions to social problems. (Will assures his readers that "not for years have sensible socialists believed in public ownership of the means of production and exchange.") But ideology is incidental. What counts is that, in portraying the country as one-dimensional and his own citizenship as unproblematic, the columnist establishes that exerting moral pressure isn't his game. Would I badger you? asks each of his pieces obliquely, through its tone. We, the vast majority, are in this together. *We* take cabs, *we* avoid the subway, *we* know no workers, *we* live high on the hog. A flicker of moral ambition may incite one of us at moments to chat up an interesting charity, or to allude, with a show of anxiety, to a culture of "lightly regulated selfishness." But we know better than to pursue this. No sermons, no manufacturing of spurious guilt. At our core, to one another and with ourselves, we're urbane, honest and without moral airs. Another way of putting it: we're people of charm.

And people of humor. On camera George Will seldom smiles, and occasionally he adopts—for a patch of seconds—a lecturer's tone, but it's the humorous side of things that he savors, particularly the unconscious humor of the morally intense. They'll always be with us, the morally intense and humorless, says his customary voice. People who won't chuckle at the President's wonderfully defusing one-liners at press conferences. People who perversely insist that a decision to use public monies to support segregationist institutions can't have had "merely procedural" ends in view. The neoconservative understands these glumbodies and carefully avoids the upbeat they abhor. He's familiar with the ancient American love of the jeremiad. He's aware that the universal, pleasure-soaked affluence unifying us as one classless community has often stirred outsiders (the Pope, Solzhenitsyn) to protest, and that these protests in turn cause some insiders to question whether they too shouldn't learn the lingo of denunciation.

But while one should respect the outsiders, one should also

be wary of losing one's balance. There's a little-known American freedom—the freedom to treat entrepreneurial rapacity as entertainment—that's good to remember here. A way of achieving a modest distance, as distinguished from a ridiculous moral high. Well-meaning citizens who forget this freedom become overheated and fret about divorce rates, or the startling sight of their grandchildren, eight-year-old twins, giggling at an X-flick on cable. They find it difficult to remain undisturbed about such a phenomenon as, say, the $4 billion U. S. porn industry. They might even rush to conclude that the porn industry is a foreshadowing—a warning about the ultimate destination of our demented, inflaming, everything-is-permitted capitalism.

But if people of this sort would only remember the freedom to be entertained, they'd see their own foolishness. Will's piece about porn hucksters presents the industry as less distasteful than diverting—a "pioneering and heroic rascality." The columnist notes, humorously, that the United States "has beat [out] a foreign cartel—an OPEC of porn exporters." He quotes "an entertaining report by James Cook" in *Forbes* magazine that "at least in the pornography business the American gift for economic growth survives." The *Forbes* report observes that the porn trade managers are unhappy because their audience is limited to people over 35, but that too is humorous to Will: "Cook says (drolly, I think) that [that] is 'merely a marketing problem,' and it will be tackled by 'someone from Hollywood, *Hustler,* or the Harvard Business School.' "

Nobody adequately inward with the easing effect of light irony will feel obliged to press on past the drolleries to inquire into the connection between alienated sex and the structures of social and economic dynamism. Wisdom doesn't brood about the waste land, or imagine different destinies; it cools itself with wry thoughts about the endless inventiveness of our ineluctable American hustle.

It does the same with advertising. George Will on this subject begins with an acknowledgment that public lying may breed cynicism—but at once shifts to the theme that more often than not public lying breeds wit: "When . . . half a class of third-graders, asked to spell 'relief,' write 'R-o-l-a-i-d-s,' alarmists cite the power of advertising. I merely admire the wittiness of American youth." Wisdom doesn't brood on the moral impact of corrupt enlargers of expectation; it cools itself with wry thoughts of the kiddies' increasing proficiency at parody. Implicit throughout Will's writing is the thesis that alarmism about extravagant consumption, advertising, and the rest is rather worse than the things themselves. At the end of the column about advertising, an ad for "a very small bank for sale" is quoted from a banking magazine. The quoted copy names the price and location, adding the information that the bank is situated in a "dreary little town." There you are, says the columnist, smiling, truth in advertising after all—"a sterling example of candor in commerce." Non-candor is a non-problem. Have light irony, can cope. Relax.

Rodeo Drive is equally recreational. A soul of simple faith roused by Pope John Paul II's summons to a life "less partial and distorting than the pursuit of pleasure" might know no better than to feel a quiver of outrage at the sight, in a shop window, of a fox fur bedspread priced at $42,000. But yet once more: the soul is overreacting. Paying $42,000 for a bedspread is wrong, but not very wrong. We need to retain the sense of proportion. Exercise humorous tolerance, as with thousand-dollar place settings. "Some facets of American civilization are—let us face facts—less than excellent. The saxophone, for one. Football halftime shows for another. Frozen French toast, for a third. But there is, I insist, a form of excellence for almost anything, even excess. So let us now praise (sort of) two and a half blocks of Rodeo Drive here." May the hungry sleep well.

At the level of ideology, needless to say, such writing cancels out that early mimicry of left criticism of capitalism, inflamer of appetite. But here too ideology is immaterial. What counts is the emerging psychological profile, the soothing, binding gestures of wry acceptance, the agreeable perception of the world as a comfy mirror of self. New Tory, it appears, possesses both sensitivity and the proportioning sense of humor. Smoothly he moves from momentary concern (illustrative of fine feeling) to relaxing smiles (illustrative of balance), from Marx on the inflamers to moderating chuckles about saxophones, frozen French toast and $42,000 bedspreads; from worries about the defacing of the environment to good-humored acclaim of Ray Kroc of McDonald's as a genius. As there is, essentially, only one class of people in America, so there is, essentially, only one kind of domestic problem, that which can swiftly be teased away by the kind of humor natural to a man who includes, in himself, the whole of that one class.

And George Will is, at this level, catholic—some sort of miniature Peaceable Kingdom of taste in himself, a center wherein the shoddy and the well-made, the sophisticated and the provincial, the brilliant and the mindless, the knowing and the square, Sir Thomas More and John Wayne, mingle nonjudgmentally in further proof of the seamlessness of the American state. Will's many badges of gentility (the most conspicuous is an intermittently priggish Anglophilia) are never out of sight for long. The columnist admires the BBC ("sublime") and treasures Oxford (the lovely eccentrics, the ancient lawns, the enthusiasm for teaching). Anthony Powell's *A Dance to the Music of Time* "provided the greatest reading pleasure of my first forty years." C. S. Lewis and Lewis Carroll are passions, and, on a single page, we find quotations from Disraeli, Walter Bagehot, George Eliot and Jonathan Swift. Here and there the writer extends a pinky, overworking such terms as *tiresome, jolly* and *enchanting*. (There's an "enchanting" novel by G. K. Chesterton, an "enchanting" refrain in a country music song, and an "enchanting" defense of Hamilton Jordan by friends of Jimmy Carter's "blue-denim Presidency.") Propriety of dress is taken for granted as a value; those uniforms Nixon bought weren't a bad idea and, for unspoken reasons that everyone who counts will understand, Jimmy in jeans was absurd.

But the urbane Anglophile elitist coexists in these pages with another figure—a country boy of plain and wholesome Midwestern origins who is given to celebrations of wife and babes, camping expeditions and baseball. George Will's rural self never quarrels with the cosmopolitan professorial-comer. Enthusiasm for "The Great State" (Illinois) is regularly leavened with self-protective capital letters, memories of school days at Oxford, allusions (suitably vague) to Donne and Baudelaire, comparisons of the crude city of Washington, D. C. with European centers one has known: "In a mature capital, like Paris or London, there are many old, established, confident elites, in industry, finance, the arts and universities. In Washington, nothing is old . . ."

But there are no conflicts of values, and middle America never recedes as a source of good. Will delights in the "quintessentially American" Mormons, lovingly celebrates a football-mad Nebraskan who carves cheerleaders' jargon (GO BIG RED) on his mother's tombstone because she liked the game. There's a booster piece about male and female West Point cadets: "When I was there [at the Academy] last fall it was grand to hear, as the cadets assembled for dinner, soprano voices in the football pep rally: 'Napalm North Carolina!' " And Will, the Baudelaire buff, nevertheless places himself with the plain folk as a hater of modern art, modern music and modern sex education, as a fan of Big Macs and little girls who want to grow up to be nurses rather than doctors.

On its face this is a complicated—some may say impossible—array of tastes. Who, one asks, can digest a Crackerjack box filled with George Eliot, Phyllis Schlafly, Dean Swift and the Chicago Cubs? But to ask that question is again to miss the point. George Will's catholic posture has the effect of draining substance from the social world; it supports the assumption that in America class differences—people significantly dissimilar—don't exist. This heartland Anglophile, Big Mac boulevardier, highbrow-middlebrow, hip-square hero replaces *We* and *They* with a compendious *I*; there's no place in his world for conflict, no ground for rage at injustice. In yesteryear, propertied defenders of privilege were a predictably sniffish lot, all polo and couture, perpetual detourers around Salt Lake City and Omaha, given to making others feel shame at their grossness. But this new spokesman for the crowd is rather more agile, alighting for the length of one column on this or that snobbish base, but racing off in the next to a different–brow–politics entirely, from which a kindly idolatrous attitude toward America the Absolutely Square can be taken up. New Tory isn't merely calm, well disposed, isn't merely amused and amusing; he's meant to be understood in addition as our quintessentially mobile man. He chides not, neither does he mock. Whoever we are, wherever we are, he is, despite the vest, the pinstripes, one of us. His chief function—like that of the politics to come—is to drain the world of difference.

PART TWO

Exploring the Substructure

1. Beyond Conflict: Three Modes of Erasure

Many factors unmentioned in Part One figured in the pre-9/11 flight from politics, probably the most obvious being the sordor of Clinton/Lewinsky, the special prosecutor and the impeachment proceedings. The columnist E. J. Dionne held that repugnance for politics inspired by Clinton/Lewinsky was responsible for patterns of truncated commitment among the college-aged. (Even youngsters who engaged in volunteer work with political overtones in the Nineties did so with the understanding that the activity belonged to a pre-career moment when indulgence and caprice were affordable— hadn't to do with the serious undertakings of grownup life.)

Historians connect apoliticality with the decline of organizations that sustained civic literacy at levels supportive of vigorous democratic life. Theda Skocpol points out that before the first World War a variety of national federations with state and local branches and million-plus memberships were teaching Americans about the interaction of micro and macro governmental entities. (Today the only two organizations of comparable size are the Christian Coalition and Mothers Against Drunk Driving.)

Other social scientists stress the failure of political leaders to explain and dramatize, to working–class constituencies, the roles that government has played and could play again in reenergizing working–class opposition to success-obsessed, middle class materialism. (See Andrew Levison's remarkable essay, "Who Lost the Working Class?" on current opinion research regarding core working class values, in The Nation, *May 14, 2001.)*

None of the causal factors commonly cited in explanations of rising apoliticality is inconsequential—but the phenomenon in question is no simple thing. It floats on a sea of vague opinions, assumptions and intuitions about abstract subjects—"difference" in America, success and failure, the nature (and whereabouts) of the good life and the ideal society, the relative unimportance of political choices as compared with choices of sexual identity, consuming behavior, and "style." Boomlets for civility or character education or faith-based initiatives are best understood as adaptive responses— efforts to translate murky anxieties and evasive impulses into gestures and policies that seem harmlessly activist and in tune with popular beliefs.

As for those popular beliefs: they are shaped and discovered in venues remote from think tanks or committee hearings. Hour by hour, season after season, masses of material designed to entertain audiences and/or move goods contribute to the large national enterprise of complacency-building. Days of terror can interrupt. Responsible voices can speak up about the need to reassess values. But mainstream cultural production—smoothly optimistic and tonally egalitarian—underpins an extremely durable structure of feeling. Much (not all) of junk politics rests on this structure.

Part Two probes in its initial section selected examples of that production. A major theme of the material is the sameness of rich and poor, black and white. (Abolish difference and you abolish conflict; abolish conflict and you abolish the tensions with which genuine politics brings a society to terms.) The denial of difference drives a thousand stories to their upbeat conclusion, namely that people hung up on difference are benighted—have simply not kept up. In these tales America sees itself, time and again, as faction-free—composed of good and bad human creatures none of whom has a social context or supra-personal cause, none of whom represents anything beyond themselves. Where such happy likemindedness rules, who needs politics?

Put on a Happy Face: Masking Differences Between Blacks and Whites

At the movies these days, questions about racial injustice have been amicably resolved. Watch *Pulp Fiction* or *Congo* or *A Little Princess* or any other recent film in which both blacks and whites are primary characters and you can, if you want, forget about race. Whites and blacks greet one another on the screen with loving candor, revealing their common humanity. In *Pulp Fiction*, an armed black mobster (played by Samuel L. Jackson) looks deep into the eyes of an armed white thief in the middle of a holdup (played by Tim Roth) and shares his version of God's word in Ezekiel, whereupon the two men lay aside their weapons, both more or less redeemed. The moment inverts an earlier scene in which a white boxer (played by Bruce Willis) risks his life to save another black mobster (played by Ving Rhames), who is being sexually tortured as a prelude to his execution.

Pulp Fiction (gross over $100 million) is one of a series of films suggesting that the beast of American racism is tamed and harmless. Close to the start of *Die Hard with a Vengeance* (gross over $100 million) the camera finds a white man wearing sandwich boards on the corner of Amsterdam Avenue and 138th Street in Harlem. The boards carry a horrific legend: I HATE NIGGERS. A group of young blacks approach the man with murderous intent, bearing guns and knives. They are figures straight out: of a national nightmare—ugly, enraged, terrifying. No problem. A black man, again played by Jackson, appears and rescues the white man, played by Willis. The black man and white man come to know each other well. In time the white man declares flatly to the black, "I need you more than you need me." A moment later he charges the black with being a racist—with not liking whites as much as the white man likes blacks—and the two talk frankly about their racial prejudices. Near the end of the film, the men have grown so close that each volunteers to die for the other.

Pulp Fiction and *Die Hard with a Vengeance* follow the pattern of *Lethal Weapon* 1, 2, and 3, the Danny Glover/Mel Gibson buddy vehicles that collectively grossed $357 million, and *White Men Can't Jump*, which, in the year of the L.A. riots, grossed $76 million. In *White Men Can't Jump*, a white dropout, played by Woody Harrelson, ekes out a living on black-dominated basketball courts in Los Angeles. He's arrogant and aggressive but never in danger because he has a black protector and friend, played by Wesley Snipes. At the movie's end, the white, flying above the hoop like a stereotypical black player, scores the winning basket in a two-on-two pickup game on an alley-oop pass from his black chum, whereupon the two men fall into each other's arms in joy. Later, the black friend agrees to find work for the white at the store he manages.

White (helpless): I gotta get a job. Can you get me a job?
Black (affectionately teasing): Got any references?
White (shy grin): You.

Such dialogue is the stuff of romance. What's dreamed of and gained is a place where whites are unafraid of blacks, where blacks ask for and need nothing from whites, and where the sameness of the races creates a common fund of sweet content.* The details of the dream matter less than the force that makes it come true for both races, eliminating the constraints of objective reality and redistributing resources, status, and capabilities. That cleansing social force supersedes political and economic fact or policy; that force, improbably enough, is friendship.

Watching the beaming white men who know how to jump, we do well to remind ourselves of what the camera shot leaves out. Black infants die in America at twice the rate of white infants. (Despite the increased numbers of middle-class blacks, the rates are diverging, with black rates actually rising.) One out of every two black children lives below the poverty line (as compared with one out of seven white children), Nearly four times as many black families exist below the poverty line as white families. More than 50 percent of African American families have incomes below $25,000. Among black youths under age twenty, death by murder occurs nearly ten times as often as among whites. Over 60 percent of births to black mothers occur out of wedlock, more than four times the rate for white mothers. The net worth of the typical white household is ten times that of the typical black household. In many states, five to ten times as many blacks as whites age eighteen to thirty are in prison.

The good news at the movies obscures the bad news in the streets and confirms the Supreme Court's recent decisions on

---

* I could go on with examples of movies that deliver the good news of friendship: *Regarding Henry, Driving Miss Daisy, Forrest Gump, The Shawshank Redemption, Philadelphia, The Last Boy Scout, 48 Hours I-II, Rising Sun, Iron Eagle I-II, Rudy, Sister Act, Hearts of Dixie, Betrayed, The Power of One, White Nights, Clara's Heart, Doc Hollywood, Cool Runnings, Places in the Heart, Trading Places, Fried Green Tomatoes, Q & A, Platoon, A Mother's Courage: The Mary Thomas Story, The Unforgiven, The Air Up There, The Pelican Brief, Losing Isaiah, Smoke, Searching for Bobby Fischer, An Officer and a Gentleman, Speed,* etc.

busing, affirmative action, and redistricting. Like the plot of *White Men Can't Jump*, the Court postulates the existence of a society no longer troubled by racism. Because black-white friendship is now understood to be the rule, there is no need for integrated schools or a congressional Black Caucus or affirmative action. The Congress and state governors can guiltlessly cut welfare, food assistance, fuel assistance, Head Start, housing money, fellowship money, vaccine money. Justice Anthony Kennedy can declare, speaking for the Supreme Court majority last June, that creating a world of genuine equality and sameness requires only that "our political system and our society cleanse themselves . . . of discrimination."

The deep logic runs as follows: Yesterday white people didn't like black people, and accordingly suffered guilt, knowing that the dislike was racist and knowing also that as moral persons they would have to atone for the guilt. They would have to ante up for welfare and Head Start and halfway houses and free vaccine and midnight basketball and summer jobs for schoolkids and graduate fellowships for promising scholars and craft-union apprenticeships and so on, endlessly. A considerable and wasteful expense. But at length came the realization that by ending dislike or hatred it would be possible to end guilt, which in turn, would mean an end to redress: no more wasteful ransom money. There would be but one requirement: the regular production and continuous showing forth of evidence indisputably proving that hatred has totally vanished from the land.

I cannot tell the reader how much I would like to believe in this sunshine world. After the theater lights brighten and I've found coins for a black beggar on the way to my car and am driving home through downtown Springfield, Massachusetts, the world invented by *Die Hard with a Vengeance* and America's highest court gives way only slowly to the familiar urban vision in my windshield—homeless blacks on trash-strewn streets, black prostitutes staked out on a corner, and signs of a not very furtive drug trade. I know perfectly well that most African Americans don't commit crimes or live in alleys. I also know that for somebody like myself, downtown Springfield in the late evening is not a good place to be.

The movies reflect the larger dynamic of wish and dream. Day after day the nation's corporate ministries of culture churn out images of racial harmony. Millions awaken each morning to the friendly sight of Katie Couric nudging a perky elbow into good buddy Bryant Gumbel's side. My mailbox and millions of demographically similar others are choked with flyers from companies (Wal-Mart, Victoria's Secret) bent on publicizing both their wares and their social bona fides by displaying black and white models at cordial ease with one another. A torrent of goodwill messages about race arrives daily—revelations of corporate largesse, commercials, news features, TV specials, all proclaiming that whites like me feel strongly positive impulses of friendship for blacks and that those same admirable impulses are effectively eradicating racial differences, rendering blacks and whites the same. Bell-South TV commercials present children singing "I am the keeper of the world"—first white child, then a black child, then a white child, then a black child. Because Dow Chemical likes black America, it recruits young black college grads for its research division and dramatizes, in TV commercials, their tearful-joyful partings from home. ("Son, show 'em what you got," says a black lad's father.) American Express shows an elegant black couple and an elegant white couple sitting together in a theater, happy in one another's company. (The couples share the box with an oversized Gold Card.) During the evening news I watch a black mom offer Robitussin to a miserably coughing white mom. Here's *People* magazine promoting itself under a photo of John Lee Hooker, the black bluesman. "We're these kinds of people, too," People claims in the caption. In the current production of *Hamlet* on Broadway, Horatio is played by a black actor. On *The 700 Club*, Pat Robertson joshes Ben Kinchlow, his black sidekick, about Ben's far-out ties.

What counts here is not the saccharine clumsiness of the interchanges but the bulk of them—the ceaseless, self-validating gestures of friendship, the humming, buzzing background theme: All decent Americans extend the hand of friendship to African Americans; nothing but nothing is more auspicious for the African American future than this extended hand. Faith in the miracle cure of racism by change-of-heart turns out to be so familiar as to have become unnoticeable. And yes, the faith has its benign aspect. Even as they nudge me and others toward belief in magic (instant pals and no-money-down equality), the images and messages of devoted relationships between blacks and whites do exert a humanizing influence.

Nonetheless, through these same images and messages the comfortable majority tells itself a fatuous untruth. Promoting the fantasy of painless answers, inspiring groundless self-approval among whites, joining the Supreme Court in treating "cleansing" as inevitable, the new orthodoxy of friendship incites culture-wide evasion, justifies one political step backward after another, and greases the skids along which, tomorrow, welfare block grants will slide into state highway-resurfacing budgets.

Whites are part of the solution, says this orthodoxy, if we break out of the prison of our skin color, say hello, as equals, one-on-one, to a black stranger, and make a black friend. We're part of the problem if we have an aversion to black people or are frightened of them, or if we feel that the more distance we put between them and us the better, or if we're in the habit of asserting our superiority rather than acknowledging our common humanity. Thus we shift the problem away from politics—from black experience and the history of slavery—and perceive it as a matter of the suspicion and fear found within the white heart; solving the problem asks no more of us than that we work on ourselves, scrubbing off the dirt of ill will.

The approach miniaturizes, personalizes, and moralizes; it removes the large and complex dilemmas of race from the public sphere. It tempts audiences to see history as irrelevant and to regard feelings as decisive—to believe that the fate of black Americans is shaped mainly by events occurring in the hearts and minds of the privileged. And let's be frank: the orthodoxy of friendship feels nice. It practically consecrates self-flattery. The "good" Bill Clinton who attends black churches and talks with likable ease to fellow worshipers was campaigning when Los Angeles rioted in '92. "White Americans," he said, "are gripped by the isolation of their own experience. Too many still simply have no friends of other races and do not know any differently." Few black youths of working age in South-Central L.A. had been near enough to the idea of a job even to think of looking for work before the Rodney King verdict, but the problem, according to Clinton, was that whites need black friends.

Most of the country's leading voices of journalistic conscience (editorial writers, television anchorpersons, syndicated columnists) roundly endorse the doctrine of black-white friendship as a means of redressing the inequalities between the races. Roger Rosenblatt, editor of the *Columbia Journalism Review* and an especially deft supplier of warm and fuzzy sentiment, published an essay in *Family Circle* arguing that white friendship and sympathy for blacks simultaneously make power differentials vanish and create interracial identity between us, one by one. The author finds his exemplum in an episode revealing the personal sensitivity, to injured blacks, of one of his children.

"When our oldest child, Carl, was in high school," he writes, "he and two black friends were standing on a street corner in New York City one spring evening, trying to hail a taxi. The three boys were dressed decently and were doing nothing wild or threatening. Still, no taxi would pick them up. If a driver spotted Carl first, he might slow down, but he would take off again when he saw the others. Carl's two companions were familiar with this sort of abuse. Carl, who had never observed it firsthand before, burned with anger and embarrassment that he was the color of a world that would so mistreat his friends."

Rosenblatt notes that when his son "was applying to colleges, he wrote his essay on that taxi incident with his two black friends. . . . He was able to articulate what he could not say at the time—how ashamed and impotent he felt. He also wrote of the power of their friendship, which has lasted to this day and has carried all three young men into the country that belongs to them. To all of us."

In this homily white sympathy begets interracial sameness in several ways. The three classmates are said to react identically to the cabdrivers' snub; i.e., they feel humiliated. "[Carl] could not find the words to express his humiliation and his friends would not express theirs."

The anger that inspires the younger Rosenblatt's college-admission essay on racism is seen as identical with black anger. Friendship brings the classmates together as joint, equal owners of the land of their birth ("the country that belongs to [all of] them"). And Rosenblatt supplies a still larger vision of essential black-white sameness near the end of his essay: "Our proper hearts tell the truth," he declares, "which is that we are all in the same boat, rich and poor, black and white. We are helpless, wicked, heroic, terrified, and we need one another. We need to give rides to one another."

Thus do acts of private piety substitute for public policy while the possibility of urgent political action disappears into a sentimental haze. "If we're looking for a formula to ease the tensions between the races," Rosenblatt observes, then we should "attack the disintegration of the black community" and "the desperation of the poor." Without overtly mocking civil rights activists who look toward the political arena "to erase the tensions," Rosenblatt alludes to them in a throwaway manner, implying that properly adjusted whites look elsewhere, that there was a time for politicking for "equal rights" but we've passed through it. Now is a time in which we should listen to our hearts at moments of epiphany and allow sympathy to work its wizardry, cleansing and floating us, blacks and whites "all in the same boat," on mystical undercurrent of the New Age.

Blacks themselves aren't necessarily proof against this theme, as witness a recent essay by James Alan McPherson in the Harvard journal *Reconstruction*. McPherson, who received the 1977 Pulitzer Prize for fiction for his collection of stories *Elbow Room*, says that "the only possible steps, the safest steps . . . small ones" in the movement "toward a universal culture" will be those built not on "ideologies and formulas and programs" but on experiences of personal connectedness.

"Just his past spring," he writes, "when I was leaving a restaurant after taking a [white] former student to dinner, a black [woman on the sidewalk] said to my friend, in a rasping voice, 'Hello, girlfriend. Have you got anything to spare!' " The person speaking was a female crack addict with a child who was also addicted. "But," writes McPherson, when the addict made her pitch to his dinner companion, "I saw in my friend's face an understanding and sympathy and a shining which transcended race and class. Her face reflected one human soul's connection with another. The magnetic field between the two women was charged with spiritual energy."

The writer points the path to progress through interpersonal gestures by people who "insist on remaining human, and having human responses. . . . Perhaps the best that can be done, now, is the offering of understanding and support to the few out of many who are capable of such gestures, rather than devising another plan to engineer the many into one."

The elevated vocabulary ("soul," "spiritual") beatifies the impulse to turn away from the real-life agenda of actions capable of reducing racial injustice. Wherever that impulse dominates, the rhetoric of racial sameness thrives, diminishing historical catastrophes affecting millions over centuries and inflating the significance of tremors of tenderness briefly troubling the heart or conscience of a single individual—the boy waiting for a cab, the woman leaving the restaurant. People forget the theoretically unforgettable—the caste history of American blacks, the connection between no schools for longer than a century and bad school performance now, between hateful social attitudes and zero employment opportunities, between minority anguish and majority fear.

How could this way of seeing have become conventional so swiftly? How did the dogmas of instant equality insinuate themselves so effortlessly into courts and mass audiences alike? How can a white man like myself, who taught Southern blacks in the 1960s, find himself seduced—as I have been more than once—by the orthodoxy of friendship? In the civil rights era, the experience for many millions of Americans was one of discovery. A hitherto unimagined continent of human reality and history came into view, inducing genuine concern and at least a temporary setting aside of self-importance. I remember with utter clarity what I felt at Mary Holmes College in West Point, Mississippi, when a black student of mine was killed by tail-gating rednecks; my fellow tutors and I were overwhelmed with how shamefully wrong a wrong could be. For a time, we were released from the prisons of moral weakness and ambiguity. In the year or two that followed—the mid-Sixties—the notion that some humans are more human than others, whites more human than blacks, appeared to have been overturned. The next step seemed obvious: society would have to admit that when one race deprives another of its humanity for centuries, those who have done the depriving are obligated to do what they can to restore the humanity of the deprived. The obliga-tion clearly entailed the mounting of comprehensive *long-term* programs of developmental assistance—not guilt-money handouts—for nearly the entire black population. The path forward was unavoidable.

It was avoided. Shortly after the award of civil rights and the institution, in 1966, of limited preferential treatment to remedy employment and educational discrimination against African Americans, a measure of economic progress for blacks did appear in census reports. Not much, but enough to stimu-late glowing tales of universal black advance and to launch the good-news barrage that continues to this day (headline in the *New York Times*, June 18, 1995: "Moving On Up: The Greening of America's Black Middle Class").

After Ronald Reagan was elected to his first term, the new dogma of black-white sameness found ideological support in the form of criticism of so-called coddling. Liberal activists of both races were berated by critics of both races for fostering an allegedly enfeebling psychology of dependency that discour-aged African Americans from committing themselves to indi-vidual self-development. In 1988, the charge was passionately voiced in an essay in *Harper's Magazine*, "I'm Black, You're

White, Who's Innocent?" by Shelby Steele, who attributed the difference between black rates of advance and those of other minority groups to white folks' pampering. Most blacks, Steele claimed, could make it on their own—as voluntary immigrants have done—were they not held back by devitalizing programs that presented them, to themselves and others, as somehow dissimilar to and weaker than other Americans. This argument was all-in-the-same-boatism in a different key; the claim remained that progress depends upon recognition of black-white sameness. Let us see through superficial differences to the underlying, equally distributed gift for success. Let us teach ourselves—in the words of the Garth Brooks tune—to ignore "the color of skin" and "look for . . . the beauty within."

Still further support for the policy once known as "do-nothingism" came from points-of-light barkers, who held that a little something might perhaps be done accompanied by enough publicity. Nearly every broadcaster and publisher in America moves a bale of reportage on pro bono efforts by white Americans to speed the advance of black Americans. Example: McDonald's and the National Basketball Association distribute balloons when they announce they are addressing the dropout problem with an annual "Stay in School" scheme that gives schoolkids who don't miss a January school day a ticket to an all-star exhibition. The publicity strengthens the idea that these initiatives will nullify the social context—the city I see through my windshield. Reports of white philanthropy suggest that the troubles of this block and the next should be understood as phenomena in transition. The condition of American blacks need not be read as the fixed, unchanging consequence of generations of bottom-caste existence. Edging discreetly past a beggar posted near the entrance to Zabar's or H&H Bagels, or, while walking the dog, stepping politely around black men asleep on the sidewalk, we need not see ourselves and our fellows as uncaring accomplices in the acts of social injustice.

Yet more powerful has been the ceaseless assault, over the past generation, on our knowledge of the historical situation of black Americans. On the face of things it seems improbable that the cumulative weight of documented historical injury to African Americans could ever be lightly assessed. Gifted black writers continue to show, in scene after scene—in their studies of middle-class blacks interacting with whites—how historical realities shape the lives of their black characters. In *Killer of Sheep*, the brilliant black filmmaker Charles Burnett dramatizes the daily encounters that suck poor blacks into will-lessness and contempt for white fairy tales of interracial harmony; he quickens his historical themes with images of faceless black meat processors gutting undifferentiated, unchoosing animal life. Here, say these images, as though talking back to Clarence Thomas, here is a basic level of black life unchanged over generations. Where there's work, it's miserably paid and ugly. Space allotments at home and at work cramp body and mind. Positive expectation withers in infancy. People fall into the habit of jeering at aspiration as though at the bidding of physical law. Obstacles at every hand prevent people from loving and being loved in decent ways, prevent children from believing their parents, prevent parents from believing they themselves know anything worth knowing. The only true self, now as in the long past, is the one mocked by one's own race. "Shit on you, nigger," says a voice in *Killer of Sheep*. "Nothing you say matters a good goddamn."

For whites, these works produce guilt, and for blacks, I can only assume, pain and despair. The audience for tragedy remains small, while at the multiplex the popular enthusiasm for historical romance remains constant and vast. During the last two decades, the entertainment industry has conducted a siege on the pertinent past, systematically excising knowledge of the consequences of the historical exploitation of African Americans. Factitious renderings of the American past blur the outlines of black-white conflict, redefine the ground of black grievances for the purpose of diminishing the grievances, restage black life in accordance with the illusory conventions of American success mythology, and present the operative influences on race history as the same as those implied to be pivotal in *White Men Can't Jump* or a BellSouth advertisement.

Although there was scant popular awareness of it at the time (1977), the television miniseries *Roots* introduced the figure of the Unscathed Slave. To an enthralled audience of more than 80 million the series intimated that the damage resulting from generations of birth-ascribed, semi-animal status was largely temporary, that slavery was a product of motiveless malignity on the social margins rather than of respectable rationality, and that the ultimate significance of the institution lay in the demonstration, by freed slaves, that no force on earth can best the energies of American Individualism. ("Much like the Waltons confronting the depression," writes historian Eric Foner, a widely respected authority on American slavery, "the family in *Roots* neither seeks nor requires outside help; individual or family effort is always sufficient.") Ken Burns's much applauded PBS documentary *The Civil War* (1990) went even further than *Roots* in downscaling black injury; the series treated slavery, birth-ascribed inferiority, and the centuries-old denial of dignity as matters of slight consequence. (By "implicitly denying the brutal reality of slavery," writes historian Jeanie Attie, Burns's programs crossed "a dangerous moral threshold." To a group of historians who asked him why slavery had been so slighted, Burns said that any discussion of slavery "would have been lengthy and boring.")

Mass media treatments of the civil rights protest years carried forward the process, contributing to the "positive" erasure of difference. Big-budget films like *Mississippi Burning*, together with an array of TV biographical specials on Dr. Martin Luther King and others, presented the long-running struggle between disenfranchised blacks and the majority white culture as a heartwarming episode of interracial unity; the speed and caringness of white response to the oppression of blacks demonstrated that broadscale race conflict or race difference was inconceivable.

A consciousness that ingests either a part or the whole of this revisionism loses touch with the two fundamental truths of race in America; namely, that because of what happened in the past, blacks and whites cannot yet be the same; and that because what happened in the past was no mere matter of ill will or insult but the outcome of an established caste structure that has only very recently begun to be dismantled, it is not reparable by one-on-one goodwill. The word "slavery" comes to induce stock responses with no vital sense of a grinding devastation of mind visited upon generation after generation. Hoodwinked by the orthodoxy of friendship, the nation either ignores the past, summons for it a detached, correct "compassion," or gazes at it as though it were a set of aesthetic conventions, like twisted trees and fragmented rocks in nineteenth-century picturesque painting—lifeless phenomena without bearing on the present. The chance of striking through the mask of corporate-underwritten, feel-good, ahistorical racism grows daily more remote. The trade-off—whites promise friendship, blacks accept the status quo—begins to seem like a good deal.

Cosseted by Hollywood's magic lantern and soothed by press releases from Washington and the American Enterprise Institute, we should never forget what we see and hear for ourselves. Broken out by race, the results of every social tabulation from unemployment to life expectancy add up to a chronicle of atrocity. The history of black America fully explains—to anyone who approaches it honestly—how the disaster happened and why neither guilt money nor lectures on personal responsibility can, in and of themselves, repair the damage. The vision of friendship and sympathy placing blacks and whites "all in the same boat," rendering them equally able to do each other favors, "to give rides to one another," is a smiling but monstrous lie.

The nearer at hand the perfect place and good life can be made to seem, the more needless politics becomes. Year by year the media feed refines and deepens its power to create experiences of seeming adjacency to ideal life—complacency-building experiences of beauty, glamour, personal transformation, ecological order. Statehouses are dark and drab but the sun and sea radiate from Lauren and Nautica spreads, from the billion-plus Pottery Barn and Tiffany catalogs that choke mailboxes even in downscale zips, from high end car ads, high tech commercials, glossy magazine layouts, counters at numberless upscale malls. One of the first and purest visions of quasi-spiritual fulfillment through browsing-consumer fantasy was produced in Depression-era America. After L. L. Bean came the flood that made the promesse du bonheur *contrived by earnest, small print utopians seem as desperately shabby as a turn of the century Monty Ward wishbook.*

The Wooing Air of Beanland

The L. L. Bean catalog out of Freeport, Maine is in some sense "just" a catalog. Issued six times yearly, it describes GumShoes, "field watches," swim suits, duffles, camp bags, gaiters, "pixie slippers," PolarGuard booties, canoes, parkas, dickies, Cedar Dog Beds, Georgia fatwood in a burlap sack, the works. Mail the order form with check or card number, and goods move. But I am not fooled thereby. I may leaf through the catalog on a utilitarian errand. I may tell myself I'm looking for wool undies or a fly rod. I may send off for a hunting knife or a flannel sheet—but what I actually locate is something else. I locate a special identity, a special vision of the relation between me, others, manufactured stuff, and true fulfillment. I live for a time in a remarkably coherent imaginative world.

The fundamentals of this world—call it Beanland—are easy to summarize. It's a holiday world, not an everyday world. It's a world in which nothing cuts me off from my natural self. It's a world wherein my customary feeling is anticipation. In Beanland I'm forever frozen at the edge of takeoff, forever caught up, like a figure on Keats's Urn, on my way to the fun: the icy river, the misting lake, the mountain hut. No bad weather, no postponements, no accidents, no distracting bickering with spouse or child. And, inevitably, it's a world stripped clean of vexing social realities. Elsewhere I hear of oppressed minorities clamoring for Justice, and of pro- and anti-nuke factions vilifying each other. Not here. Troubling murmurs subside as I turn these pages. Recollected unpleasantness vanishes. I'm beyond numbing office routine and urban gridlock. Repugnance at rave parties and cable porn cannot touch me.

Live free or die.

All this is obvious, though—and insufficiently inward with the imaginative experience in question. Structurally speaking, the Bean catalog is an intricate assemblage of subtly interlocking themes, and both their nature and the modes of their interdependency bear inquiry.

Starting with the theme of History. Past and present are beautifully continuous in Beanland. I read of fine old human-scale companies none of which—contrary to talk in business journals—faces pressure from marauding conglomerates or Taiwan. "Bean's Child's Pull Sled [is] made for us by Paris Manufacturing Company of South Paris, Maine, sled makers since 1861." Bean's Shetland sweaters are "knit in a small plant in Nottinghamshire," each sweater receiving "individual attention." Bean's "Women's felt hat [is] made in the town of Atherstone where fine wool hats have been made for 300 years." Bean's "Hudson's Bay Point Blankets . . . are identical to those traded nearly two centuries ago." Bean's Mackinaw was designed by C. C. Filson "in 1897 for use in the gold fields during the Alaskan Klondike Gold Rush."

My sense of comfortable continuity, my feeling for the attractive accessibility of the past, is strengthened in a variety of ways. The history that the catalog remembers is invariably familiar history—nothing recondite or Third Worldish. The period in favor is World War II: who can forget WW II? Gloves, leather jackets and crew neck sweaters are linked with, respectively, Austrian ski troops, the U. S. Naval Air Corps, and "the British S. A. S. Commando regiment . . ." Scattered about in Beanland dreamdust is the unfaded amaranth of intimate reminiscence. "Bean's Chamois Cloth shirt . . . is the shirt Mr. Bean used on his hunting and fishing trips. It has been in our line since 1927." Who can forget old Mr. Bean? The word *traditional* tolls two, three, four times a page. "Traditional lasts." "Traditional designs."

Nor is tradition influential only upon styles or production standards; it shapes domestic life as well. In my father's country children were not problematic; so it is still in Beanland. Children here are not considered, debated or regretted, they exist. They occasion pride. The pleasure taken by a smiling mother in her pleasantly frecklefaced lad is as relaxed and easy as that of the well-fixed Mom in Renoir's "Madame Charpentier and Her Children." And the children themselves are exuberantly healthy and merry, witness the rosy-cheeked toddler waving on the cover. Beanland sex, to come to that, is nowhere haunted by the gamy scent of the illicit. Regard this illustrated couple in plaid flannel nightshirts, he in grey, she in red. His hand rests gently on her shoulder, both figures take in the camera straightforwardly. No snigger, no slyness. Stance, eyes, teeth and skin tone bespeak a happily unselfconscious, contentedly conventional sexuality. No kinky videos for this pair, thank you very much. And, by the same token, when I am resident in Beanland, I not only know the difference between men and women, I can assert my satisfaction in that difference without offending any organized sector of the electorate. "Men's . . . has self-closing pockets; Women's has slash hand-warmer pockets;" we are not the same.

Equally crucial to the catalog's thematics is the readiness of Beanland upholders of tradition to stand on the side of discipline and authority. The voice of Beanland does not shirk, speaks of holiday things in sternly prescriptive tones and condemns those inclined to dogging it. The catalog tells me, firmly, precisely, *how* each item should be used or worn. This "sturdy well-made sled [is] for pulling one or two small children, supplies, or icefishing gear . . ." This parka is "designed for ski touring, bicycling, hiking or backpacking." The terry cloth back of this ski glove is "for wiping cold noses." This hunting shoe is "for use in hard hilly terrain where wet and cold conditions are . . . encountered."

And I am meant to like hard hilly terrain—hard anything, in fact. I'm meant to put out, meant to subject my gear to rough use. No flummery pursuit of the easy way here. The "River Driver's Shirt" is for "strenuous activities." The Northlands Parka is "rugged and durable," as my case demands. The Lined Work Gloves are made of buckskin that's been "degrained to expose the toughest, most dense part of the hide. Originally used by western ranch hands for stringing barbed wire."

A true holiday world, pardner, is quite unlike the familiar everyday world of enervating, neurasthenic luxury. We're talking *degrained*.

Tradition, strenuousness, the demanding way—these are the major themes of the catalog. But shaping and controlling their interaction is a yet more moving master theme, Ventilation. The authors of the Bean catalogs place me as a person *obsessed with breathing*, and everywhere they commend my obsession. The leitmotif, air, surfaces at or near page one of every catalog ("goose down breathes for comfort"), and ceaselessly returns thereafter. In 1984 I read of "breathable" Anorak Parkas and "breathable" Windpants and "breathable" Ski Touring Pullovers and "Breathable" Cross Country Gloves and "breathable" Thinsulate Gore-Tex Parkas and "breathable" Gore-Text Pack Jackets and "breathable"

Gore-Tex Overalls and "breathable" Women's Larkspur Jackets and "breathable" Women's Polo Shirts and "breathable" 50/50 Channel Comforters. The Women's Eskimo Parka "breathes," the Men's Rainier Boot is "lined for Breathability," Bean's auto seat cover of Merino sheepskin "allows free air movement around your body. . . ."

In 2001 I read of a "tropics shirt [that's] highly breathable," of "Cool weave shirts" that have "fresh air woven right in," of "Ventilation Shirts" that allow for "maximum airflow for the hottest days on the trail."

What's more, I'm presented year after year with chances to seize grander air, to breathe yet more freely. These buttons can be *opened*, this zipper can be *unzipped*. "4 Inch rib knit collar . . . opens for ventilation." "12 inch coil zipper at neck for ventilation." "Convertible turtleneck . . . can be opened up for ventilation." "Double-thick shawl collar . . . can be worn open for ventilation." At the core of my nature is a kind of Lear-like lust to unbutton, profound hunger for oneness with each stirring of the common wind. Other themes in Beanland carry practicalities; this one is purest poetry. You love best your freshness, it tells me; Spontaneity is your god.

About the connection between what's called reality and the world of L. L. Bean little need be said. In *The Fashion System*, a semiological study, Roland Barthes held that we make a mistake when we brood about a cultural object's authenticity or lack thereof. Every cultural object, Barthes claimed, has a "semantic vocation," and that's what matters most about it. We clothe ourselves in signs, not in garments. "The ten gallon hat (rainproof, sunproof) is nothing more than a sign of what is 'Western;' the sport jacket no longer has an athletic function but exists only as a sign, opposed to the *dressy*; blue jeans have become the sign of leisure . . ." My Bean gear, in a word, encodes my desire.—I desire to be a man or a woman whose sexuality is without ambiguity, a parent whose nurturing gift is warm and strong, an American whose mind and heart flood with faith in the nation's virtue and generosity, a citizen whose relation to society is untormented by suspicion that I abhor those unlike me, a physical system draining great cleansing drafts from the radiant atmosphere, a player-worker of passionate intensity, a moral being aloof from commerce, hardsell, profit, advantage-seeking, meanness. I wish to be good, in sum. I wish to be straight. I wish to be pure.

Can Beanland slake that many desires? Wrong question. Ad copy doesn't slake desires, it gives them voice, lifts them into sight, causing me thus to comprehend that I *am* my desires. What is identity, finally, except clarity about what I want? Reading the Bean catalog I become one who not only wants to believe in his own purity and straightness, but wants also to believe in the purity and straightness of everybody else. And, to repeat, it's the catalog that shows me these desires of mine. The L. L. Bean people assure me that I am one of them—not a mere customer in a money-maddened age, but an oldtimer, seasoned, bone-hard, downright, part of the human fraternity of roughwear that could not care less about chasing a buck. "We appreciate any suggestions," the Bean catalog asserts. "We consider our customers a part of our organization and want you to feel free to make any criticism you see fit. . . ."

Of *course* these longings of mine can be dismissed as silly, naive, reductive, mindless. Of *course* there are others besides the Bean folks who bring such longings to life for their profit (the Ralph Lauren folks, for example). And of *course* it's true that the themes shaped in the catalog have a long history in American culture. Anti-modernist protesters against the tyranny of the shoddy and the soft, the degradation of work, the commercial exploitation of human relationships started sounding off on these shores in the 1880s or thereabouts, developing ideologies of arts and crafts, scouting, the Simple Life, the Strenuous Life, and so on. (A splendid recent study of the breed, by Jackson Lears, is called *No Place For Grace.*)

But although the dream of escape from meretriciousness and stultification has its mindless side, it's clearly senseless to knock it, or to deprive it of its literary due. When faith disappears, we're left with our overwhelming need for signs that life might be otherwise than it is. In another age politics met that need by giving voice to dreams of social transformation. Beanland pastoral meets the need by telling us an untruth that makes only a fantast's day: the world we *know* we live in isn't really here at all.

A *highly effective complacency-builder—firm foundation for belief in American goodness ("a nation of kind hearts")—is an experience of ideal order: a perfect place that seems at once near at hand and compellingly authentic, yet dependent solely on raw fact, unimproved by the imagination's sentimental wand, and possessing more than negligible duration. Movies lack duration and so also does the glossy catalog. The gap between fantasy and the real world, between Frank Capra-style daydreams and things as they are, can be briefly forgotten at the multiplex or while studying the Lauren life, under the lamplight, in the Sunday* Times *magazine. But only briefly. Book-length evocations locating the ideal order in the dailiness surrounding us—in non-fiction reality—are less interruptible, hence less fragile.*

As it happens, the late 20th century was strikingly inventive on this cultural front. For long decades representations of mainstreet America as utopia had been left to the likes of Capra, Norman Rockwell and "editors" of the Reader's Digest, *and gradually enthusiasts of all three were taught to sneer at themselves as softies. But the Nineties brought to life a new genre which, pretending to belong to plain facts reportage, spoke at powerfully extended length, with best-selling influence, on the theme that here and now—in this particular American home place, this particular American schoolroom or corporate computer lab or home for the aged—human life was reaching an apex of decency, dignity, and love. The advent of the form lifted self-satisfaction in educated sectors of the population wherein, for a half-century the* Reader's Digest *had been a joke. Tracy Kidder, author of* Hometown *(1999). pioneered the new, apolitical, upbeat-documentary genre.*

It's a Wonderful Life

The city of Northampton, Massachusetts (pop. 30,000), a county seat in the Connecticut River valley, is located ninety miles west of Boston, three hours north of Manhattan. Until fairly recently it was best known as the home of Smith College. Two decades ago the *National Enquirer* and the news weeklies brought the city fresh notice by declaring it to be friendly to homosexuals (the *Enquirer* called it "Lesbianville, USA"). To cultural historians, Northampton has meaning because Jonathan Edwards preached fire and brimstone here (until his parishioners cast him out, in 1750); activists are aware of the place because the two most recent generations of feminists have been led by women—Betty Friedan and Gloria Steinem—who graduated from Smith. Casual visitors notice the density of ethnic eateries, "boutiques," young people on the streets (three other colleges and one university are located in the immediate vicinity), and preceptorial bumper stickers (PERFORM SENSELESS ACTS OF BEAUTY. MY KARMA ATE MY DOGMA, etc.).

The city is the setting and subject of *Home Town*, by Tracy Kidder—the fourth work of nonfiction that this writer has situated in Northampton or neighboring towns (Leeds, Holyoke, Amherst). The three other works—*Old Friends* (1993), *Among Schoolchildren* (1989), and *House* (1985)—deal respectively

with life in a nursing home, in an elementary school classroom, and on a construction job. *The Soul of a New Machine*
(1981), the book that earned Kidder his first fame, reported on
the design and building, by Data General, of a fast new computer, and is set at corporate headquarters near Boston.

With an exception or two, these books have received smooth
rides from reviewers, commercial success, and prizes (*The Soul
of a New Machine* won a Pulitzer for nonfiction). Like the earlier works, the new one has a cultural interest, owing to links
with New England's (and the nation's) self-mythologizing past
and doggedly vain present. At a moment when the star of the
Northeast—"The Spirit of America," as Bay State license plates
call it—isn't rising, the old regional myths of special identity
and superiority undergo local resuscitation, and prove service-
able to the broader society.

As spokesperson for these myths, Tracy Kidder, Andover- and
Harvard-educated, is unassuming and retiring—no flamboyance, no reminders of the super-hyped reportage of the Sixties.
He presents himself as a diffident student-apprentice, eager to
learn and troubled about intruding; a typical "Acknowledgments" section thanks dozens for "letting me into their lives, for
putting up with me, for teaching me."

Autobiographical snippets reveal the writer has down-to-
earth recreational tastes (carpentry and computer games); his
statements of general views reveal a positive thinker, preoccupied with good conduct, and self-secure:

> Many people find it easy to imagine unseen webs of
> malevolent conspiracy in the world, and they are not
> always wrong. But there is also an innocence that con-
> spires to hold humanity together, and it is made of people
> who can never fully know the good that they have done.
> The central problem of life at [a nursing home] is,

after all, only the universal problem of separateness: the original punishment, the ultimate vulnerability, the enemy of meaning.

If civilization implies more than TVs and dishwashers, more than artistic achievement and wise rules, it implies just this, a place with a life that shelters individual lives, a place that allows people to become better than they might otherwise be—better, in a sense, than they are.

In keeping with sentiments of this sort, Kidder country is a quiet place, inhospitable to celebrity, investigations of civic wrongdoing, noisy eccentrics, polemical politics, anger at hierarchy and injustice. Kidder describes what people do and how they relate to others in their work as computer designers, home builders, architects, teachers, cops. And he holds the focus steady on people he admires—whose thought and action, he feels, radiate goodness. He's willing to "hang around"—his phrase—for months or even years, waiting for a real-life, suspenseful narrative pattern to emerge.

But suspense is incidental. What counts in his often shapely narratives is the continuous unfolding of the major characters' qualities—self-reliance, reverence for craft, concern for others, generosity, faithfulness, and absence of greed. The writer's readiness to subordinate himself—the sustained authorial self-effacement that's integral to his themes—chimes with his characters' lack of presumption and creates an impression of a coherent and harmonious human world. In *The Soul of a New Machine*, Tom West, the computer engineer who heads up a successful crash program to build a wizard computer, keeps his team motivated to the end despite ill-judged harassment from above. And he is fiercely modest: he won't seek or accept public credit for his accomplishment. Jim Locke, ascetic carpenter-craftsman-contractor in *House*, is dedicated to an uncompromising "pursuit of quality" that's almost totally oblivious of the bottom line. Lou and Joe, seniors thrust together by a nursing home in *Old Friends*, repeatedly—and touchingly—put personal interest aside to care for each other and for their neighbors in the home. Lou has "great sympathetic capacity"; Joe tirelessly serves his fellow residents: "[Joe] had entered a little society founded merely on illness, and, accepting it for what it was, realizing it was all there was for him, he had joined it and improved it."

Many of the most carefully controlled scenes in these books invite readers to live with presumed virtue as it experiences guilt. In *Among Schoolchildren*, a gifted elementary schoolteacher named Chris Zajac is obliged, because of the disruptive behavior of a black fifth-grader, to consent to a disciplinary committee's decision to pack the youngster off to a special class for the unruly—a probable life sentence of loserdom. Kidder tracks Zajac's loving concern for the lad and her subsequent self-arraignment—her over-conscientious distress that defects of hers as a teacher could be responsible for her pupil's fate. On the last day of school, months after his banishment, the boy looks in the doorway at his former teacher and old class:

> In the midst of [her] reverie, sudden, untoward motion on the perimeter, that sense of something out of place, made Chris turn her head, and there in the opened doorway to the playground stood the familiar figure of Clarence. Brown-skinned and wiry with huge eyes. The knees of his jeans had holes in them. He wore a dirty white T-shirt. He stood there, dismounted, holding on to the handlebars of a ten-speed bike, and gazed in at the children with his mouth slightly ajar.
>
> "Hi, Clarence!" said Chris. "How *are* you?"
>
> He looked at her and smiled. Those dimples! And he

looked so small! In her mind, he had grown much larger. Could this have been the most difficult student of her career? He was only four and a half feet tall.

"Come on in!" she said to him.

Clarence, she noticed, still stuttered sometimes at the starts of sentences. "Nuh nuh no I can't. Gotta go someplace." But he lingered in the doorway, and his mouth came ajar again as he gazed at his old classmates. They were all looking back at Clarence now.

"Oh," she thought. "I feel bad for him."

"Don't you want to come in and talk to any of them?" asked Chris. It would be sweet and fitting for him to pass the last of this afternoon with them, as if perhaps he'd never been sent away. . . .

[She] sat in her chair, turned toward him. She smiled at him. Probably he wanted to join them, but was feeling shy. Maybe she could coax him. "Don't you want to come on in?" said Chris again.

"No," said Clarence. "Not today." He smiled at her, and again he went back to gazing at the children while Chris gazed at him.

"Oh, well," said Chris offhandedly. But she had to try once more. "Sure you don't want to come in?"

"No. Bye," he said.

He turned away and sped off on his bike, so quickly she hardly saw him go. It was like the time, months ago, when Clarence was supposed to stay after school, and she turned her back for only a few seconds and turned around again to find that he had vanished. The doorway was empty. She turned back to face the room.

Determination to do well by the pupil in greatest need, shame at the thought one may have quit too early, longing for speech sufficiently kind to purge the momentary sense of oneself as uncaring—all are sharply lighted in this portrait of a teacher's virtue. Less vivid in *Among Schoolchildren* is the complex of forces that limit the potency of teachers working in overcrowded, underfinanced classrooms. But Kidder's subject is Chris Zajac, not the "problems of urban education"; in this book as elsewhere his effort is to construct situations as stages on which personal conduct, good and bad, can be experienced and assessed without distraction. Detaching teachers, architects, carpenters, nurses, and engineers from the workings of civic finance or of the banking, housing, computer, and "nonprofit" aging-care industries, his books erase the conditions of moral performance. The understanding is that, whether or not minority ghettoes are expanding in Holyoke, Massachusetts, a teacher's individual goodness creates a world of its own.

Home Town's dominating figure of rectitude doesn't stand alone but shares the stage with a multitude of others of comparable "secularized virtue." Kidder attempts to examine—as he hasn't hitherto—the role of external influences, especially that of the past, in shaping the moral examples under scrutiny. And there's one other difference from the earlier works: the book's subject shifts quite early from figures of rectitude to the sanctified place that their character and actions bring into being: Northampton, Massachusetts. With that shift the tone turns celebratory, literary interest declines, and cultural interest expands.

At the start, Tommy O'Connor, home-grown police-sergeant hero, is *Home Town*'s prime representative of uprightness. The man is self-deprecating: praised for saving an injured child's life, he tells his commenders he's tried and failed twenty times before at mouth-to-mouth resuscitation ("Hey, now I'm one for twenty-one!"). He upholds the policing system without self-righteousness: when friends or former classmates ask him to fix tickets for traffic violations, he pays their fines himself. He's patient and sympathetic with the suicidal, with drunks and druggies, even with a relatively bigtime drug dealer whom he sends up for forty-five years. His commitment to his wife, Jean, is absolute, as is his commitment to his widowed father (the son plows the father's driveway when it snows, cooks dinner and eats—with his wife—at his father's house most nights, dreams of taping the old man's stories so he can pass them along to his own children when they arrive).

And this policeman is racked, like Chris the schoolteacher, by wrongheaded guilt that nevertheless does him credit. When another police officer charged with abusing his own daughter confesses his heinous crime to O'Connor, the latter, obedient to his professional obligation, passes the confession along to a local prosecutor specializing in rape cases. Torment follows. O'Connor can't stop reproaching himself—he imagines in his nightmares being called on to lock up his friend. Did he have to tell the prosecutor what the officer friend admitted in confidence? Self-doubt, pity for the convicted child molester, outrage at the crime itself conjoin with O'Connor's self-mockery and humorous impiety to fill out a portrait of likable rectitude.

Similar portraits abound in the book. Not just O'Connor playfully skidding his cruiser in the midnight snow but the police chief, as well, incarnates likable rectitude. Also the mayor, who is "incorruptible . . . shy, big-hearted, thoroughly competent, imaginative, and garrulous." Also a presiding judge, who is incorruptible and "didn't like sending people to jail, because he didn't like jails." Also funny, charming Frankie, a drug dealer-police informer who cooperates with cops partly for money, partly out of feeling for Sergeant O'Connor and for the greater social good ("If they only knew, wouldn't every citizen of Hamp applaud Frankie's work on their behalf?"). Also the representative of studentdom, a scholar who, after wrestling with "the fading doctrines of the deconstructionists," decides their ideas aren't "right," and stays up all night in ecstasy reading *Paradise Lost* ("The poem's majestic, oceanic music carried her so far off that when she lifted her eyes from the book, she was startled to find herself in her apartment"). Also the academic administrator—a kind heart who regularly goes extra miles on behalf of the weak who are threatened with flunking out.

Before the end, indeed, figures of virtue are multiplying intolerably in *Home Town*, like luxe mail-order catalogs in an upscale zip. There's "the person who planted pansies in the scraggly ground beside a pair of public steps," and "the youthful anarchists who retrieved the stolen plaque from the front steps of the First Church," and "the man who goes out early in the morning and tears down the posters illegally attached to light poles, mailboxes, and other public property." There are the sensitive Northampton motorists compulsively forcing the right of way on pedestrians and hesitating "to honk at another driver, perhaps thinking, 'I might know that idiot's wife.'" Thoughtful Northampton shopkeepers who "didn't cover their windows with steel grates after hours . . . left things outside that could easily have been defaced—flower boxes by the sidewalks, canvas awnings over storefronts." Shy, benign Northampton rich, plus the local, self-abnegating upper middle class:

> Wealthy people here tended to live on remote hilltops, far away from inquiring eyes, or else discreetly, in houses with plain exteriors but interiors that contained kitchens good enough for restaurants, and private libraries, and art collections of great worth. The wealthy of Northampton drove good cars but not the very best. They didn't have live-in servants, though some maintained the equivalents of staffs, in caterers, cleaners, gardeners. One tier below, there

was a much larger prosperous class, the upper middle by local standards—academics, business owners, various professionals. Many people had given up a little something to live here, forsaking their chances to maximize profits.

Bashful rich, gracious motorists, kindly drug dealers—all are as they are, the writer explains, because of the saving hand of the past. And that explanation exacerbates the book's developing problems. Kidder is creditably wary of certain mystical accounts of Northampton's past and present—he smiles gently at a Christian lay preacher who tells his flock that from time immemorial "an angel guarded Northampton from 'the malice power,' the evil influences that wanted to migrate up the river valley, from the cities to the south and into Northampton's streets." But sane skepticism deserts him elsewhere, as when he gushes about aristo lineage (the gift of background). Jean O'Connor, the detective sergeant's wife, is a person of distinction because she's "descended on both sides from some of the first English settlers of the Connecticut valley" (her "face had an heirloom quality," her "eyes had what seemed like an ancestral steadiness").

Worse, this writer believes in the impact, on present character and behavior, of mid-nineteenth-century egalitarians, abolitionists, and revolutionaries—men and women who tried "to establish an ideal place inside Northampton," and had to settle for less, namely a century and a half of living, radical influence:

> They dreamed of sexual, racial, and economic equality, and they wanted to show the world that a society built on such principles could thrive materially as well as spiritually. . . . The utopian community had contributed to a continuing tradition here, a tradition of secularized virtue that fed on dreams of ideal places.

Through the moral agency of Smith College (an "ideal place within a place"), the effects of yesteryear's utopianism pulse through the decades into contemporary veins "like [the effects] of distant ancestry." The continuing tradition puffs nothing up, to be sure—no person, no place. Kidder's miniaturizing rhetoric enfolds city and citizenry alike in caressing diminutives that celebrate "little acts of courage and kindness and simple competence" performed by "little people" of the kind, Sergeant O'Connor believes, big city doctors don't care about. All remains in human scale—the "little airfield in the Meadows," the "little council chamber" for the city councillors, "little mountain ranges," "a little island" floating out in the middle of a pond.

Can design govern in a place so little? It governs here. "No committee had sat down and arranged the watches of the town," the author writes, "and yet they functioned as if by grand design, so that one's doing this allowed the other's doing that, even if the one didn't know or didn't like the other, even if neither the one nor the other was civic-minded."

Pure panegyric prepares the way for this "grand design"—floods of flattery. Northampton resembles "Plato's ideal city-state" (it has "thirty thousand souls"). Northampton resembles the ten similar-sized cities Leonardo da Vinci had in mind to build in order "to relieve the squalor and congestion of Renaissance Milan." Northampton also resembles the famous garden cities invented in the late nineteenth century by Ebenezer Howard. (The "perfect garden city," Kidder explains, "was neither quite a city nor a country town. It combined the best of both. It wasn't an American-style suburb, but a truly self-sufficient place, with farms and rural scenery, urban entertainment and variety. Northampton had become a place rather like that, where many people went for weeks without leaving because they found some of everything they needed and wanted here.") Northampton's downtown resembles the "ideal urban neighborhood" Jane

Jacobs extolled. "It was used at almost every hour, and this ensured not just liveliness and profit but also the constant presence of 'eyes on the street.' "

Caution: Paradise City is good not because it's secure but secure because it's good. "Regionally renowned for its peacefulness and safety," it is above all "a moral place," hence capable of bringing off great deeds. On his penultimate page, Tracy Kidder takes testimony from a young black resident concerning one great deed:

> Often when he passed other black people downtown, ones he didn't know, [the young black] smiled at them and they smiled back, little smiles that seemed to say, "Isn't this place weird?" and, "What are *you* doing here?" And yet he had begun to feel something like a booster's pride. This past winter he'd attended a lecture by two famous black intellectuals, delivered at Smith. He'd listened with mounting anger. "White man bad. Black man good." That, he thought, was the lecturers' central message. He felt offended, not personally, but on behalf of his fellow townsfolk. "How dare you talk that way *here*," he'd wanted to say. "These are some of the nicest white people you'll ever meet."

Race is no problem in the moral place. The nicest whites have licked it cold.

The question of whether a small college town in western New England is paradise received some play in the news, arts, and letters columns of the local daily paper (the *Hampshire Gazette*) soon after *Home Town* appeared. An editorial columnist saluted the book—on the paper's front page above the fold—as the first recognizable portrait of the town he lived in (a welcome change from the badmouthing of Northampton in the news weeklies and the *National Enquirer*). The *Gazette*'s back pages ran a trashing review by a sharp-witted city writer, Tzivia Gover; Gover called *Home Town* a "sophisticated version" of the kids' world chronicled in PBS's *Mr. Rogers' Neighborhood*. Letters went back and forth, for a while, on whether *Home Town* was fiction or "documentary," and at summer picnics people who had read the book were called on to stand and deliver.

I was among them—no authority on the city but a resident of neighboring towns for several decades and acquainted with some Northampton townsfolk and institutions. The matter of interest wasn't whether I or any other local thought *Home Town* was "right" about Northampton. My opinion of the city's hospital (high) or of the citizenry (low: this moral place allowed its public high school to sink to a condition of decrepitude before a frantic bumper-sticker campaign persuaded it to finance renovations); my judgment of Smith College (mixed: Smith is the least provincial of the five local institutions of higher learning but is also the only one lately afflicted with declining standards); my judgment of local "tolerance" (mixed: Northampton seems safer than many other places for homosexuals, but a friend who's homosexual was badly beaten on the town's streets not long ago)—all this is beside the point.

The matter of interest about *Home Town* is, simply, how could a man who has lived in a town gull himself into such preposterous claims for it? What renders a talented journalist susceptible to this degree of extravagance? The author's earlier books, true, betray strong leanings toward hero worship and affiliated sentimentalities. And, true again, the country's pop past is seductively chockablock with big paydays for small-town mush (Norman Rockwell, the *Reader's Digest*, Capra, Saroyan, Wilder, Keillor, others beyond counting). But such answers face away from what's central.

The case is that there's no mystery about the origin of works like the one at hand. *Home Town* draws on a perfectly conventional mythology of national integrity that's often localized, but rarely to any purpose except to roll the whole. The miscellaneous bits from which the present hallowing of New England is fabricated (Pilgrims, Puritans, Boston Tea Party, Paul Revere, City on the Hill, Underground Railway, Massachusetts alone for McGovern, etc.) are easy to identify. And it's worth noting that New England nationalism, cultural imperialism, and sense of sectional superiority have closest to their core, as a brilliant recent study of the region's myth-making demonstrates, the "erasure by whites of the historical experience of local enslavement."*

But the point of moment is that Kidder's Northampton descends neither from the secularized virtue of yesteryear's local utopians nor from their self-inflating claims to purity and nobility, nor from the visions of their heroes, such as Emerson. (The self-congratulating author of *Self-Reliance*, arguing for confiscating Southerners' property after the Civil War: "You at once open the whole South to the enterprise & genius of new men of all nations & *extend New England from Canada to the Gulf, et to the Pacific.*") This ideal, light-bringing place—this paradise of ordinary broken parking meters and ordinary public meetings about banning barroom smoking that end in shouts of "Nazi! Fascist!"—was born in national fantasy: the dream that the virtues of the virgin land remain intact, available for consultation, pick up your pass at the gatehouse.

The map tells the story. Such a tiny, tiny section of the land, way off there on the upper right, barely enough of it to make one state much less six. . . . Size isn't it, though, you understand. Probity

---

*Joanna Pope Melish, *Disowning Slavery: Gradual Emancipation and "Race" in New England, 1780-1860* (Cornell University Press, 1998), p. 3.

counts. Probity radiates and elevates. It's the national moral energy source. Probity keeps sending out waves to all four corners, bringing us back to our best selves, showing us the way that sometimes we seem for a second, just for a bit, to have lost. As long as it's intact, as long as we can hear those little *morally cleansing beeps*—

Our national bedtime story. Begat by virtue, surviving through virtue, flourishing and earning the right, by reason of an inviolable innocence, to correct the world: this is our bailiwick and base—the pure Spirit of America become every Yank's hometown.

2. The Culture of Celebrity: Insiders & Outsiders

One major support shoring up apoliticality is the mass of cultural production, books to movies, representing America as friction-free—a place where an unparalleled combination of abundance and one-mindedness renders politics needless. An equally potent support is the mass of cultural material that provisions the country's celebrity culture.

Discussion of celebrity culture regularly patronizes it, not without reason, as a mindless, trivializing distraction. Bread and circuses. But the standard indictment mistakenly ignores the culture's political functions. The badmouthing of politics from on high implicitly deprecates loyalty to party, class, occupation and ethnicity—but can't erase the appetite for association. Celebrity culture eases this problem. It creates an arena of extrafamilial relationships wherein the appetite for association can be slaked without risk of stimulating the formation of ideologically coherent groups.

Individual celebrities often slip the bonds of apoliticality, to be sure, becoming spokespersons for Positions. Lennon, Springsteen, Fonda, Beatty, Reagan, several Kennedys—dozens of similar crossovers come to mind. But it would be wrongheaded to place any of these, regardless of influence, as defining figures of celebrity culture. The manufacture and marketing of Names—proliferating entertainment weeklies, instant showbiz updates on cable and Internet, daily personality columns in newspapers of record, the guests industry, the endorsement and testimonial industry—is a vast enterprise. An individual celebrity with a political cause is a marginal phenomenon—a minuscule cog in a giant machine that dwarfs all causes.

And shapes mentalities and moralities. Partly because the machine exists, patterns of attention and indifference have markedly changed over the past few decades. A new value, insidedness, attains striking esteem. Market society bromides—Winning is the Only Thing—become rules of conduct. Pride in participation in the public square vanishes. The celebrity culture calls into being a state within the state—a kingdom closed upon itself.

The subjects of this kingdom inhabit it in individual ways, shifting interest and allegiance often; generalizations about ruling norms of thought and feeling are unsafe. On rare occasions someone gifted caught in the tangle of longings for fame brings to life, at book length or some similar sustained performance, the texture of the experience of celebrity worship, even dealing directly with the onset of contempt for traditional politics. (The third essay in this section treats one such work, by a youngster who hungered for celebrity and attained it.)

But such guides are rare indeed. Probes of the relation between celebrity culture and no-politics politics inevitably lean heavily on guesses and intuitions: speculation about fans' motives, feelings, peculiarities of response. The upcoming piece, for instance, studies goings-on at a Citrus League ballgame played some twenty years ago, for hints about the functions, for fans, of the experience of recognition. It argues that that experience, far from being a mere distraction or diversion, is a mode of pseudo-democratic self-assertion: a means of separating oneself from the herd of the unknowing, ground for personal pride of a kind not known to our elders.

Recognition Scene

The pre-season Yanks-Rangers night game was half over when Howie Cosell arrived, and for a while there wasn't any fuss. Nelson Briles, the Rangers' starter, was in process of being knocked out (homers by Jackson and Chambliss) and the good-sized crowd, mostly Yankees fans, had cause to keep its mind on business. Once the shelling subsided, though, the crowd's attention shifted quickly to the box beside the Yankee dugout. Autograph hounds who had lined up earlier—besieging the Yanks' owner, George Steinbrenner, and Cosell's announcing partner at ABC, Chris Schenkel—materialized again in greater numbers for a greater prize: Cosell himself. The Carlton Fisk fan across the aisle from us, a blond, beer-flushed, hoarse-voiced twenty-year-old who couldn't be distracted, even during the blasting, from noisy taunting of Thurman Munson, the Yanks' catcher, scuttled purposefully down the stairs to join the latest autograph line. Two men behind us, older than the Munson heckler, one from St. Louis, the other from Worcester, who had kept up an informatively detailed conversation about lifetime batting averages and forgotten, interesting trades of yesteryear, fell silent, focussed like the rest of the nearby crowd on the Steinbrenner-Cosell box.

A new entertainment began.

It wasn't a shapely or dramatic entertainment, to be sure. Cosell in the front row, hearing a sally from Steinbrenner behind him, swings round, grins. Cosell and Schenkel face each other, speak animatedly for a moment. Cosell says a word of greeting to Munson, who's headed for the on-deck circle; Munson nods, pauses, smiles in his mutton chops at a second Cosell offering, then replies. Cosell calls Jimmy Wynn, a lively-eyed black man, over to the box—Wynn is on *his* way to the on-deck circle. After an exchange or two Cosell pats this ballplayer, a first-class power-hitting outfielder just traded to the club, on the top of his helmeted head. A blessing. Double play on the field, side retired. Cosell accepts and signs a piece of paper presented to him from the dugout by another auto-graph-hunter—the Yankee batboy. Cosell rises, leaves the box, ascends the stairs as the adjacent rows watch and a group above, at the beer counter, sets up a chant—*How*-weee. *How*-weeee. Cosell returns shortly, and, as the assemblage watches him descend the stairs, the *Howie-Howie* chant resumes. After another inning it picks up again, stops, picks up once more.

It's neither hostile, the chanting, nor exactly affectionate—more like involuntary, or sheepish, or both. Cosell, teased over the years by a thousand homemade banners slung from foot-ball stadium railings, behaves as though used to it. No doubt he's aware that the so-called "celebrity culture," like the Grape-fruit League itself, is widely understood to be a kind of joke—weightless, theatrical, semigenuine. George Steinbrenner, a cheerful *moyen sensuel homme* to judge from his appearance, is a ship-building executive, contributes heavily and illegally to the Nixon campaign, is fined $15,000 for so doing in 1974, buys a ball club, and overnight becomes an object of interest to autograph hunters. Amusing. Cosell, a toupéed gent whose voice is a mechanically variegated monotone, holds a mike to the lips of athletes humiliated or triumphant ("Did he hurt you? Did he hurt you at any time?"), and becomes a household word, a "personality" whom brilliantly coordinated athletes allow to tap their heads condescendingly. Amusing. A celebrity is a person famous for being well-known: witty remark. Historians who bother to comment on these phenomena—Daniel Boorstin, for example—speak of pseudo-events and the image. Novelists—William Gaddis, for example—work up metaphors of forgery and counterfeiting. A light tone prevails. Everyone is assured that there are no real hazards, that as long as people bear in mind where they are, no serious damage can be done.

Yet despite the seeming good sense of taking all celebrity worship lightly, this intermittent semi-genuine chanting at a semi-genuine game didn't finally come off, for some reason, as innocuous. It was a joke, yes, but the third or fourth time round it was a habit as well—a habit of sheepishness, of unwarranted deference, of behaving as though celebrities really are different from us. And it was out of keeping. Florida ball parks—Bradenton, Lauderdale, many of the rest—take you back. They're smaller even than most Double-A parks and much more intimate than the friendliest big league stadium. Wood is what they're made of, often, and the grass is grass; the feelings stirred are green, clean, fresh. The child beside you is yourself. Eskimo Pie is as it was. No sleaze. But listening and watching the celebrity and his fans introduces the illicit and the sly. Neither party has met the other, yet each feigns familiarity, closeness. The air becomes knowing and cynical. Cosell gestures once or twice at the chanters, raises his chin to them, smiles as though in bonhomie, as though assured of the quality of the relationship between the chanters and himself as private persons. Perceiving this, the chanters grow for a moment more raucous—more daring? more mocking? And the rest of us are transformed into voyeurs, forced to try to read an unreadable primal scene, an obscure play of faked personal relations. It's like catching a scent, on a forest walk in crisp air and golden sunlight, of putrescence, and realizing, at once, that you won't be able to hold your breath long enough.

Celebrity Cosell passed near us as he climbed the stairs from the owner's box. The gait was leaden and ungraceful, and a certain superficial arrogance was unmistakable. But the true look in the man's eye was furtive.—*If they* think *I'm different from them, mustn't I be? Am I really?* In the celebrity culture fan and hero are caught in the same jam, share the same fear—that of being found out—and the consequence is confusion of feeling, ceaseless shuttling between pugnacity and shame. At any hour the world could change. At any hour it could decide, suddenly, no notice, to recover responsiveness to talent, developed gifts, well-made objects, accomplishments (athletic, medical, diplomatic, editorial, other) as opposed to fluff. What if it happened? Best to stand ready, best to run scared. Best to chant *Howie-Howie* in a neutral tone.

As for the ballgame, some of it was beyond spoiling. (Line drives, fast-ball pitching, men on in every stanza; the Rangers were blown out, 10–4.) But the sound sticks in the memory anyway—the automatic, unwilled quality, the utter absence of conviction, the squandered self-respect. *How-weee . . . How-weee.*

It's well understood that no-politics politics and celebrity culture favor the same yardsticks of evaluation: likability, "sensitivity," won-lost record. Not so well understood is the effect of these standards on attentiveness to content of performance. Down the stretch they come—competing opinions on tax cuts, welfare reform, school financing—but the terms, the logic, the democratic appropriateness, the meaning and worth of the opinions aren't to the point. The race is all; the worth of the opinions equals their win and place standing—their probable order of finish. Celebrity culture and no-politics politics teach each other how to be content-free: how to fix the public gaze on the scoreboard not the issue. The result is fascination with victories minus matter, defeats minus marrow.

The first person narrator of the piece ahead is a celebrity handicapper, knowledgeable about moment to moment league standings everywhere, but nowhere acquainted with or interested in what's at stake—except finishing first—in the races he follows. Schooled by the star system, fiercely committed to competition, possessing a tragicomic dimension, he's a model citizen for any no-politics regime.

Who's on First?

The mind of this country, taught to aim at low objects, eats upon itself.

—Emerson

I follow the columns, the media-type celebrities, but I have a confession. Carefully as I follow, picking up on a tremendous amount of grist, I still never once in my life saw a word written about what interests me most with these people on the air. You read about the difference between the real person and the image. The money. Also the hype, how much it takes to make a nothing a household word. (On public TV, which I watch a lot, and this surprises me, it took $2 million worth of advertising to make Carl Sagan a household word. A known fact. Arco-Richfield saw *Cosmos*, they said to themselves this Scientist fellow should be a household word, and put on $2 million worth of advertising. So roughly $2 million is the cost.) Also changes at the top. Back in '72 Walter topped the Trustometer, most trusted man by poll, and here, a decade later, courtesy *Ladies' Home Journal*, comes the survey that the person America wants to be is Alan Alda, the Hawkeye Pierce of *M*A*S*H*.

Which is interesting, I don't deny. The information is informative. But still, actually, I don't care, it doesn't do it for me. It doesn't come to grips, not with what I follow on the air. Do I care who's first in the polls? With the media guys I'm thinking exclusively how they handle themselves and vice versa. This is the key, the ultimate. Him against them, how does he do? Them against him, how do they do? This is politics, this is work, the whole story of work, the family, America, especially America. Am I unique?

Take Dick on the old *Cavett* show. Lots of nights the show was Howdy Doody. No sock. Dick has on the London playwright who falls all over him.—Gee, Dick, wonderful to be here with you, what can I tell you. And Dick says, Hey, what is it with you writers, you smoke too much, and London looks ashamed and says, Gosh, Dick, you're right, I'll quit tomorrow. A zero.

But not always, not always. I remember one night Dick had on four guys at once, book reviewers, three book reviewers named John and Jim and Jack, John from the *Times,* Jim from the *Voice,* and Jack from *The New Republic,* I don't know their last names. Plus a professor named Al Kaline or something. Kazin? Dick is The Thumb, right, and they're all fingers, but oh no, wait till you see.

Two seconds into the show this Al puts a move on them. He gives a speech, he tells the other fingers which guy's work he likes best (Al likes John's work at the *Times* and John grins), and then Al explains writing and America and they're listening like it's Louis Pasteur, and where's Dick? He's The Thumb but forget it, not tonight. This Al is all over the lot and Dick is squirming. How do you get back in, whose show *is* this? Oh wow does Dick squirm. And finally he thinks up a question and he says it to Al straight and Al looks at him like at a cretin. I don't understand that question, says Al, cool, like, frankly, it's the dumbest question Al ever heard. Al says, Frankly, I don't know what that question could mean.

Dick looks around. Where are these other guys, John and Jim and Jack? He looks around like, hey, one of these turkeys is supposed to come in on cue and say, Wait a minute, it's Dick's baseball, don't jerk Dick around or he'll go home. But no, the three just sit there grinning: Al wins. All four came in equal, see, four fingers under The Thumb, and the other three Jims or whatever are thinking all through the show, Hey, Mom, here I am on TV, look at me. But not this Al. No way. Al knows you only go around once, let's see your gusto. He delivers. The wife says to me, What's it to you who delivers, but she's wrong. Next time I see something written by Al I'll take notice because the guy made an impression. Out of the pack comes one horse and it stands to reason you'll remember.

But that's not the point. The point is it's not Monday night with Cosell or the Rangers or the playoffs but you still got people making their move and it's more real. This is life. You've got matchups, you've got muscling. There's a lot going on not to be missed.

On some shows, of course, they horse around with the matchups, which can be fun, too. *Carson*, for example. Mostly John and Ed and Doc and Tommy and the audience give it the humorous treatment. Standing up for yourself, handling yourself in front of somebody bigger in such a way that you keep your position—John keeps making it into a joke. He runs the number of Tommy as Mr. Personality, and Tommy stands and takes it with this sappy grin on his face, and it's funny because nobody is that much of a pushover, willing to put up with any insult to keep his job. Or John puts a move on the audience. How come you want to wait hours in the rain just to touch my hem? Or on Ed. The joke is that Ed fights for position. That is the premise. H-e-e-e-e-r-e's Johnny! But from then on Ed may—it depends—slip into needling to get his own back after John has commented once again on Ed's drinking. The minute Ed tries to needle, John gives him the warning glance, plenty announcers looking for work these days, John hears, and so on. And then it's up to Ed to handle that with dignity, laughing heartily.

So it can be funny, handling yourself, not giving ground. Some shows should use the humorous approach more, and I am thinking *60 Minutes* at the head of the pack. Yes, now and then Morley, Dan, Mike, and Harry have on a celebrity who could make a move. But mostly the only handlers-of-themselves you see on *60 Minutes* are Morley, Dan, Mike, and Harry. Not only do our heroes always win, they never look ruffled. Everybody's cowed. It can be good, sure. It's nice knowing every week you have a chance to see four rich famous fellows go riding out into the world full of nuts and stuntmen and social disease and dope runners and religious fanatics and phony franchise promoters—week after week you see these fellows go into that jungle and get results as easy as Coop or McCrea. Always they handle themselves better than anybody they have on. If Dan is coming to New England, the cold country, to do a story in somebody's colonial home on a Sunday afternoon, he changes out of the highrise collar and tie and climbs into a plaid shirt open neck so nobody welcoming at his hearth can say, Hey, fella, how come you're overdressed for New England, the cold country? You don't know better?

Or Mike. Whenever Mike sets up the investigation sting, bringing the camera into the room with the con about to swindle the straightarrow businessman and housewife—when that happens, Mike *stays on his feet*. The others you see sitting down, and are they surprised. Mike *Wa*llace! CBS News? Give me a break! So surprised they can't move. But Mike moves, you better believe it. He's all over that place, on his feet, pointing, shaking his head, opening the closet door and out pops the police chief stationed as the helper for CBS News.

It's predictable but I don't knock it within limits. It's like church. But after a while these patsies they have on got to have a *little* moxie, don't they? They're so amazed at Morley & Mike. I would like to see maybe the equal of an Al the Professor on

Cavett. Or a Joan Embery, the zoo gal on *Carson,* acting as though what the hell, these animals are every bit as important as you and don't forget it. Not sassy, just maintaining position. Joan has her degree and a job, why should she kowtow too much.

And of course your trained physicians on *60 Minutes*—they give nobody nothing. It's wonderful to see, the pride, when you have one on with Harry Reasoner. A physician. The Pope couldn't get a kidney specialist to give ground if he hit him with his bat. These guys know their worth. Stay out of my space. Very courteous, but still: out of here. As Frenchy the other barkeep says: *Quant-à-soi.*

But most *60 Minutes* it's no contest. Morley has on some dopey English broad that trains dogs for the BBC in twenty minutes and doesn't even know who Morley is, so, while the lady is at least no pushover, what does it mean? She never knew where she was in the first place. Week after week it's Mike saying to the businessman who got fleeced, How come you don't know better, Jack? I mean . . . you didn't even *read* the contract? I thought you were in business. Shit, fella . . . Mike pushing these guys with D & B's probably up there half a million and them taking it like kids.

What I really love, and see if you agree, I love the wrap-up show. The convention is over and the election and we have the wrap-ups—TV at its finest. The roundtable where the newspeople sit down to fan. Dan, Morton, Phil, Bruce, Bob, Bill, Leslie, plus Walter as editor-in-chief until retired. Each one in the roundtable has a problem. You want your time first—why should the other guy get more than you? You want your shot. But no hogging. People can tell when somebody's hogging, so you have to remember—get your shot but no hogging. Plus show respect because you're not The Thumb.

In the Walter days Walter was The Thumb, and the fun was, you watch the others muscle for their shot. People in there maintaining position, showboating, fighting for it with smiles but no sucking up, maybe eyeing each other but always on the lookout to say the insightful thing that will put the others in a response-to-you situation. They may not like it, the others, if you hit, but if it's good Walter came back to you and made them eat it anyway. Walter heard what you said as long as you weren't hogging. "Bruce, there was something you said a minute ago that really struck me—" Zingo, you're off and running.

I eat it up.

Now, about Dan. I would have said, frankly, Dan sucked up too much. It got worse after Dan beat Roger out and it was so flagrant you wondered. I was positive they would go back on themselves about Dan. Just say to the guy, Dan, you're sucking up too much, The Thumb-to-be doesn't suck up.

But win or lose, up or down, it's drama. No one can forget it was Roger's insisting on maintaining position that brought Teddy down. Sure, you bet it cost Roger. You pay for your space sometimes, comes with the territory. Roger has one thought: We have a president already, a Democrat, so how are you, Teddy Kennedy, under a cloud, coming forth at such a moment and lousing up the other guy's act? Does it mean anything except you're one of these would-be prima donnas up on the hill? That was Roger's way but without the acting-style aggression of a Mike. And of course it spilled over into Chappaquiddick and pretty soon we the reviewers are seeing one thing: this Roger just is *not* sucking up. It's always there with Roger, the guy has an air. You see the way he carries himself. The chin. Looks you up and down. Over to you, brother. I'm talking to the man inside, not the Senate leadership majority. Roger knows politicians *cannot* be trusted, and that coming across makes the great show. Two people muscling each other and hanging in there for tension.

It's a dynamic thing on the good shows. Changes from day

to day. Handle yourself one way tonight, different tomorrow. Brinkley takes the day off and it's Sam being Thumb and muscling George and Sander and Miss Gorgeous on the *L.A. Times.* Yesterday on *Agronsky & Co.* Elizabeth was inside, close to the administration. "I have it on good authority," and people have to listen. Today it's George on good authority. Hugh is the senior correspondent and we go to Hugh first, Hugh with the hands and the shininess on his forehead and the small tight smile. Hugh calling Martin "Martin" and then Jack calling Joe Kraft "Brother Kraft," and oh! is it hard for the guests on this show to get in and hold ground.

Haynes Johnson of the *Post,* for example. Haynes is The Thumb on *Washington Week in Review,* moderated by Paul, Triple-A League. When Haynes is on *Washington Week,* the others salute. It's tricky, oh yes. Rick is the *Times,* so might outrank. Al Hunt is the *Wall Street Journal,* a respected publication, and has the Donahue hair and real feeling for himself. And there's the woman, or *a* woman, scared of her ass no matter who she is, but she's trying. But on *Washington Week* Haynes is Numero Uno, yet only a guestshot on *Agronsky,* so that both he and Brother Kraft when they're had on are earning their spurs. Don't hog it, don't suck up, show respect, and it's Haynes muscles them out of there by the middle of the show.—Last word, Haynes. Whereas Brother Kraft keeps trying but doesn't make it, because you think, Joe, Joe, stop hogging it, fellow. Hey, stop proving yourself. Definitely Joe needs to be more laid back.

Always it's there, push with the shoulder, butt in, butt out, handle yourself with class but dammit get your time. *Quant-à-soi,* as the man says. On the spot. You have these anomalies, not just changes from who's inside and outside but plain looniness sometimes. The other day I'm home with the nasal congestion and I watch *Donahue* and—amazing!—his people forgot him. The whole show collapses and they go after each other as though Numero Uno left the room. All the fingers acting Thumbs. This day they had on Joan the runaway mother with eight kids she left, and Joan—Jesus, the woman behaved like *she* was Donahue, the pinky playing The Thumb, and then forget it, the roof falls. The nonrunaway mothers are furious at Joan, yapping at her for leaving her kids behind, how could she, it's against love and caring, a bunch of utopians, forgetting the whole point of the up and down of the show, muscling and beating out. They're acting like the story of life is in one person, Donahue rushing the mike from this corner to the other and the crowd not even looking at him. Absolute chaos, all they have on their brains is together we defend the family. Regular anarchy.

It can happen.

Or you get the situation that can't be doped out not because the people want to pretend to be one person and forget differences, but because one person on the show is so far removed, so far away, a stranger, he's talking to God and he doesn't want a thing. *Wall Street Week* it happened lately. Lew had on Granville the investment adviser that broke the market wide open last winter. Lew has a guest after you hear the volume and the elves. Everybody goes off into the other room to welcome the guest and they sit down on the leather couches, glad to have you here, hi how are you, the whole bit. The club atmosphere. Lew doing the little pun about silver, and remember, folks, we're not guaranteeing anything here. You could lose your shirt and what a laugh. Up yours. Lew is The Thumb and the regulars, Frank and Carter, who will guest host, almost never muscle. They're *inside*.

But now here's Granville and they're calling him Joe and getting on him because who knows where Granville fits? Is he maybe bigger than any of them? Could *they* say Sell and break the market wide open? So Lew begins about Granville's mistakes, guy is wrong a lot, missed this rally, lost the downturn, and Granville sitting biding his time, saying the same words no matter what, saying like Scripture *We put you in at the bottom and we take you out at the top. Over and over. We put you in at the bottom and we take you out at the top.* That is all ye need to know. No sucking up, it was as though he wasn't in their ballpark, playing their game. Didn't even want to be a finger. Didn't care. I mean—

—What? Well, Christ, what do you think? Of course it's all one man against another. One on one. What about it? What are you thinking, all for one, one for all? Sure we should have that, I agree. One for all certainly. Where the people are not standing up to each other, muscling all day—let's work for the good of everybody. I buy it. Wonderful. Only tell me where it is, is all I'm asking. Show me where it is, and I'm for it. The trouble is you can't. The most important thing is stick up for yourself or who will. Friend, the bottom line is not one for all. We are talking Democracy. Pictures of the democratic way of life night after night. Where else do you see it, where else do you feel it? Walking to the train I'm a bullet, I see nobody, I don't want to see anybody. They crowd you and you're in trouble if you notice. You know it's going on, of course you know. They're in behind you with BJ behind closed doors, the accountants or upstairs.—Hey, look, we carried the guy so long and frankly what is he producing, BJ, the numbers are not right. But it's hidden, it's hidden.—BJ? He's my boss.

On the shows it's different. Less masks. You see the battle unfold. The obligations. The celebrity remembering he's not so big because this is America, no kings. The underman remembering no matter how hungry, he has got to not show it because he's equal to begin with. Night after night, if you watch with me, this is what you see. You see scrambling. Guys struggling to be at the same time kind of proud and kind of humble. You can look for it anywhere else but you're not going to see it because people hunker down. They're scared. They act like, Who me? I'm a happy guy, want nothing. Money's no problem. Terrific. I love my job. Bullshit! They're all waiting and wanting but wanting to not let you see it, wanting to not suck up or look down or lose position. But on the shows it's America. Guys and girls looking out across the air toward the other person even-steven *no matter what is going on inside.* What I am, what we are—I'll keep watching for it even if nobody ever writes it down. I mean, what is the message, what are they putting, what are you *supposed* to see if it isn't this? Am I missing something? Am I unique?

For a time—as noted earlier—no full length autobiographical account of the celebrity-obsessed sensibility existed. But the year 2000 brought a massive self-study by the young writer Dave Eggers, which abruptly altered the situation. The work in question is built on a number of assumptions illuminating relations between the rise of celebrity-obsession and the rise of apoliticality. Among the assumptions are the following:

- *Claims by political officialdom that it exerts influence on common life are absurd; celebrity culture is far more potent.*

- *The entire generation now in its twenties is in the habit of imagining itself in leading roles in films, rock group performances and other entertainments; it seldom fantasizes about political eminence.*

- *The standard issues that oldstyle politicos fret about—race is the big one—are in fact pure hype; nobody cares about them, and that includes the faking politicos responsible for the hype.*

- *The crucial test of individual human value has zero to do with participation in the public realm; it centers solely on how intensely and honestly you observe your own thoughts and feelings, especially feelings about fame.*

The Politics of Dave Eggers

I n little over a month, in the early Nineties, a twenty-one-
year-old college senior named Dave Eggers lost both his
parents to cancer. Eggers's older brother and sister were
launched on business lives and postgraduate education, so he
took over as de facto guardian of the family's youngest child,
eight-year-old Christopher (nicknamed Toph).* At the same
time he became the family memoirist, describing—in a
journal that serves as the basis of A *Heartbreaking Work of Stag-
gering Genius*—his parents' terminal illnesses, his own performance as quasi parent of a younger sibling, and concurrent
episodes in his sputtering career in San Francisco, as founding
editor of a satirical journal called *Might* and would-be cast
member of the MTV series *The Real World*.

Enthusiastically reviewed and widely promoted, A *Heartbreaking Work* turned up on best-seller lists the week it appeared
and remained on them for months thereafter, winning rank as
a cultural event (paperback rights brought a reported
$1,400,000). "It's been a long time," said one author, Robert

---

*Eggers's sister Beth argues, in interviews, that her brother exaggerates his role
as guardian and unfairly deprecates her own contribution. See "Et tu Beth?"
Harper's, August 2000, p. 23.

Polito, "perhaps as far back as *Gravity's Rainbow*, since I've seen so many people on the subway reading a serious hardcover book and talking about it." Eggers emerged as a Manhattan presence, highly visible in media interviews, humor pieces in the weeklies, and as the editor of a literary journal (*McSweeney's*) praised by other editors and literary people.

Some strongly felt memories of dysfunctional family life breathe in *A Heartbreaking Work* and there's an affecting although sketchy and evasive portrait of the writer's mother. A short inventory of elements of the book's success would begin with intensive reader flattery—especially the assurance that readers are too smart to need a linear narrative. Other items in the inventory would include authorial rage to ingratiate, stylized bitterness and stoicism in the manner of Heller, Vonnegut, and Salinger, a smug, ill-informed apoliticality, dismissal of race issues, scorn of elders, messianic leanings, "postmodernism" reduced to shtick, and a conviction that shamelessness confessed is shamelessness absolved.

Described in a dust jacket blurb as "endlessly self-ironizing," Eggers directs a steady flow of initially amusing criticism at himself for ignorance, stalling, and the like. He also directs—in thirty-plus pages of prefatory fine print and elsewhere in his book—much sedulous if prankish compliment at readers. The latter are imagined as persons of much creative patience, eager to puzzle out contextless snippets omitted from the body of the work ahead, notes on passages in the work that should be skipped, rules and suggestions for reading, "guides to symbols and metaphors," and other anti-novelish bits. The pages in question shuttle from awkwardly intricate self-scrutiny ("his knowingness about his self-consciousness of self-referentiality") to slapdash mucker-posing ("until last spring [I] thought Evelyn Waugh was a woman and that George Eliot was a man") to formal salutes to the sophisticated ("The author wishes to acknowledge your problems with the title. He too has reservations"). Tongue-in-cheek promises of five-dollar rebates to the first two hundred shoppers who submit proof of purchase of the book are elaborately particularized and spliced into acknowledgments that this "seemingly endless [introductory] screwing about, interminable clearing of one's throat, can very easily look like, or even *become*, a sort of contemptuous stalling." But Eggers stresses that the stalling itself is a form of considerateness to the reader: "a device, a defense, to obscure the black, blinding, murderous rage and sorrow at the core of this whole story, which is both too black and blinding to look at— *avert . . . your . . . eyes!*"

At readings the author performs passages from his work to musical accompaniment by a guitarist friend. (Members of the audience choose the passages to be performed, calling out page numbers to the performers.) He also hires go-go dancers and charters buses that carry selected attendees to bars and art galleries (paintings by elephants were the attraction at one gallery). "Friends mean everything to me," he observes. "I cling to them with white knuckles and beady eyes."

Eggers speaks often of himself as having a message but is wary of spelling it out, seemingly concerned about being perceived as a moralizer or pedant. ("A few good friends," he tells an interviewer, "wrote 'No! No!' in the margins every time I started pontificating," and he cut the passages.) Countering suspicion that he's a goody-goody, he reports in *A Heartbreaking Work* on his masturbatory habits, and argues for exhibitionism as a value ("If you don't want anyone to know about your existence, you might as well kill yourself"). And he regularly flashes his hip bona fides, establishing that he sees through almost everything, wasn't overattached to his mother, doesn't want the pity or sympathy his losses stir in the compassionate, and is above all complex (embodies extremes, is a mass of contradictions). The book's prefatory screwing-about is followed by an account of the late stages of Heidi Eggers's struggle against stomach cancer. Her pain and despair are movingly evoked—the hopelessness of the struggle, the reek of the blood draining unstaunchably from the dying woman's nose, the inability of her children to comfort her. But as the forty-page chapter proceeds, its formulaic, deadpan bitterness commences drawing attention to itself. (" 'Is [your nose] still bleeding?' I ask, sucking on my popsicle.") Reflecting on the external intravenous feeding bag and tube that have replaced his mother's stomach, Eggers writes:

> It's kind of cute, the IV bag. She used to carry it with her, in a gray backpack—it's futuristic-looking, like a synthetic ice pack crossed with those liquid food pouches engineered for space travel. We have a name for it. We call it "the bag."

Studying the fish tank in the sickroom where his mother lies—fish died in it weeks before and the tank is gray and moldy with feces—Eggers notes:

> I am wondering about something. I am wondering what the water would taste like. Like a nutritional shake? Like sewage? I think of asking my mother: *What do you think that would taste like?*

Imagining his mother's last hours—the stream of visitors, the mindlessly chatting relatives and family friends—he entertains himself with comedy about a meaningless priest:

> There will be baked goods. There will be Father Mike, a young red-haired priest assigned to us—how do they

assign the priests? I picture something like a police dispatcher, barking commands—"O'Bannan, you've got the disaster on Waveland"—with the priests groaning once given their orders.

Close to the end of this almost four-hundred-page work the author allows himself an extended grief aria for his mother (flights of angels transport her heavenward from her funeral)—but before then lapses into tenderness are rare, as Eggers himself acknowledges. When he collects his mother's "cremains" from a funeral director and broods—on the Lake Michigan shore—about an appropriate interment, he writes, "Look what I'm doing, with my tape recorder and notebook, and here at the beach, with this box—calculating, manipulative, cold, exploitive." (The cremains venture ends with Eggers the clumsy mourner involved in black comedy: "I open the canister. . . . Inside is a bag of kitty litter, tied at the top. Fuck. Someone switched the ashes with this fucking kitty litter. This is not it. Where is the ash, the ash like dust?")

As already noted, echoes of old masters of helpless bitterness resound throughout *A Heartbreaking Work*: Eggers acknowledges having devoured Kurt Vonnegut in high school. But his purposes in warding off pity and suspicion of niceness are clearly his own. "I wanted more than anything," he tells an interviewer, "to make my recent self seem ridiculous and annoying."

Explaining his willingness, at age twenty-one, to take a younger brother in tow, Eggers cites the fringe benefits of guardianship— among them, improved opportunities for sexual scoring. He was dutiful about attending school functions, he reports, not to show orthodox parents that his young charge had a competent adult protector but for another reason: "My goal, a goal I honestly thought was fairly realistic, was to meet an attractive single mother and have Toph befriend the mother's son so we can arrange playdates, during which the mother and I will go upstairs and screw around while the kids play outside." In addition: for a Victor Frankenstein type like himself, there was the pleasure of shaping a zombie to his own will:

> [My brother's] brain is my laboratory, my depository. Into it I can stuff the books I choose, the television shows, the movies, my opinion about elected officials, historical events, neighbors, passersby. He is my twenty-four-hour classroom, my captive audience, forced to ingest everything I deem worthwhile. He is a lucky, lucky boy! And no one can stop me. He is mine, and you cannot stop me, cannot stop us.

As for those stuffed opinions: corporate America and officialdom worldwide are gripped by absurd delusions of power. Viacom Inc. is "wealthier and more populous than eighteen of the fifty states of America, all of Central America, and all of the former Soviet Republics combined and tripled." But regardless of the size of:

> such companies . . . and how many things they own, or how much money they have or make or control, their influence over the daily lives and hearts of individuals, and thus, like ninety-nine percent of what is done by official people in cities like Washington, or Moscow, or Sao Paulo or Auckland, their effect on the short, fraught lives of human beings who limp around and sleep and dream of flying through bloodstreams . . . is very, very small, and so hardly worth worrying about.

Race is an uninteresting subject overhyped by politicos.

Speaking warmly of his nearly all-white suburban home town (Lake Forest, Illinois), Eggers remembers that the only black children he saw, as a schoolboy, were Mr. T.'s daughters (the performer had recently moved to Lake Forest) and "Steve the Black Guy":

> He was just this average guy, not incredibly popular, but nice enough. And so people liked him, and people I guess thought it was this odd novelty that he was different, odd in the same way that it was odd that one kid had a crewcut, or that one girl, I forget her name, she hung out with the basketball players, was a dwarf. So he was Steve the Black Guy.

Postpublication, the writer sought to moderate the impression of unconcern left by various remarks in his book. "Part of me," he told an interviewer, "thinks the issue is so boring and old and silly (race can be such a waste of time, such a pointless diversion from deeper things), but another part of me finds it absolutely electric and vital."

Middle-aged and older Americans alike are lifeless and strikingly irresponsible:

> We are new and everyone else is old. We are the chosen ones, obviously the queens to their drones—the rest . . . are aging, past their prime, sad, hopeless. . . . They are over. They are walking corpses. . . . [We are] ready to kick the saggy asses of the gray-haired, thickly bespectacled, slump-shouldered of Berkeley's glowering parentiscenti!

Eggers reports himself "too stunned to speak" when, in his hearing, a suburban mother in stretch pants preens herself for letting her tenth-grader smoke pot at home. "She should be jailed," he writes. "And I should raise her children. Maybe I'm the only one qualified to raise all these kids—so many of these parents are too old, dusty."

Questioned about "what structural notion" he had in mind as he wrote, Eggers responds in part:

> I guessed I wanted more than anything else for the book to defy any linearity. . . . When I began the narrative in earnest, I was appalled again and again by how linear it was becoming. Of course, I didn't really intend to leave many parts as they were left. I really wanted to dig in again and revise and couch everything in more and better devices—I had a few dozen stylistic and formal tricks I wanted to use when reshaping some of those passages—but in the end I found it really hard to deal with some of that material in any way. . . .

In the fifty-page audition-interview for the MTV show *The Real World* that is the centerpiece of *A Heartbreaking Work*, Eggers holds forth on his qualifications as spokesperson and as "inspiration and cautionary tale." Conducted by a producer named Laura, the interview opens with reflections on the causes, among twenty-somethings, of "pure insinuating solipsism." (Solipsism is "the main by-product of . . . comfort and prosperity . . . the absence of struggle against anything in the way of a common enemy—whether that's poverty, Communists, whatever.") There's comment on the difference between inward-turning and outward-turning self-obsession. (Inward-turning obsessives, unresponsive to others, lack interest in anything but their own "haunted house of a brain." Outward-turning obsessives command respect because, although self-absorbed, they believe in the possibility of teaching by example—"think their personality is so strong, their story so interesting, that others must know it and learn from it.")

There are patches of sonority on Generation X preoccupation with fame, the "media," and personal looks:

> . . . We've grown up thinking of ourselves in relation to the political-media-entertainment ephemera, in our safe and comfortable homes, given the time to think about how we would fit into this or that band or TV show or movie, and how we would look doing it. [We] are people for whom the idea of anonymity is existentially irrational, indefensible.

And there are hard-sell bits, wherein the author talks marketing to media moguls, showing he knows the angles, grasps "the demographic," is fully aware of the "bottom line":

> I represent everyone who grew up suburban and white, but then I've got all these other things going for me. I'm Irish Catholic, and can definitely play that up if you want. And then the Midwest thing, which I don't need to tell you is pretty valuable. And if you want to go hardcore rural, play that angle, I went to school in the middle of a cornfield, have seen cows, smelled their waste every day there was a south wind. Oh and: it was a state school. So, I can be the average white suburban person, midwestern, knowing of worlds both wealthy and central Illinoisian, whose looks are not intimidating, who's self-effacing but principled, and—and this is the big part—one whose tragic recent past touches everyone's heart, whose struggles become universal and inspiring.

At the end these separately pitching characters—sociologist, culture critic, high school bright boy, and so on—are overpowered

JUNK POLITICS

by a voice that's apostolic, prayerful, and evidently half-desperate for alms and a Name. "Reward me for my suffering," Eggers pleads, apparently believing that, as a cast member of a "real-life" TV show, he could tell his story. "Put me on television. Let me share this with millions." Confessing, keening, supplicating, Whitmanizing, insisting that "everyone must know," promising that he'll perform "slowly, subtly, tastefully," averring he's earned a shot at the multitude ("I deserve this. I have this coming. . . . I give you these things, and you give me a platform. So give me my platform. I am owed"), the would-be TV star becomes for long pages at a stretch a caterwauling, cross-sectional messiah:

> Give me something. . . . I promise I will be good. I will
> be sad and hopeful. I will be the conduit. I will be the
> beating heart. Please see this! I am the common multi-
> plier for 47 million! I am the perfect amalgam! I was
> born of both stability and chaos. . . . I am bursting with
> the hopes of a generation, their hopes surge through
> me, threaten to burst my hardened heart! Can you not
> see this? . . . I am the product of my environment, and
> thus representative, must be exhibited, as inspiration
> and cautionary tale. Can you not see what I represent? I
> am both a) martyred moralizer and b) amoral omni-
> vore born of the suburban vacuum + idleness + televi-
> sion + Catholicism + alcoholism + violence. . . . I need
> community, I need feedback, I need love, connection,
> give-and-take—I will bleed if they will love. Let me try
> . . . . Pass over me at your peril! I could die soon. . . . I
> need to bring this message now. . . . I need to grab this
> while I can, because I could go at any minute, Laura,
> Mother, Father, God— . . . Let me be the conduit. . . .
> Oh, I want to be the heart pumping blood to everyone,
> blood is what I know, I feel so warm in blood, can swim

in blood, oh let me be the strong-beating heart that
brings blood to everyone! I want—

Here as everywhere self-ironizing persists ("my hardened heart," "I
will be sad and hopeful"); the writer wants it understood that he's
conscious of his excess, critical of his absurdities—isn't to be confused with the shameless crawler-before-the-media-gods who
happens to bear his name. When MTV rejects him, he falls quickly
into bluster mode. ("Fuck it. Stupid show. . . . We don't need *The
Real World*, we don't need any crutches, we don't need an ongoing
role on a television show with a massive worldwide audience and
an unquantifiable kind of influence over the hearts and minds of
the young and impressionable of the world. No. We will continue,
against the odds, with only these simple tools, these small hands.")

The sour grapes and the preceding hyperbolics are two sides of
a single coin. But even as he grins at the extravagance of both,
the writer clings, "against the odds," to the rhetoric of mission
and message. It's plain that at some level he believes that he's
owed and that he has lessons to teach.

What message, what lessons? A lengthy chapter in the second
half of *A Heartbreaking Work* is devoted to the staging, by the editors of *Might*, of a hoax about the death of a celebrity—a TV actor
named Adam Rich. Presumably intended to teach a lesson about
the vacuity of celebrity worship, the chapter lacks focus and
urgency. But Eggers's chuckling preoccupation with—and
defiant candor about—his own crass ambition and fantasies of
fame may have sharpened his book's attractiveness to readers in
their twenties or younger. Popular literary characters in the
recent past—Roth's Portnoy and Salinger's Holden Caulfield are
examples—spoke with unapologetic frankness about subjects
their elders proscribed, thereby charming large audiences.
Eggers's elders tell themselves that schoolboy murderers, rock

groupies, toddler beauty queens (and their coaches) are freaks. But hunger for renown is now ever more broadly diffused; commodified fame creates a near-universal itch for stardom. And in dealing with the itch with as little embarrassment as his literary predecessors dealt in their time with adolescent libido, Eggers appeals to an audience that hears in his voice hitherto unarticulated and widely shared anxieties about ascent from nonentity.

The problem is that, in *A Heartbreaking Work*, these anxieties and cravings are less vividly alive than the subjects from which they divert the author's imagination. There are, to repeat, several strongly felt moments in the work, namely those recounting Eggers's panic when his demented alcoholic father roars up the stairs to beat him (the lad's mother saves him in a scene not shown to the reader), Eggers's extreme anxiety at the thought that a babysitter he's hired to care for his brother may be untrustworthy, Eggers's pain at the realization, at his mother's funeral, that the large crowd of mourners he had hoped for and expected won't materialize.

Had Eggers been less rigidly bound into the culture of knowingness, less obedient to the counsel of friends overdisposed to see through everything, these experiences might have led to a ponderable message. Some possible themes: mortal pain and suffering in a loved one can't be seen through or managed by hard-nosed, distancing irony; grownup acquaintance with the weight of responsibility for the well-being of a child clarifies the sacred character of the obligation; gauging the depths of the roots of injustice on earth is easier if one has learned something, through contention with one's own grudgingness, about the infrequency with which genuine human worth in others earns more than perfunctory regard.

But to bring to life such themes the memoirist needs to place himself differently in relation to both his material and his audience. He needs to shed his terror of banality. He needs to acknowledge that, if the misfortunes of his life have provided him access to some truths hidden from most of his immediate contemporaries, that access has been owing to an elder's selflessly courageous devotion. (Although her story is marginalized in this work, sealed off in undramatized corners, one gathers that Heidi Eggers was uncommonly brave, fought her drunken husband times past counting, protected her children at immense cost, and tried with passion to teach them not to whine.)

Beyond this, Eggers needed to seek a language rich enough to overcome inhibitions about giving domestic heroism like his mother's its full due—an idiom capable of calling up the true costs and benefits of self-forgetful surrender to the claims of others. More committed than he knew (despite the brandished self-consciousness) to screwing around, this "perfect amalgam" and "common multiplier"—this "charming"/ugly, loving/loutish, self-touting scourge of sentimentality—never embarked on that search. Out came a blockbuster instead.

3. Tomorrow: The Only Winning Ticket

Probably the most potent cultural force driving no-politics politics is the ever-stronger public conviction that the present has zero to learn from the past—and traditional politics belongs to the past. Public opinion about the relative uselessness of the past reflects in part the impact of technological revolutions: advances that transform medicine, manufacturing and communications year by year, confirming the outmodedness of yesterday's "product" (vaccines to voting machines) and directly promoting certainty that new means better—or at least more interesting. New faces—a John McCain, say—freshen the national political scene at the quadrennial elections. The primaries become horse races in which worn labels (Republican, Democrat) count for less than proper names. Well-advertised, once a decade "third party challenges" flourish for a time before commencing to founder in their own versions of junk politics.

But nothing in the contemporary political world can begin to match the ceaseless electric manufacture of the new in the worlds of entertainment and fashion. Here alone new victors are announced weekly (box office and rating figures). New drugs are sniffed, new remedies tested, new packages, art forms, methods of teaching and learning are marketed, new skills honed—and all the while, less and less dutifully reported in the media, politics lumbers on: a tired mix (for the most part) of decrepit parties, bespoke candidates, arcane committees, goppy idioms and buildings ("Will the gentleman yield?"), none of it touched by the glamour of the new.

Among the more influential chroniclers and celebrators of this glamour in recent decades is Tom Wolfe. The author of Bonfire of the Vanities *has helped persuade two generations that tomorrow is all ye need to know, and at the turn of the millenium, he launched—with near monomaniacal fury—an effort seemingly to clean the clock of everybody who ever dared to resist this theme. Not excluding one of* his *own former selves.*

Caught in the Curve

T he title piece in Tom Wolfe's latest collection looks back jeeringly, from a not very distant tomorrow, on today's American costumes, affluence, and linguistic, intellectual, and sexual behavior. There's an account of the life of the "average electrician, air-conditioning mechanic, or burglar-alarm repairman" —"a life that would have made the Sun King blink":

> He spent his vacations in Puerto Vallarta, Barbados, or St. Kitts. Before dinner he would be out on the terrace of some resort hotel with his third wife, wearing his Ricky Martin cane-cutter shirt open down to the sternum, the better to allow his gold chains to twinkle in his chest hairs. The two of them would have just ordered a round of Quibel sparkling water, from the state of West Virginia, because by 2000 the once-favored European sparkling waters Perrier and San Pellegrino seemed so tacky.

A page or so later we're at the entrance of "one of the forty-two Good Buildings" on Manhattan's East Side. The doorman, dressed "like an Austrian Army colonel from the year 1870," holds the door for a "wan white boy," "teenage scion of an investment-banking family." The lad wears

> a baseball cap sideways; an outsized T-shirt, whose short sleeves fall below his elbows and whose tail hangs down over his hips; baggy cargo pants with flapped pockets running down the legs and a crotch hanging below his knees, and yards of material pooling about his ankles, all but obscuring the Lugz sneakers.

Elsewhere in *Hooking Up* there are notes on casual contemporary coupling in high school hallways, with attention to related Oval Office sport:

> Thirteen- and fourteen-year-old girls were getting down on their knees and fellating boys in corridors and stairwells during the two-minute break between classes. . . . In the year 2000, boys and girls did not consider fellatio to be a truly sexual act, any more than tonsil hockey. It was just "fooling around." The President of the United States at the time used to have a twenty-two-year-old girl, an unpaid volunteer in the presidential palace, the White House, come around to his office for fellatio.

In other pieces in this collection books and ideas as well as manners surface—but they rarely lead away from the present. The culture of Intel is probed, and the invention of the Internet, and the leading concepts of sociobiology and neuroscience. The author hails E.O. Wilson's *Consilience* (1998) and, in a piece entitled "Sorry, but Your Soul Just Died," extols brain imaging. ("If I were a college student, today," says Wolfe, "I don't think I could resist going into neuroscience.") He reports on a squabble in academe between "traditional humanists" (the National

Association of Scholars) and Stanley Fish, Judith Butler, *et alia*. There's a lively counterattack on the writers—Updike, Mailer, and Irving— who savaged Wolfe's novel *A Man in Full* (1998), plus a seventy-page novella detailing a sting operation, by a *60 Minutes*-style TV producer, on three US Army combat veterans guilty of homophobic murder.

Yesterday has a walk-on in the closing section—two pieces on *The New Yorker* and William Shawn first published thirty-five years ago. But the book scurries back into the present at the end, to comment on more recent portraits of the Shawn and post-Shawn eras—Lillian Ross's *Here But Not Here* (1998) and Renata Adler's *Gone* (2000). Approaching his seventieth year, Tom Wolfe stands forth, rather more unrelentingly even than in his past, as a committed specialist in Now.

In writers who possess large talent and energy—Wolfe has both—present-mindedness and observational intensity often conjoin to produce insight as well as amusement. Any competent catalog-copy hack can detail the "features" of a wan white boy's cargo pants—but those yards of material "pooling" around the teenage ankles in *Hooking Up* point suggestively to a defiantly mindless, diaper-pining dishevelment; they attest that a writer's spirited concentration on contemporary surface and circumstance can pay off.

Certainly it pays off in the pieces about *The New Yorker* and William Shawn that elevated Wolfe to notoriety. Not sight but sound—better, a relative absence of sound—turns up the observational wattage in these reports. In the mid-Sixties, at firsthand or otherwise, Wolfe noticed the quiet of the magazine's corridors and cubicles; absent a bulging file of other facts about the place, he built an edifice on the quality of the whispering, and arrived thereby at an intimation of the deepening piety, the nearly choking hush, of *The New Yorker*'s pre–Tina Brown self-reverence. Attentiveness and rudeness fused to produce perspicacity.

As for the style Wolfe contrived for chronicling cultural news: it clearly served both his own irreverence and the larger cause of immediacy—and it transformed the journalistic palette. Among Now-specialists the assumption came to be— witness the front page of any issue of the *New York Observer* or any "style" page of the *New York Times*—that if the object in view really is distinctively new and of the moment, its presentation requires unique lingo, rhythm, exclamation. The features of the style visible in *Hooking Up* include *in medias res* openings and bullying italics (*"Omert...!* Sealed lips! *Sealed lips*, ladies and gentlemen!"), saturation bombing by brand names (Lugz sneakers, Quibel sparkling water, etc.), and fashion page gush ("Hottest fields in science" . . . "hottest field in the academic world" . . . "hottest and most intensely rational young scientists"). Smacking readers in their dozing eyes, the idiom pushes the cultural beat implacably but entertainingly, and does nobody irreparable harm.

Still, unrelenting present-mindedness can create problems. The minor problems in *Hooking Up* include excessive confidence that "hot" status details are an adequate substitute for penetration of character and moral dilemma, and credulousness regarding whatever mode of "scientific" intellection is advertised as the latest. The major problem is declining proficiency in distinguishing the counterfeit from the real.

No small measure of Wolfe's readability as a novelist depends on his gift for producing fast-paced scenes of confrontation between figures fighting for place in American bigmoney hierarchies—witness the scrap, in *A Man in Full*, between the tycoon Charlie Croker and Harry Zale, a fiercely adamant Real Estate Asset Manager to whose bank Croker owes half a billion and change. It's the remembered verve and fiery ole boy–Willie Stark diction of these scenes, together with Wolfe's adeptness at choosing the slackest work of Updike-Mailer-Irving when illustrating their alleged remoteness from the "raw, raucous, lust-soaked rout" of America here and now, that lends his counterattack on his contemporaries initial credibility.

But the very obsession with status—the insistence on engaging that subject as though little of large significance lay beyond it—thins and lames Wolfe's fictional characters and situations in *The Bonfire of the Vanities* (1987) and *A Man in Full*. And the obsession weakens Wolfe's performances both as fiction writer and as critic in *Hooking Up*.

Setting up the standard in the book by which to knock down his perceived competitors, he argues that the key content of naturalistic fiction consists of

> the notation of status details, the cues that tell people how they rank in the human pecking order, how they are doing in the struggle to maintain or improve their position in life or in an immediate situation, everything from clothing and furniture to accents, modes of treating superiors or inferiors, subtle gestures that show respect or disrespect—"dissing," to use a marvelous new piece of late-twentieth-century slang—the entire complex of signals that tell the human beast whether it is succeeding or failing and has or hasn't warded off that enemy of happiness that is more powerful than death: humiliation.

He holds, further, that the greatness of great novels has to do with shrewdness about social gradation (*Anna Karenina* becomes "Tolstoy's incomparable symphony of status concerns, status competition, and class guilt within Russia's upper orders"). The weakness of weak novels—John Irving's *A Widow for One Year* (1996), for one—is their preoccupation with people "encapsulated in their neurasthenia": people who, as they drive through a seaside Long Island town, refuse to "take a look, just one look, at a $125,000 show-circuit hunter pony in the pasture over there at the Topping Riding School." Further still, Wolfe contends that a prime disadvantage of movies is their inability to render "status details": "When it comes time to deal with social gradations, [movies] are immediately reduced to gross effects likely to lapse into caricature at any moment: the house that is *too* grand or *too* dreadful, the accent that is *too* snobbish or *too* crude."

A view of *Anna Karenina* that sees mainly status concerns—forget anguish about moral disorder, broken vows, lost darlings—isn't a lot less blinkered than a gaze held oblivious of a six-figure show pony in Sagaponack. But Wolfe is on a reductive tear, uninterested in qualifications and counterpositions. He moves directly from anatomizing Updike's and Mailer's obliviousness to social fact to a swatch of his own fiction, *Ambush at Fort Bragg*, as though assured that it will back up the argument—and the piece fails him.

The theme of status does indeed dominate its pages—but so also do stereotypes and glibly bypassed moral dilemmas. In *Ambush at Fort Bragg*, Irv Durtscher, the point-of-view character, is a TV news producer and director who's unhinged by jealousy of his show's star interviewer. Irv can't bear his own obscurity:

> Suppose [Irv thinks] he hit the jackpot. Suppose the three [homophobic] soldiers hung themselves on that videotape. Who would get the credit? All the newspaper stories, the editorials, the Op Ed pieces, all the pronouncements

by the politicians, all the letters from the viewers, would talk about this big, gross, aging blonde sitting up in this chair with her regal posture as if she actually ran the show. All anybody would talk about would be Mary Cary Brokenborough [the star interviewer].

The tale harps ceaselessly on Irv Durtscher's bitterness:

Why couldn't he come on at the very beginning of the program, the way Rod Serling used to in *The Twilight Zone* or Alfred Hitchcock used to in *Alfred Hitchcock Presents*? Yeah, Hitchcock . . . Hitchcock was just as short, round, and bald as he was. More so. He could see it now . . . The titles come on . . . The theme . . . but then he lost heart. They'd never go for it. On top of everything else, he looked too . . . *ethnic*. You could be Jewish and still be a star in television news, an anchorman or whatever, as long as you didn't *seem* Jewish.

The climax of the novella is an explosion of rage—Durtscher's rage at the star interviewer's mate, an eye surgeon guilty of taking an upstaging emergency beeper call during an advance showing of the sting footage:

That son of a bitch! Him and his Dr. Daring stage whisper! *Corneal-scleral laceration—meeeeeyhah!* Probably beeped himself and then faked the call! A pathetic failure at the dinner table who couldn't even pick up, much less carry, his end of the conversation—and so now he has to try to steal the scene by playing Emergency Medical Hero during the very climax of his own wife's triumph—as orchestrated by me, Irv Durtscher! Why, that ice-sculptured *son—of—a— bitch!*

Implicit in the characterization—as in those of many of the city detectives, black activists, rich women, and assorted Masters of the Universe in Wolfe's other fiction—is impatience with the tugs of appetite, conscience, self-distrust, and the rest that loosen stereotypes and sharpen the sense of intimacy, in readers, with literary characters and their psychosocial crises. And one element in that impatience is, as I say, the conviction of the decisive influence of current position on the status ladder—hot status detail. My self and the truth of my moral situation at any given hour *equals* the sum of my resentments.

The celebrations in *Hooking Up* of sociobiology and brain-imaging neuroscience are interesting partly because their view of human innerness as Wolfe represents it—namely, innerness is a myth—chimes with the view embodied in Wolfe's characterizations. In passages marked by strong leanings toward determinism and misanthropy, the writer makes clear that he prizes the new disciplines for their lack of sanctimony about "our own precious inner selves"—their freedom from solemnity regarding individual responses and aspirations:

> Since consciousness and thought are entirely physical products of your brain and nervous system—and since your brain arrived fully imprinted at birth—what makes you think you have free will? Where is it going to come from? . . . I doubt that any Calvinist of the sixteenth century ever believed so completely in predestination as these, the . . . most intensely rational young scientists in the United States in the twenty-first.

Wolfe announces that "I love talking to these people [the young scientists]—they express an uncompromising determinism." Just ahead, he predicts, lies a time when everybody will believe that "this ghost in the machine, 'the self,' does not even exist and brain imaging proves it, once and for all." After the coming sociobiological triumph, "all knowledge of living things will converge . . . under the umbrella of biology. All mental activity, from using allometry to enjoying music, will be understood in biological terms." Quoting E.O. Wilson, Wolfe adds: "The humanities and social sciences would 'shrink to specialized branches of biology.' Such venerable disciplines as history, biography, and the novel would become 'the research protocols,' i.e., preliminary reports of the study of human evolution." Farewell characters, flat or round.

But it's the conduct, not the substance, of the argument about sociobiology, happy dispatcher of "precious inner selves," that's symptomatic. Having anointed E.O. Wilson as "Darwin II" in a piece called "Digibabble, Fairy Dust, and the Human Anthill," having saluted Wilson's *Consilience*, with small-boy glee, as "a stick in the eye of every novelist, every historian, every biographer, every social scientist— every intellectual of any stripe, come to think of it," Wolfe, in the following piece, "Sorry, but Your Soul Just Died," sticks it to Wilson himself—by suggesting that this "terribly polite, terribly reserved" Alabamian is nearing obsolescence. Cheers for sociobiology and neuroscience now give way, in short, to a faster-breaking story—news that an "Ultimate Skepticism" about these disciplines and indeed of all else in science has begun mounting among scientists:

> Over the past two years even Darwinism, a sacred tenet among American scientists for the past seventy years, has been beset by . . . doubts. Scientists—not religiosi— . . . have begun attacking Darwinism as a mere theory, not a scientific discovery, a theory woefully unsupported by fossil evidence and featuring, at the core of its

logic, sheer mush. . . . The scorn the new breed [of Ultimately Skeptical young physicists] heaps upon
quantum mechanics ("has no real-world applications"
. . . "depends entirely on goofball equations"), Unified
Field Theory ("Nobel worm bait"), and the Big Bang
Theory ("creationism for nerds") has become withering.
If only Nietzsche were alive! He would have relished
every minute of it!

A comparable catch-the-curve impulse—also recognizable as
plain fickleness—figures in Wolfe's decision to present himself
in *Hooking Up* as an enthusiast of life reduced by science to
theory, abstraction, predictable formula. Once "every action
and reaction of the human brain has been calibrated and
made manifest [by neuroscience] in predictable statistical formulas," he writes, we'll be able to

> dial up the same formulas and information and diag-
> nose the effect that any illustration, any commercial,
> any speech, any flirtation, any bill, any coo has been
> crafted to produce. . . . Something tells me, mere
> research protocol drudge though I may be, that I will
> love it all, cherish it all, press it to my bosom.

In yesteryear those who tried to reduce experience, "vision," and
"evocation" to formula infuriated Wolfe. He attacked critics and
painters whose theories yielded only "an abstraction of an
abstraction, a blueprint of the blueprint, diagram of the diagram," and denounced the alleged philosophy of Abstract
Expressionism everywhere in *The Painted Word* (1975):

> No more realism, no more representational objects,
> no more lines, colors, forms, and contours, no more

pigments, no more brush strokes, no more evocations.
. . . Art . . . came out the other side as Art Theory! Art
Theory pure and simple, words on a page, literature,
undefiled by vision, flat, flatter, flattest. . . .

The impression of push-the-beat swerving, role to role, view to
view, is sharpened elsewhere in *Hooking Up* by a variety of passages in which Wolfe (who by report is finishing a novel about
academe) plays pop lecturer, spieling "dazzling" rubbish
about the past:

The nineteenth century began with the American and
French Revolutions of the late eighteenth. The twentieth
century began with the formulation of Marxism, Freudi-
anism, and Modernism in the late nineteenth. And the
twenty-first began with the Great Relearning—in the
form of the destruction of the Berlin Wall in a single day,
dramatizing the utter failure of the most momentous
start-from-zero of all.

Even his lively answer to the strictures of Updike and Mailer
loses its way, straying from the aesthetics of naturalism to current market and gym standards, as Wolfe taunts his enemies
for poor sales and failing health (Updike has an "aging
bladder," Mailer "support[s] himself with two canes, one for
each rusted-out hip").

The tyranny of Now allows small space to resisters. Yet this
writer is capable of resistance. Moments in his career have been
marked by sustained responsiveness to the genuine—most
memorable of them the moment that produced *The Right Stuff*
(1979), Wolfe's report on the astronauts. And some continu-
ities exist between that book and his current work. The hero-
worshipping impulse that powered *The Right Stuff* is in

evidence no less in the sketches of the Intel founder and of E.O. Wilson in *Hooking Up* than in the portraits of rich, hard-driving men "in full" in his novels. The eye for costume that studied the pooling cargo pants (and that leads Wolfe to enjoy chatting with talk show hosts about his thirty-two white suits) is the same eye that lingered long and pleasurably on the "stylish" bridge coats worn by heroic navy officers to the funerals of fellow heroes burned to cinders in crashes ("big beautiful belly-cut collar and lapels, deep turnbacks on the sleeves, a tailored waist . . . ").

The discontinuities, however, warrant more attention. *The Right Stuff* is shot through with episodes that talk back eloquently to brand-name/status culture. There's splendid fury in John Glenn's voice when he learns—for one example—that officialdom is harassing his wife Annie, a stutterer, trying to force her to do interviews in the couple's house with LBJ and the networks. Glenn calls his wife, tells her he's on her side "all the way, one hundred percent"—not to let Lyndon Johnson or any of the rest of them "put so much as *one toe* inside our house!" The subject in view is the pure proud solidarity of lifetime mates and Wolfe does it justice. The same holds for his book's treatment of heroic codes. The pilots in *The Right Stuff* possess little—pittance pay and a thousand square feet or so of shelter for wife and child—and endure by choice fearful peril day by day. The finely disciplined asceticism of the group as a whole, together with the feelings of joint moral responsibility to the confraternity of the brave, might well have stirred Conrad himself; Wolfe's high admiration, persuasively bestowed, bespeaks a sense of the worthy which, when the book appeared, seemed likely to serve him in the future.

But recall the hour: the tide that lifts all boats was rising. Lawyers going broke on a million a year, private jets hung with pricey paintings, layer upon layer of fascinations: Lugz upon Air Jordan, Quibel upon Pellegrino, Dr. Hot-Ticket upon Dr. Wilson, late Wolfe upon early Wolfe, merger mania, whirling dot-coms, Jacuzzis in every pot, gold chains on every electrician, values by the dozen shelved with merciless sell-by dates . . . Until the eve of the Eighties, apparently, one could hope—as long as one stayed ahead of the curve—to recognize and speak up for the genuine when it emerged. But the Reagan Era brought a famous proliferation of wrong stuff—irresistible attractions—and it became harder for the Now-specialist to see beyond the pony.

Hostility to yesteryear is, of course, no mere matter of distaste (except on nostalgia nites) for bygone moralities, hits, costumes, scientific theories. The hostility has other kinds of outmodedness in view. Racism, classism and sexism: these too are seen as belonging to the past—and traditional politics is tightly associated with them. Still more important for many is repression: prejudice after prejudice, mad rule upon mad rule, marked the repressive past (and yet again, politics is of that past).

On its face it seems implausible that the opinion driving enthusiasm for "getting beyond politics," for "setting politics aside," for running against Washington and for mocking the Beltway, has any connection with the sexual revolution. Most assuredly the connection isn't direct and causal. But states of mind and whole ways of seeing and interpreting don't abide rigid boundaries. For many millions of Americans the most powerful experience of release—of blessed freedom, the thing itself—in the past half century came as the result of the extraordinary changes in that period in domestic values and behavior. Those changes were represented without exception as victories over the darkness and superstition—the stupid severities and dimwitted disciplines—of yesteryear. They simultaneously created and mirrored a culture-wide sense of the past as a burden to be shed—a constraint, a needless limit on possibility.

And that culture-wide sense can't be fenced off from attitudes toward conduct in the large, including political conduct. The exhilaration of escape from foolish concealments, inhibitions, enforced loyalties—the delight in triumph after triumph over shame and bondage—these moved like a tide through the general society, leaving in their wake scorn for everything enslaved by convention, habit, loyalty. New languages were spoken, pieces of which shape today's touchy-feely talk: caring, involved, fully functioning, open to experience, lifestyle, interpersonal, getting it together . . . Carl Rogers, the "non-directive" psychotherapist who popularized the language, imagined himself to be lifting the great cloud of pessimistic severity spread over the world by the elders—Sigmund Freud in particular. (My theory, Rogers wrote, "places greater stress on the

*emotional elements, the feeling aspcts, than upon the intellectual aspects
. . . [It] places greater stress upon the immediate situation than upon
the individual's past . . . [It] lays stress upon the therapeutic relationship itself as a growth experience [and strives to increase] the client's
unconditional personal regard.")*

*At its weirdest the sexual revolution produced "serious," pseudo-
scientific claims for something called "positive incest"—attempts to
distingush "a positive, consensual, nondamaging incest" from "abusive assault." Absurdities mounted. But so also did the certainty that
today and tomorrow were times of emancipation and that the past
was some kind of prison.*

*No brief effort to call back the hour when Now was freshly felt as
revelation—as proof that all must change—can succeed; the best
that can be done is to revisit one or another phase of the experience,
and trust it to function as a reminder of the experience as a whole:
the permanent zapping of respect for the past. The piece ahead,
written a quarter-century ago, attempted to cast light on the efforts
of individuals to engage the new: people troubled, depressed, excited
by change, now wrangling with it, now relishing it. The reporter,
myself, was already a father and grandfather at the time; the vote
ambivalently for the past that I cast at the end is open now, as it was
then, to the charge of sentimentality.*

*But that charge misses the point. Whatever its defects of perspec-
tive, the piece bears witness, through the voices of those it quotes, to
the strength of the belief that a world was ending, and that every
institution would therefore need to think of changing its shape. This
belief, together with growing intergenerational suspicion and fric-
tion, deepening public dispute about "lifestyle" and the advent of
"radical licentiousness" in the media, encouraged national leaders
to bypass secular issues. Stepping forth as moral exemplars—
defenders of heterosexual unions, spokespersons for the moral
majority (American goodness once again, the nation of virtuous
kind hearts)—they widened the opening for no-politics politics.*

After the Sexual Revolution

I don't write the songs and for a long time I'd been uneasy listening to them. The new domestic music . . . My children of childbearing-childrearing age, sons and daughters alike, declaring against having children. A friend, father of three, seeming to take his own divorcing casually. (He: "Jane and I are through." I [over-pious]: "I'm sorry, I really—" He [lightly]: "Not at all, not at all. Should've happened ten years ago.") A friend, bored with the search for euphemisms, settling on the term "um" to denote members of an unmarried couple. (The friend says parents of these couples depend on that sound when alluding to their child's partner. "My daughter's . . . um . . . friend." "My son's um . . .") Anti-weddings, wherein clerics scrap the language, "in sickness and in health," in favor of "I do my thing, and you do your thing. I am not in this world to live up to your expectations. And you aren't in this world to live up to mine." Sonny and Cher with the running joke the other season, from Sunday to Sunday, in the family hour, about Cher's *sportif* pregnancy. A women's magazine polling 10,000 mothers on whether they would choose to have children again and reporting that 70 percent said No. Couples in their mid-thirties talking as though marriage were a survival epic, theirs the only union not on the rocks in a whole circle, neighborhood, college class. (Grimly, through clenched teeth: "It's not going to happen to us.") Our former neighbor Herb, down from his retirement home in Maine, coming in for a drink and telling us he's here for a wedding, to give away the bride. Herb has no daughters—is he giving away a niece? No, says Herb with an amused grin, his daughter-in-law. She's remarrying. She's the mother of his grandson and has just divorced his older boy. The girl is remarrying and she wants her father-in-law, Herb, to give her away.

New domestic music.

If I sound condemnatory, that isn't how I feel, or how I felt. A certain stiffness before the journey I'm writing about—but not condemnation. The stiffness was traceable, moreover, to confusion and muddle and frustration, not to moral clarity. Sometimes, during conversational and other encounters of the sort I mention, I'd feel myself slipping into the stock response to new music, new anything, among people like myself—WASPs in their forties and fifties. The stock response is disgust, a feeling that leads on through posturing and highmindedness toward eventual emotional freeze-up. Or, in short, to another evasion.

My problem was, quite simply, that I believed a right and decent way of thinking or responding—a place to stand regarding the New Everything—truly did exist, in me, in everyone. Not a revelation or brilliant stroke, merely a decent way of thinking. Something unmysterious capable of cutting away these clogged contradictory feelings . . . disapproval, worry about being prudish, vague hypocrisy, simulated disgust. Something which, if said out loud, wouldn't make me wince when I heard it, or feel false—softer or holier or dumber than I am.

Something with a bit of breadth, and available on demand.

Believing in the existence of this golden inner text, though, wasn't sufficient to produce it. For whatever cause—swallowed up in the bad old middle-class silence?—the "right response" was some kind of an inexpressible. No birds sang.

A far-out thing to do with such a problem is to take it seriously, take time off and work on it. Treat it as worth wrestling with. Try to loosen yourself up. Read relevant books. Rent some money and travel with the problem in mind—talk to old friends, to experts and specialists if you can locate your trouble as part of a "field." Go find the strangers who write the songs, and talk to them. I thought, too, of looking in on my kids at some point, the three who are twenty-one-plus—catching them and myself by surprise, being the visitor for once, instead of the visited. Surprise is your only teacher, said Charles Sanders Peirce.

Laziness, embarrassment, and self-mockery intervened, naturally. Also an inside voice distracting me from my own purposes by pompously inflating the subject. Futurology kept seducing me, as though what I was after was a prediction, news about things to come. Is our age a period of transition; are we moving from A to B? The inside voice insinuated that the true source of my discomfort was only that I couldn't see the direction (B); that I was aware only of loss and deprivation and people behaving as though tomorrow is all; that my real need was for another issue of the magazine *Daedalus* on the year 2000, or a futurology seminar. As the sequel proved, there was plenty to be done before I could go on the road to any purpose. But the first step was grasping that futures weren't my business. What mattered to me was the missed inner connection—the lack of an unphony language to think and feel in when I heard the new tunes. For tripping itself to be better than another evasion, I had to know the nature of my need.

On the road I went to singles bars, talked to creeps and

mucho-machos, listened to Home Ec and Family Life specialists, spoke with marriage counselors and militant feminists,
with friends who've recently been divorced, with "career
women" and "young marrieds" hopeful and dour, with militant male feminists, with graduate students in "guidance,"
education commissioners, university chancellors, school
supers and principals, my editors, my students, my kids. I visited some newish institutions like day-care centers, marriage
clinics, a "human resource" college, schools for pregnant
unmarried teenagers, and "one-stop multi-human-service centers," moving up and down the coasts, and from Lauderdale to
Laramie.

I heard about torments, triumphs, gains, and losses that
were new to me (maybe not to others).

I fumbled with questions which, I admit, seldom had an
edge, since they were in essence only attempts to locate a
missing cue.

And, despite my awareness that I needed to stay on my own
beam, I was often beguiled away from personal need by
irrelevancies—negatives and positives, affirmation and despair
about The New Manners, The New Domesticity, The New Nurture.
(This figures below as one–hand–other–hand–ism.)

Gradually the mists burned off. Pieces began coming
together. Hints, cues. One midsummer Saturday morning in
the heartland, I heard three rural women fighting for their self-
respecting life against some militant eastern sisters. As I listened, a button was touched under the map and I felt a dozen
lighted-up links among places I'd been in the past few months,
and among people I'd talked to. Epiphany. I woke up the next
morning with something unlocked inside, and afterward
everything was easy.

That, though, was up the line from where I started. First
came books and numbers, weekends in the library.

"Wake up, I got news for you," says the Janis Ian song. "Nobody needs you anymore."

On the money, the numbers say.

Last year more than a million U.S. couples were divorced—twice as many as in 1966, three times as many as in 1950. (Children under eighteen in these marital breakups numbered about one million in 1975, as in each of the three previous years.) Between 1970 and 1975, households with a female head increased by 30 percent and the number of people under thirty-five maintaining a household alone doubled from 1.5 million to 3 million. There were fewer marriages in 1975 than in any year since 1969, and a steep, if difficult to measure, increase in "unmarried but living together" pairings. The fertility rate for women of childbearing age dropped to 1.8 births, less than the 2.1 rate necessary for replacing the population. In 1960, according to the Office of Population Research at Princeton, 13 percent of the married women aged twenty-five to twenty-nine were childless; last year the percentage rose to 21.

The most interesting discussion by academic intellectuals of issues related to these trends still depends heavily upon Hegel, Marx, and Engels. But all commentators, regardless of school, and regardless of whether they float light loads of knowledge or heavy, in short words or long, toward mass audiences or learned clubs, enter sooner or later into warfare about whether the domestic trends in question are Good or Bad. Among the major battles are these:

Faith vs. Consciousness. When the former First Lady, Betty Ford, gave hesitant approval to the "living together" syndrome, Ethel Kennedy countered with church-based moral disapproval in a *Family Circle* interview.

Mrs. Kennedy: " . . . the *feeling* you got [was] that maybe she [Mrs. Ford] thought, 'Well, it's a new generation and maybe it's okay.' "

Interviewer: "Do you think it's a new generation and it's okay?

Mrs. Kennedy: "No. I think it's a new generation and it is definitely not okay."

A variety of spokespersons filled out the First Lady's position, before and after it was taken—among them Gail Graham Yates, women's studies professor at the University of Minnesota. Professor Yates hailed the new conventions as signs that intelligent, rational commitments will soon be the norm. Marriage today, she added, "is becoming stronger because it's more deliberate. The assumption that you have to be married is changing very rapidly. This generation of college students is going to decide—really decide—to get married rather than just drift into marriage, as was more the pattern of even a decade ago. . . . "

Fidelity-as-Creation vs. Fidelity-as-Suicide. The porn merchant's message is that a little secret dirty fun nowadays costs peanuts; the pop philosopher's message is that the road to promiscuity is also the road to spontaneity, in-touchness with one's physicality, and honesty about human nature itself. Each is part of a saturation-coverage Heed-Your-Instincts campaign—heed your instincts, forget your inhibitions, advance from prudery, break your marital contracts—seemingly designed to reach everybody in America regardless of class, income, educational level, sex, age, or taste. (Other anti-fidelity campaign workers include poets, novelists, ministers, and seers.)

The secular resistance to this tide starts not from the Decalogue but with critiques of modish values like spontaneity and honesty. Conceding that fidelity is widely perceived as a symptom of evasive conventionality and spiritlessness, they hold that this perception is wrongheaded. "Fidelity is extremely unconventional," according to Denis de Rougemont in *Passion and Society*, ". . . not in the least a sort of conservatism but rather a construction." Indeed, in this view it's the only kind of truth human beings can construct. Heed your creativity, say the new moralists, not your instincts; reject the adultery bandwagon.

Egomania vs. Caring. A secondary operation but interesting. On this front the fight is between those who read the statistics as evidence of heightened self-absorption and ego-obsession and those who see, instead, a movement toward broader, less "privatistic" modes of concern. Edwin Schur, a New York University sociologist, holds that we're falling into an "ethic of self-preservation" which teaches that, since you and I "are surrounded by self-interested schemers," we had "better fight fire with fire"; the product is a "kind of interpersonal *laissez-faire.*" D. Keith Mano, *National Review* columnist and novelist, claims that people are beset by fantasies about secret talents and undiscovered gifts, and that these fantasies, which induce a rage to "discover 'the true self,' " are responsible for contemporary disparagement of "conventional roles . . . the husband and the wife, the mother and the father."

The opposition counters that what's in progress is the growth of wider sympathies than were practicable under the rigid, priggish rule of Family—a new concern for "problem population groups" . . . an "age of caring." Yesterday a high school girl who became pregnant was expelled from school; today she transfers to a special school and studies infant nutrition. Yesterday divorced people raising children alone were solitary in their alienation from social norms; today an organization with thousands of local chapters helps them to share their experiences and problems with people like themselves. Yesterday a young mother with sexual problems or a physically abusive husband had nowhere to turn for aid; today many communities have agencies and hot-lines providing immediate assistance. Yesterday young married couples thinking positively about improving their marriages had no assistance from outside; today a dozen organizations sponsor "marriage retreats," with professional counselors in attendance, in every section of the country. New occupational categories in "people worker" fields—male mothers, marriage savers, rehabilitation counselors, death therapists, divorce therapists, and the like— are constantly surfacing, all signifying the opposite (so goes the claim) of ego-obsession.

"New Luddites" vs. "New Lifers." Some observers tie marriage and birth-rate declines to an outbreak of cavalier attitudes toward life, citing in particular developments in medicine: molecular engineering, prenatal screening, psychosurgery, genetic manipulation, abortion, and euthanasia. Doctors perform abortions on no other ground except that the child's sex is in the parents' view wrong . . . The *New York Times*'s Op-Ed page entertains the argument that homosexuality is a sane means of controlling population growth. And some New Luddites are persuaded thereby that the most momentous event of our age is the murder, by technology, of awe.

Other New Luddites indict not only science proper but industrialization-modernization in the large, focusing on the obliteration of family life and functions by industrial capitalism. The classic twentieth-century statement on the subject is a 1930s essay by Max Horkheimer called "Authority and the Family," detailing stages in the reduction of parental function to subpersonal status. Horkheimer held that even at the time he wrote, owing to the "demands of extensive industrialization [which] do away with the present home," there was no longer any possibility of a private familial existence with its own intimacies, satisfactions, and values; soon children would cease to be regarded "in the old way, as 'one's own.'" More recent works, as for example the psychoanalyst Herbert Hendin's *The Age of Sensation* (1975), trace a relationship between "home

life as a factory for producing people who fit into the economic system" and the advent of a "generation of young
people who are trying to stop their own romantic impulses in
the suspicion that intimacy may end in disaster."

New Lifers, on the other hand, are all cheer, excited by
visions of new emotional possibility and sexual gratification—
newly expressive lives. . . . Their academic spokesman, Professor Edward Shorter, a specialist in family history, in *The
Making of the Modern Family* (1975) spiritedly welcomed the
age of "the free floating couple. . . ."

Other specialists in his field have challenged Professor
Shorter's theses, and one of them, Professor Christopher
Lasch, slated the man, in *The New York Review of Books,* as "the
Helen Gurley Brown of social history." But the high optimism
of the New Lifers, their positive sense of change, hasn't been
deflated by academic sniping.

"The constant impression [liberated women] make," says
Elizabeth Janeway in *Between Myth and Morning: Women Awakening* (1974), "is sheer enjoyment of life and good feeling with
each other . . . overwhelmingly energetic, cheerful, funny and
good-natured." "What a vast laboratory . . . is being conducted
by our young people," says Carl R. Rogers in *Becoming Partners*
(1972). "Unheralded and unsung, explorations, experiments,
new ways of relating, new kinds of partnerships are being tried
out, people . . . inventing alternatives, new futures, for our most
sharply failing institutions, marriage and the nuclear family. . . ."

The key (and archetypically American) theme here is, as
often as not, that of the new start. Time and again it resounds
in the media, in self-help manuals, in a flood of upbeat
renamings—for example, divorce as "breakthrough" or "act of
creation." A summer ago it filled an issue of *Harper's Bazaar,*
billed on the cover as "Your Complete After-Divorce Guide to
a Happy, Healthy, Successful *New* Life," and offering writer

after writer noodling round the theme. "Divorce may be exactly what was needed," beamed Rollo May, "to bring you a new life—more enriching than the one that is past."

Today is the first day of the rest of your life. I learned a lot in the library about the principal domestic wars now raging, came upon much heady suggestive writing. Most of it, however, felt over-generalized and class-bound, too tendentious, too heady. Too far out, too far behind, too spiky, too beamish, too Coruscatingly Brilliant, speaking to genuine needs, no doubt, but not to mine.

Time to fly the maze and try talking to people.

An attractive, soft-featured woman in her early thirties, diffident in manner, an Ohioan, mother of three, Ellen has been divorced since 1972. I've known her for a dozen years, and when I looked her up and told her my problem, she produced a bottle, ice, glasses, put her cigarettes on the table, and talked for close onto an hour and a half with few stops. She'd just been, as it happened, to a Parents Without Partners meeting, a chapter meeting—her first and, as she claimed ruefully, her last. Why had she gone? She'd had a dream, Ellen told me. She wrote a box number in the local paper, got back a newsletter that told about activities for parents and kids and that also had "little boxes with numbers in them." In the newsletter, it seems, there was a squib about how many children grow up in single-parent families. Two out of every five kids born in the seventies will spend at least five years with just one parent. Twenty to thirty million children.

"I never saw the figure before," Ellen said. "So, suppose you go to these things, the hayrides, the trampoline, whatever . . . Wouldn't it maybe teach them—my brood—something? I mean . . . they'll see they're not all that different, not freaks?"

PWP members are good people, Ellen insisted. The meeting

was held in a Sunday school classroom with a mid-fifties man in a sky-blue knit suit signing up new people at a card table, and when you sat down people introduced themselves to you. Forty or fifty in the room; a dozen newcomers, all women, in their twenties and thirties, but the others, except for two or three men, were old—"I mean stooped and white-haired and trembling hands, widows and widowers. Their kids would be thirty and forty if they're a day."

The meeting started with the reading of the PWP "Preamble."

"It was nice," Ellen said. "Simple, dignified language. It said the group's only reason for being was to help the single parent with his children; children were hurt the worst by death or divorce; it's the overriding responsibility of the parent to lessen—to try to lessen—the hurt. It was decent and good and hopeful. I felt something, honestly. A shiver. It wasn't just some kind of unreal joining-a-club thing. Rotary or Kiwanis. There was—for an instant—a thrill. I can't explain. You're not just joining. You're singled out, you've singled yourself out. You've had a loss and now you aren't going to hide it anymore, you admit something—"

Ellen shook off her words impatiently.

"It wasn't a joke. For that one minute when I was going in . . . I felt shy and *very* exposed and very hopeful. Just to go out and admit something—my failure, my need. My feeling outside of everything. My feeling new and wanting to express it. They may be naive and simple but they do know what you're feeling. They work so hard to be hearty, to make you welcome and feel accepted. It's like going to the altar to be saved. The congregation's happy for you and rooting for you and they're solicitous, they know how you feel—you feel you've maybe done something a little crazy. You're embarrassed and they worry about that. They care about you. They enjoy being solicitous. Oh, it's a moment."

Ellen let out her breath. Another frown.

"The trouble is there's nothing afterward. That's it. You're saved and it's all over. You go from that one moving moment where you see yourself so clearly and are seen by other people, where it doesn't matter about the knit suit or about anything, it's all about people and real things. You go straight from that into a committee and it's all bureaucracy from then on. Not even a singles bar. Just a committee. It's all about raising money and slates of officers and last names beginning A through B bring salads and K through P bring desserts and Camilla wants people to promote Stanley Products, have a Stanley party—

"It lasted about one minute: my experience. It was like a confession. One minute afterward I was standing around collecting invitations. Camilla—she was absolutely huge. Would I come to her house party? She was the ham raffler and the knife seller. The spark plug. The vice president said, 'Any more business?' An old lady—the front row—said she'd sent a card to Lois. 'Lewis who?' the vice president said. I almost wept right then. I was in a daze. How dare I come there in the first place? How could I have believed—"

She brightened.

"Outside I was getting into my car and somebody called out at me from across the street. 'Hey, Ellen, you ever see the insides of a mobile home?' It was the man in the sky-blue knit. I went for the tour. It would have been worse not to go. He showed me everything. He showed me how it 'slept eight.' We looked into every closet, every drawer. I saw the ashtray from his Nassau cruise. Monarch line. I felt so detached. I got an explanation of toilets in mobile homes. 'You have two kinds of toilet.' He demonstrated his toilet for me. I mean the flushing mechanism. Twice.

"I should have raced out of there. The last thing I wanted or needed was something pathetic. It was foolish. They do so much for each other. They tell each other they're handsome and 'self-possessed' and that they're having fun, and of course if helps them. But I don't care. I said, 'You have a very nice place, a very nice—mobile home.' 'All it needs,' he said, 'is a girl who can cook.' He was really nice. But I don't care. It's pathetic when people need so much so badly they can't know any more about each other than to say, "All it needs is a girl who can cook.'"

In my first days on the road the "learning" consisted mainly in this: the breadth of variation, among divorced people, in need and desire to tell whole stories, to share—with one's child, with one's own new beloved, with a stranger—the full, tortured intricacy of a complex attachment shredding itself.

One afternoon, heading east from Rochester, New York, on the plaza by the mini-serve island of Bill's Mobil, W. Kulakowski, Prop., the owner—"I'm just a dumb Pole"—passes along in minutes the story of his own separation. Stylized, to be sure, feelings in check, a comic frame . . . but I feel no holding back. The paperback on a pile of magazines beside me on the front seat is a work called *Creative Divorce* by Mel Krantzler. Coming around about the oil, Bill K. notices the book, wants to know what it is about. I tell him and he moves his head in a way that seems to cancel his interest. A big, wet-lipped, sandy-haired man in his forties.

"My wife left me," Bill says. "I gave her a bad time."

He goes on with the story. A twenty-year Army man, he'd come back to his hometown meaning to wipe out the time from Korea to his first pension check. He bought into the Mobil, married a girl eighteen years younger whom he'd met at a "St. Biddie's" bingo night, and considered himself "set." But home from the honeymoon he discovered his bride "has this mania. She sews a new dress every night." Bill's wife works in a bank as a teller and all the women tellers her age are great sewers, new outfits for every day of the week. "It kills them, they stay up all hours, three in the morning. All over the house these papers, cutouts. Paper dolls." Bill "took it" for a month, "ding-a-ling all night long after supper" while he sat in his chair. "Finally I said, 'Listen, what is it, are you going to stop?' " Bill got on her. It wasn't the money, he explains. "But every night a new dress . . . It was, like, ridiculous." So he got on her and rode her until she said he was a "dumb Pole that didn't understand creating." And "she up and left."

A whole story? The conversation lasts barely longer than it takes to pump sixteen gallons of gas. Bill finishes and I say I'm sorry about the breakup, maybe it'll still work out.

"Yeah," Bill shrugs.

Clipboard and pen to him, credit card to me.

"Have a nice day."

"And yourself." I move on.

The more I'm with you pretty baby,

a performer sings on my car radio,

> *The more I feel my love increase*
> *I'm building all my dreams around you*
> *Our happiness will never cease*
> *'Cause nothing's any good without you*
> *Baby you're my centerpiece*
>
> *We'll find a house and garden somewhere*
> *Along a country road a piece*
> *A little cottage on the outskirts*
> *Where we can really find release*

'Cause nothing's any good without you
Baby you're my centerpiece

Shining hair and shining skin
Shining as she reeled him in
To tell him like she did today
Just what he could do with Harry's House
And Harry's take home pay.

"Harry's House—Centerpiece,*" says the disc jock, his voice up and over the closing bars. "That was Joni Mitchell."

Beginning as I did with "broken homes," I was made over, within weeks, into some kind of sadness freak. People like Ellen who had bitter-funny anecdotes to tell pushed me that way, naturally. So did the odd, offhand, unprepared-for narrative like Bill's at the gas station—stories that had a detached and final quality, like a sign announcing a blasting area, firmly fencing off response. More than a few divorced people I spoke with were able to move through their domestic story from start to finish without once uttering the former mate's name, as though it had been forever wiped clean from the mind. But as you listened, the unsaid name became a nerve and the refusal to touch it made the hurt all the more palpable.

Hardest by far, though, were the Believers. "One of the most creative and transforming experiences," says the fashion magazine doctor discussing divorce. "A time to create a new more fulfilling life for yourself . . ." Believers spoke sometimes in this very idiom, fully meaning their words. A friend I'll call Dick—a prep school history master and coach—told me his story in company one evening, looking away repeatedly and lovingly, as he spoke, to the two young women on the couch opposite us—Jen and Lindsay—with whom he was making his new life. All three were Believers. Jen is his daughter, a fully matured, beautiful sixteen-year-old who's decided she's happier with her father. Lindsay is the twenty-eight-year-old art director who has lately moved up from New York to New Hampshire to live with Dick and Jen. They had "won through," Dick told me. His wife, Jess, would never have believed in "us," in Jen and Lindsay and Dick together—"in this room, in Lindsay and Jen and me being able to talk and be happy and open together, really sharing."

But his present happiness has been *earned*, Dick insisted. Beforehand, nothing but frustration. It stemmed from his wife's attitude about "the movement."—women's liberation. "I brought women's lib home myself," Dick explained. His former wife took the position that while the movement was a good thing in the abstract, it was just too much trouble for her. Dick pushed. He read the books and started them off cautiously with housework-sharing, and "it was so good in so many ways that I used to go to sleep happy and wake up looking forward," The chief benefit was self-knowledge, and Dick tried to share the knowledge with his wife—feeling that he was caring for her, reaching out, concerned about her growth as well as his—but the conversations went poorly. ("She wasn't *there*.")

He began looking differently at his own life, his own house. "I saw I was just dodging it, going over to my office, leaving things undone, not pulling my oar. Why not learn how to cook? My God, I still remember it. I was adding things to myself. I was, dammit. I mean, I wouldn't be what I am now, what *we* are, the three of us . . ."

Dick smiles across at Lindsay, and she meets his eye gently. They are in love.

"I can't disavow it. I mean, Lindy cooks, Jen cooks, I cook
. . . We all clean . . . The whole thing is shared. But it's not just
that. It's attitudes, everything was different. And I thought it
was changing things for Jess."

Dick hesitates, thinking back. There's no time like it in a
man's life, he tells us. He'll never forget it. "It dawns on you that,
holy shit, you may not be correct in your assumed view of your
wife, your partner, or of the degree to which you're sharing the
same understanding. For years and years . . . My tries at thinking
things through . . . I was sure we were together."

He began spying on his wife, watching and listening to her with
Jen and Mike, his daughter and son. "I was spying on your
mother," Dick says, looking across at Jen, "spying on her in our
own house to see if she was stupid." He actually tried to think
the worst of himself—which meant, he believed, that he was still
loyal. "Was I dumb too? I'd just happened onto a new way of
looking at things but maybe I was dumb too. Why do we all think
we're so smart? I was still loyal because the first thing I did when
I suspected Jess was dumb was instantly protect her from being
seen that way *by me*. I started knocking myself."

Recounting the sequel Dick turns wry. His "first step" had been
to run off for a month with the "nearest intellectual woman"—as
though to discover whether certified brilliance would see anything in "Richard the Jock." The intellectual woman, also married, "went along for the experiment," and, when they both
woke up—"You know what happened," Dick says to Lindsay
with a glance indicating 'we've discussed this'—"she was able
to go home, she could let herself be taken back." Dick
couldn't. Not because his wife was stony but because he himself knew that he'd turned a corner and it would be wrong—
"anti-life" is Dick's word—to turn back. "Jess believes in things
as they are." And their children were supposed to be continuous with the world as it is. The problem is simply that his

wife "can't think." She simply believes in money, authority, the right opinions. She never was private. The familiar forms are the right forms. "People couldn't live together and stay together and make full commitments to each other if they stepped out of their regular roles, the conventions . . . She couldn't reach for anything—new feelings, better feelings . . ."

Dick shakes his head at a burden that's passed.

"The greatest thing that's ever happened," he repeats. The tone is close to wonder. "It's made all the difference." To Jen: "Like coming into Seal in the fog that morning, remember? Everything suddenly has a shape and I know what I am. We know what we are. We're free. And every single word and thought for nineteen years was *wrong* . . . opposite."

Dick's eyes are moist as he looks across at "my women." Jen drops her gaze. Lindsay is steadfast, sharing again the weight of their victory. Feeling wariness somewhere close by, a sadness freak's fear of his too great hope, Dick comes back to me impatiently: "Can you begin to imagine what that's like?"

"Hi! It's Ben. How'd you like to come over for a drink, you and Sally? Sure, now, why not. Who? I'm sorry, *who*? Ned? Ah, of course, *sorry*. Of *course*, bring him along. Love to have him."

In the old pre-study, pre-journey days, I was dimmer about the Neds of this world than I've been lately. What I knew in those days was that nice Ned cooked and ate with Jim and Sal, made wine and baked pies with Jim and Sal, chose the records for Jim and Sal's dinner parties, vacationed with good old Jim and good old Sal . . . and that whenever he was part of the scene I registered a slight intensification of social ambiguity. Now, launched on my "project," however, I seem to have moved an inch forward toward—where? Well, it's come to mind that Jim and Sal and Ned are, just conceivably, A Threesome. It was last month, in my study period, reading Alex Comfort, that I learned about Three-somes, *viz*:

> People who are on frank terms say, "We're going to make love, would you care to join us?" It's better to be forth-right than to try to set someone up. A threesome starts best by gentle proximity, with the odd-sex partner in the middle. The couple then both pay attention to the guest (massage is a great start, unembarrassing between males, which can gradually become sexual). Sometimes gentle intimacy all night with mutual intercourse seems the right sequel—or it can get wildly playful. We heard of a man being tossed for by the two girls—the wife won and had the orgasm of her life. Sensible people don't pro-gram this or any other sex experience, however. It it goes wrong, they have the sense to stop, at the request of any of the three players, and switch to simple intimacy—sleep or listening to records.

I remember an old Eudora Welty story in which a sexually curious adolescent keeps asking, But what do people *do*? I see that I've taken over the kid's project. Mid-life sex education: I'm learning what people do.

Singles joint on Las Olas in Fort Lauderdale, the weekly wet T-shirt contest. (Pedantry: a wet T-shirt contest offers a cash prize to the woman contestant dressed in T-shirt and bikini bottom and soaked by hose or bucket whose breasts seem, in the opinion of the judges, more pleasing than those of the other contestants.) Today's prize is $250 and the scene feels chaotic, partly because of the jam-up in the doorway, partly because of the racket made on the amps by Springsteen's "Hidin' in the Back Streets," but mainly because of Jack, my neighbor on the next barstool. Jack has chosen this time and place to air a gripe at the state of Florida.

Here we are, my neighbor and I, enticed to this parlor by a streamer flown behind a plane above the crowded weekend beach. Girls lined up in a planter filled with sand . . . crowd in a semicircle. The girls have been dampened with pails of water amid much spluttering, merriment, shouts, exhortation. Judges arrive, Bruce wailing high—"*back streets—WAAAA-0-0-WWW* . . ."—you can feel the beat in the footrail. Jack is now shouting in my ear. We'd begun a chat earlier about porn, and Jack had started detailing, in a reasonable voice, various porn rip-offs in the Citrus State. He was only slightly sauced, but for some reason he got madder as he proceeded. A few feet from us, Honey, Bunny, Bette, and Lee stand soaked and bulging, laughing, kidding each other, with the judges peering, taking up peculiar angles of vision, clearly men of research interests, scribbling notes on their pads. ZERO-ZERO read one T-shirt. HERMANN HESSE, another. LOOK STOP TALK, another. Cheers for each girl resounding, Springsteen blotted out but returning strong.

"Hey, Bunny—wink." a voice cries from the crowd.

"Hands off, Freddy."

"Fucking Aloha," Jack shouts in my ear. The Aloha is some kind of adult motel—jelly beds, overhead mirrors, X-rates in your room. "Twenty-five bucks—"

"X is *shit*!" Jack shouts angrily. "*Deep Throat*—all you see in *Deep Throat*—"

"Wink, Bunny—"

"I mean down *here*," Jack shouts. "Florida, X is shit here."

"Number Four, please step forward. Bunny—"

Great roar.

"All you see is her head bobbing, remember? They cut it to pieces. What a rip-off!"

As the man with the hand mike announces the winner and runner-up, Jack falls silent. He seems dazed, frowns into the cheering and applause, the music. He squints at me sincerely, no longer shouting. He shakes his head at the still-dripping girls.

"They wrecked it," he tells me sadly. "Fuckers. It used to be wild. They used the beer hose, you know? What the hell they want to fuck it up with water?"

The last word. The decline of culture: no more hosing down wet T-shirt girls with beer.

When you achieve this measure of detachment, you discover just how much your culture can do for a soul surfeited with other people's absorption in each other. Along Las Olas I was on the prowl for pure nullity, and I found it in spades, shedding in the process some piety. Having laughed, cheered, and applauded with the gang—the only bad humor in the place, really, was Jack's—I left the saloon feeling the fine companionable relaxation that comes over you when you grasp with full forgiving understanding that you are part of the problem, absolutely, aren't, *can't ever be*, anything like the solution.

The following evening, in a different southern city, I eat with a married couple named Ross and Alice who have a problem but are uncertain how to focus it. They are, let's acknowledge it, Jack and Jill Armstrong WASPs in appearance, nifty clean-cut blonds, bloomy, fresh-faced, desirable-looking people. They'd met "vaguely," these two, while they were at Oberlin, but Alice was at the conservatory, and Ross, son of a philosophy prof, was pre-engineering and not thinking about girls. Alice's widowed mother had run a successful music school, secondary level, and after their southward move here, where Ross had lucked into a site-planning job with "one of the only three idealistic land developers" in the country, Alice thought of teaching—and then thought herself out of it. Being married was enough for a while. Plenty of time later to take some pupils.

But what to do, laze around, practice, or work, wasn't the problem. What comes out, slowly, as we talk, is that as people just turning twenty-five, they prefer not to be too hip too early, aren't ready for cynicism about their marriage, yet they've found, to their depression, that fending off isn't easy. They liked feeling open and unfurtive . . . and they're upset because too many things go against them. This place they'd moved into, Alice said. It wasn't a swingles place when they moved in, or, if it was, who knew? Were they so innocent? But now the kids—Ross and Alice—don't go down to the pool much anymore. Lots of spacey types down there. People smoking dope discreetly, staying apart from each other. "You're sitting there and you hear somebody talking about, *You should have been there last night at Harriet's, wow, what a scene, must have been eight or nine couples, all . . .*" And then the other day, an incident. Some girl in the house went topless at the pool and people tried to make her get dressed. She wouldn't—topless was her *cause*, you see—so they sent for the police.

It seems to be partly the inconsistency or the pretense that bothers Ross and Alice. The other tenants, swingles folk, acting as though topless was a crime—it made things feel even sinful. Everybody secretive and false, suddenly people worrying about "outsiders," "the place's reputation." For Ross and Alice the heart of the trouble was, Who wanted to know about any of this? Why did they even have to hear about it or have an opinion about it? Sleaziness and hypocrisy . . .

Listening, I think: Is it harmful to be swept into knowingness? Neither one of these two is attempting to pass himself/herself off as an innocent. But because of their past, their interests, perfectionist temperaments, Ross and Alice led lives of (more or less) relaxed asceticism until bumping into each other after college at a wedding—it was the first party either had bothered to go to for almost a year.

Alice says, "Shouldn't people be allowed to be newlyweds? What's wrong with that?" Ross answers easily with a grin. "We're allowed." But while his tone brings his bride partway back toward conversational lightness, nobody feels like laughing. The point is serious. If you value your innocence and would like for a while to continue to feel your newness before each other, shouldn't you be free to do so? Must you be hip overnight? Anyone who can remember that time of life, the lovely combination of pride, uprightness, sensual release in the first year of marriage old-style, would be touched by this couple's talk, their confused protest.

But it's not important that I'm touched, rather that I see something I'd missed. The trouble with porn, and the surrounding jungleland, is that it is contemptuous of the life cycle—jumbles the stages of human life, rushes the tempo, asks you to play ahead and behind the beat simultaneously. A fully matured person, with a stretch of variegated living to look back upon, has a clear idea—assuming self-honesty—about the quality of his moral life. He's reckoned his distance from innocence and toted his crimes and—since we're not now speaking of saints—therefore usually can't be affronted by porn. But the jungleland—the permissive, sexually liberated, "non-repressive" society— includes tens of millions who haven't matured to this clarity, who might in fact maintain touch a bit longer with an idealizing self if they weren't hounded out of it daily by porn and border porn, by X and marginal X, R, PG, by the universal tide of knowingness that tugs and nudges, thickens the air, loosens the principle, mucks up every good act by reminding it of its exceptionality. —*You should have been there at Harriet's, of course you've seen* Deep Throat, *how'd you like* Emmanuelle? *Special privileges for charter couples at Club Cupide in the Aloha!*

The precocity of the cynicism gets to you, everybody racing toward hipness. Couples in their twenties divorcing—on TV— at year's end and remarrying in January to collect a tax refund bundle and float a Jamaica holiday. Couples every age electing to be closet marrieds, hiding their wedded state for financial, social, and "image" reasons. (By report these people exist by the tens of thousands in California.) Couples consenting to be spied on by their employers, fitting familial and sexual life to the rules of The Game. (Players on National Football League contenders who are caught sleeping with their wives the night before a game are fined, and some recorded fines run as high as $2000.)

Nobody has to finger the girlie books to be aware that every month a torrent of weirdo knowingness pours through their columns. "My mistress and I," runs a recent letter in the "Playboy Advisor" column in Hef's magazine,

have practied to perfection a provocative technique that, I am convinced, produces the ultimate in male orgasm. Immediately prior to coitus, the lady employs fine-grained sandpaper to remove a thin layer of epidermis from the whole surface of my penis. The results are an incredible sensitivity and an unbelievably prolonged climax. The only difficulty is the progressive loss both in diameter and in length of my copulatory organ. Recently, I have found it necessary to notify my partner when I have entered her. Please advise.—L.H., Detroit, Michigan.

Why say anything? answers the "Playboy Advisor." *It should be obvious that you're not all there.*

Nobody has to hide out in the back streets to know that some discos in Los Angeles cater to homosexual teenagers; others, in New York, to exhibitionist odd couples and triplets. A gas. The couples and triplets mock-copulate on the white

211

plastic couches of Les Jardins on West 43rd Street in Manhattan. Nude female wrestlers, five shows daily, belt shit out of
each other in a mud pool in a Pussycat Theater, 79th Street,
Miami. Hurry on down. It's the texture of experience and you
breathe it as a kid, and the result is that the ineluctable sweet-
ness of true beginnings cannot be assumed any more.

Fighting for your innocence . . . a concept new to me.

"Sexual relations with persons other than a spouse are now
becoming common," I read on a plane, turning the pages of
Rustum and Delia Roy's *Honest Sex*. "When human need is
paramount, such relationships may serve as the vehicle of faithfulness to God."

More new domestic music.

Midsummer afternoon in the New England Berkshires, brilliant
sunshine, high clouds. Ted and Carolyn, Ted Jr., Chrissie, and
Susannah (the last three are Ted and Carolyn's children) are visiting friends who have a one-room house on the side of a hill
and this quite nice swimming pool. Ted has been helping
Chrissie, six, with a diving problem. Each time Chris pulls herself together for another try she calls out to Carolyn—
"Mommy, watch!"—and Carolyn watches, afterward
commenting encouragingly but undemandingly. Naked
intrepid Susannah, twenty-one months, pooped from running
up and down the hill from the pool to a clump of blueberry
bushes, plops down on the towel beside Ted Jr., eleven. She
puts her thumb in her mouth. Young Ted, with nothing but a
sleepy mindless love in his head, extends an arm and pats her
shoulder, without opening his eyes. "They're an item," their
mother says mildly, watching.

Chrissie's problem with the front dive is that, concerned probably about picking up a snootful of water, she can't seem to go in

headfirst. She leans over, leans still farther over, her daddy holding her gently by the waist, talking to her calmly, reassuringly. "That's it, hon, *lit*tle bit farther . . ." But then, amazingly, she does some kind of incredible somersault flip instead of just falling in, and lands on her back. Hesitant about pushing on, because these have been real hits that Chris has been taking, frowning at his inability to figure out the right words of instruction, Ted the daddy is ready to knock it off for a while. The ice is melting in Chris's Tab, how about they take a rest and try later? But Chris is remorseless, gutsy, will go again. Ted speaks to her quietly, we can't hear what they're saying, and by wit or wisdom they find the formula this time, something about being a stone and dropping herself, and, terrific, Chris does it. Headfirst into the water. 'Ray!' Chrissie Flagg's first front dive. She comes up happy to her mother's and Susannah's applause, shaking the water from her eyes. Her father is on the end of the board, hands on hips, grinning down, pleased with himself. "See how easy, hon? Didn't it feel nice?"

"That was good, Chris," brother Ted says soberly. Approval from the truly significant elder.

Bored with clapping, Susannah begins doing what Ted Jr. calls her fat walk, moving about in stately gait with her tummy hideously protruded. Nobody has specially requested this number, as Susannah becomes aware. She pauses briefly and, when everyone's glance has been drawn to her, pees studiously on the concrete walkway. "I think that was intended," Carolyn says. She empties the ice cubes from her glass, walks round to the dark spot, and rinses it away with pool water.

Susannah disappears down the hill, Ted Jr. in pursuit.

Time passes.

A tanager lights in a nearby cherry tree and everyone sits motionless. The color is stunning.

Chrissie does another dive, better than the first, asking this time for no witness.

No sound in my ear except the whir of the pool filter, a flutter of birch leaves.

This is the way life is supposed to be: how long will it last?

Somewhere on toward the middle, or institutional, phase of my tripping, a seesaw Yea or Nay motion began that soon became insufferable—a kind of entrapment. On the one hand, on the other . . . If Parents Without Partners was wrong for Ellen, other new instruments, schools, agencies, therapies kept surfacing, some of them admirable. The longer I was on the road, the surer I became that a "new nurture" does indeed exist—substitutes for traditional familial nurture, inventive new ways of helping people cope with a life in which official or received values and dailiness are wildly out of sync, and maternal and paternal authority—since it can't teach what has to be learned—is bereft of power and control.

On Long Island I visit the Ida B. Wells School, Miss Bernice Moze, principal, 92-10 165th Street, Jamaica, Borough of Queens—enrollment limited to pregnant high school girls.

It's Friday afternoon, and after I look in on classes for a while and talk with Miss Moze, I spend an hour with Constance Kelsick, the guidance counselor, talking methods and goals.

"All we do," Mrs. Kelsick tells me in her office, "is teach that *you* have to care. Nobody else is doing it, just you. You're the parent. Right from the beginning, that's where you are. All right, they can have a baby-sitter if the child's grandmother or the father's mother or somebody is willing to sit to make a contribution. Fine. They have a baby-sitter. But don't you ever forget that baby is yours—you brought that life into the world of your own free will and act and it's up to you to do some parenting, take hold and help that child grow.

"That baby is yours, that's what we teach. She's not your mother's. You have your schoolwork *and* you have your baby, yes, and it's a lot, but you're thinking about the long run, you're thinking about being able to bring in a little something at any point. So you know you have to keep up in school. Too much at stake. That little baby is yours and you're doing it to care for her, you're doing it because you're parenting, and it's your Job."

Mrs. Kelsick, a former nurse, a pretty woman with a positive, earnest manner, shows me teaching materials for that morning's class and tells me, thoughfully, how it went. It was their weekly problems discussion—her group, Veronica, Michelle, Santee, Denise, Dolores, and Rosanna. The sessions are open-ended; if a debate develops that promises to sustain its interest, discussion runs through lunch in the cafeteria and sometimes on into the first afternoon period. Today's subject was responsibility and blame. The focus was a sheet of mimeographed excerpts from a year-old newspaper horror story—a couple claimed to have lost two children in a midtown department store and later confessed, when the charred corpse of an infant was recovered from a nearby parking lot, that they had killed both.

"Whose fault was it? Who deserves the blame?" said Constance Kelsick, putting the query to me.

That was the question she put to Veronica and the others, and apparently there were plenty of hands. For a time the group pointed a finger at the city hospital. It seems that one baby had once been treated for bruises that suggested a battering, and nobody at the hospital had taken an interest in the case. No follow-up. The Doctors' fault.

But no, you can't let off the dealers and pushers. The husband had a habit, so what about the pusher? He was to blame? Veronica and Denise were quick to approve each new suggested criminal, and most of the others went along with them easily. Mrs. Kelsick pauses, looks at me.

One girl wasn't talking, she says. The girl was Rosanna. She had delivered, as they say, five months ago, would shortly be leaving Ida Wells to return to regular school. Mrs. Kelsick felt her being separate from the others, shaking her head at them as though their opinions were naive or plain wrong. The others had come back to the father with the habit again. Michelle pointing out that, according to the story, he wasn't even the real father, so maybe the one to blame was the real father and nobody knows who he is. The girls giggled, Mrs. Kelsick said. Another girl thought it wasn't the real father's fault, he didn't know anything about it, it was the man's fault because probably he was running short, the mother had other kids and then here was this new one and you know they're all short and he can't feed them so—

Mrs. Kelsick interrupted herself.

"Rosanna shut them up," Mrs. Kelsick said abruptly, nodding, looking stern. "Rosanna said, 'You know what? How come you so sure it wasn't the mother? How you know she wasn't the one that lit up those babies?'"

Mrs. Kelsick sits nodding, seemingly with her whole body. "I said, 'You're right, Rosanna. We never said one word about the mother, did we? How come we missed that?'"

Rosanna didn't want to talk further just then, said Mrs. Kelsick, so they, she and the social worker, Anna, who teaches with her, turned away from her and repeated the question to the others. How come they didn't ever think about the mother? Blank expressions. Did they think the mother could do such a thing?

"Rosanna came in again," Mrs. Kelsick said, pushing her lips out, reconstructing. "Suppose that baby's a crier. One of them. The husband, the man, he doesn't like it, but what about her? She wants to sleep. Supposed to do something. Not his worry. He's telling her, Shut that baby up. Maybe he isn't even telling her, he's out, maybe she's just telling herself . . . she doesn't know how to shut that baby up and it's getting her, Just starting to get her."

Then, said Mrs. Kelsick, Rosanna spoke the words—the perfect words for them to hear, and they hugged her for them.

" 'That baby got some rights,' Rosanna said. And I said, 'Rosanna, that's so right and good.' "

Mrs. Kelsick comes back to me.

"That was today."

It was toward the end of the sixties that the city board of education dropped its push-out policy for unmarried pregnant girls and began encouraging these students to stay in school, creating new schools offering programs in infant care, nutrition for mother and child, and homemaking in addition to the usual academic fare. Moving about among the crudely partitioned classrooms, offices, cafeteria, and library, I heard a lot that roused, simultaneously, pity, fury, frustration. Without exception, teachers, principal, and custodians address classes or groups of girls as "ladies." ("Ladies, today we're working on the run-on sentence": English teacher. Called to order, the friendly, curious eyes of a thirteen-year-old large with child turn away from the visitor. "Ladies, please, your attention, ladies . . .") Last month the class worked on Shakespeare, *Romeo and Juliet*, not for the flight into an ideal world of love but for deadly school purposes ("identify asides, soliloquies, foreshadowing").

But these are places of love, not in the end depressing. Much that is taught is the opposite of asides and foreshadowing— substantive, necessary knowledge . . . the nonpliancy of the past, the need to tie and root yourself ever more clearly to what has happened, to deeds done, the nonmalleable yesterday. No new bride to give away. Belief in "the strong for the weak" is alive in the air, in the eyes of teachers and students alike.

"I see them all afterward," says Bernie Sabel, economics teacher, talking to me in the cafeteria. "They'll be downtown with the baby and you see them coming out of the super and you stand there and b.s. with them a little about what's coming down, their problems, how's it going . . . They want to talk. They *like* school. They all want to come back to Baby Day and bring their kids. They're gone and they're back in the old school but they remember we're friends and they feel friendly. I can tell."

The seesaw was a long time stopping. On the one hand, Everything Costs, the new life, change, promise, the end of prudery . . . On the other: much good comes from change. You walk into the midst of these various ongoing sexual and sex-role and marital and abortional revolutions and recover feeling for first things, for the nature of the behavior that created the human world in the beginning. You get a reminder that the creation of the human world preceded by millennia the birth of the values of psychological self-expression and spiritual liberty. But you can also stumble not upon Jesus but upon swarms of people at each other's throats for money. Porn is money. Defacing human physicality is money. Faking relationships is money. ("Men!" cries the massage parlor ad in the Miami paper. "Linda's BACK!") Improved fucking is money.

The handy directory in the appendix of Joanna and Lew Koch's *The Marriage Savers* (1976)—it's entitled "How to Find a Marriage Counselor"—provides some thirty tightly printed pages of information on people and organizations under these headings:

Behavior Modification
Bioenergetics
Family Therapists
Feminist Therapists
Gestalt Therapists
Humanistic
Marriage Encounter/Marriage Enrichment Programs
Pastoral Counselors

Psychiatrists
Psychoanalytic Referrals
Psychodrama
Psychologists
Psychotherapists
Sex Therapists/Sex Clinics
Social Service Organizations
Social Workers
Transactional Analysis

In several major cities the stink of hard-sell competition for the troubled soul's buck rises from the newspaper ads that ask: "IS YOUR MARRIAGE BETTER THAN NO MARRIAGE? If you've begun asking yourself this question, you'll probably want to talk to us . . ." (Some entrepreneurs, like the owner-operator of a Boston service called the Divorce & Marriage Counselling Center, Inc., are quite upfront about profits. "We're business people," James Heimen of D & M tells a reporter. "We wanted to short-circuit the delayed-referral process so we went to direct advertising.") And the likelihood is that thousands will shortly be in the game. Edna Barrabee, member of the American Association of Marriage Counselors: "In this field anyone can do anything. Anyone, from any walk of life. That's how open this counseling practice is today . . . This new commercial counseling center is openly a superservice agency . . . Boy, are they smart. The next thing you know they'll be opening like those income tax places, one on every corner."

I visited a "non-profit" service in Philadelphia called Wives Self-Help, whose advertising borrows snippets from old extra-strength Excedrin campaigns:

. . . a unique and innovative service created in January, 1974 in answer to an urgent need for help to marriages on a positive, preventive basis. Two out of five marriages end in divorce. Those who are struggling to maintain viable marriages in the face of these overwhelming odds need help. Families experiencing stress and strain often do not know where to turn for counseling or are afraid to go. Furthermore, the high cost of mental health coupled with the overcrowding of many of our clinics is often a deterrent to those seeking help for marital difficulties. The immediate relief and direction provided by WIVES SELF-HELP can alleviate a stressful situation before disastrous complications result.

Throughout my interview with the president of the organization and a senior marriage counselor, a third official, the secretary-treasurer, is on the phone with a client in the same office: "Look, we're not gonna hold you up. We know. Thirty dollars a week, that's a lot of money." And the interviewees' style of address to my questions is uniformly business-brisk. I ask about first visits, clients' feelings at the time of the initial class or appointment. "Nothing," says Helene Halpern, the counselor. Helene looks to be in her late twenties, an attractive, mod-jeaned, frizzy-curled blond, a student at Bryn Mawr in psychiatric counseling. "When they come in, it's just"—she crosses her arms, index fingers on each hand pointing angrily in opposite directions—" 'It's his fault. Her fault.' 'So wait a minute,' I say, 'if he's such a bastard, why do you put up with it?' "

"They try to hang you up on their presenting problems," Maxine Schnall, the president, explains. Maxine is mid-fortyish, divorced, dresses in knit pantsuits, and is studying law at Temple. She mentions a name to Helene, who nods and grins. "The wife came in and she said her husband had a vasectomy and never told her. 'How'd you find out?' I said. 'Was he grasping himself down there in terrible pain?' " Maxine chuckles. "Well, no, actually she overheard it on the phone. Later *he* told me why—he just wanted to test himself, it was a courage test. Could he do it? But the thing is she'd come in with this as the presenting problem and later it turned out *she'd* had her tubes tied herself three years before and never told *him.*"

On her preferred methodology Helene is crisp and downright.

"What I do," she tells me, "is find out how her crap fits his crap. Okay, this guy is running but his wife is the suspicious type. 'I don't know why I do it,' he says. 'I just do.' Well, I know why. He was in an orphanage as a kid and anyway it's available—he's very good-looking—so why not? But she says, the wife, 'Well, when I was a kid I wanted to be a detective, I wanted to get to the bottom. I wanted to get to the bottom of everything!' So right away, this was how they completed each other's neuroses. But he could say, 'Hah-hah, see, it's your fault, you're suspicious so I only do it because you make me.' So I anticipated that and I warned them right off it. We're not fixing blame on one person. If you can just get them to take a measure of responsibility for the situation and move on, just see that . . ."

On overall objectives, whether to "save" marriages or junk them, Maxine is clearly a little left of center, headed toward the creative split school. ("Sustaining the marriage—oftentimes that's not what you want to do. It's not best. Divorce could be the most creative thing.") On the sources of the problems she deals with, she talks clichés: "This is the crossfire generation—thirty to thirty-six, caught between what Mother told me and *Cosmo* says—wanting more sexual freedom, satisfaction, something . . . And the media, it talks divorce and sex . . . opportunities." About the domestic future she speaks as though the issues are more or less closed: "Everybody I know is insisting their daughter have a career aspiration, not marriage and babies." And continually in the background, as I said, the secretary-treasurer was on the phone, cash-nexusing: "Ten is fine. Ten a session. It's *okay*."

A phony negative. Stock response. What that I know escapes the domination, the hegemony, the superstructure, the System, the Profit Angle? Nothing "wrong" at Wives Self-Help except the unfurnished quality, the way in which the counselors' heads *have* to view the world. The *bareness*. The client arrives naked—no family, no past. He's a spot of time, a little quick cross of relationship existing here and now. "I want to start over." When the client calls, the counselor works with what she hears, sees, picks up. Spot-check. Somebody's starting over and the point is that he or she, the client, has a decision ahead, and the counselor's energy has to gather toward that. It's the present, the state of mind here and now, that's all-consequential. This is where we are, and the weight of what has been and what the client was before this decision, this movement to "therapy," isn't in the equation. It's not even supposed to be felt, it's a distraction. Causes and backgrounds summarized in thumbnail phrases—"the orphanage" . . . constant foreshortening of the past, telescoping of it to formula, making it manageable, keeping the eyes focused on the Decision ahead, the Options.

Max Horkheimer: ". . . a process of reduction to sub-personal status occurring within the family."

Stopping off in Montgomery, Alabama, to visit my daughter Jo, a filmmaker attached to a local TV station, I discover she's in the hospital. Surprise is the only teacher. A minor operation, her friend Jeff tells me on the phone, they hadn't wanted to scare us. There was a knot in her thigh, doctor wanted to be sure, penicillin not working. It turned out to be a minor infection, possibly a spider bite, no big deal . . . We eat supper in the hospital restaurant and Jo, looking fine, tells some funny Deep South stories that break me up—people met while she and Jeff were shooting. They both talk excitedly about their current project. (They kid *my* project—"Pop's values trip.") I press for an errand when it's time to go—nothing for a concerned daddy to do?—but they can't come up with much. Jeffie's been coping, it seems. He's solved the murmur in their best camera, fed pills to Pie, Joey's cat, also ill, "done a shtick" to their house, scrubbing it top to bottom in preparation for The Return, and this morning went off and bought a new mattress and box spring for the bed they liberated "somewhere in South Carolina."

In the hall by the elevator, saying goodbye, we're another family trio. Noticing Jo leaning a little on Jeff's arm, I catch myself just in time. (*Don't* say, Take good care of her.) Later on the plane I think: They do seem to like their lives. Later still: Jeff's a good um.

The promise of growing space for variousness: this is what lies at the heart of the new nurture. To be a citizen, a worker, and an artist in a single lifetime, to hunt in the morning and be a music critic at night, to express one's sexual self, one's parental self, one's familial self, to move ceaselessly toward fuller individuation, development, enrichment . . .

Which institution is pivotal in the service of this dream? As pivotal as any, probably, is the day-care center. In her *Working Mothers* (1976), Jean Curtis separates "groovy" centers, where parents themselves play a key role from day to day, from "custodial" centers, staffed by outsiders only, stiffer and chillier in atmosphere. I've also read descriptions of day-care centers to come, like those envisaged by Elizabeth Janeway:

> . . . facilities at industrial plants, commercial centers, educational establishments—everywhere that parents go to work; *model* care facilities cosponsored by unions and

imaginative educators, with programs offered by libraries, museums, musical conservatories, theater and dance groups, the inheritors of ethnic and cultural traditions. . . . They should engage, use and entertain a coming-and-going population, directed by a professional core, of children of all ages, adults of both sexes and all the generations that could be called on, interacting, teaching each other, connecting.

Not unattractive visions. Furthermore their specificity reminded me that it's absurd to deal with day-care issues in a purified, non-economic context, as though day care had one and the same meaning in every sector of the society.

Still . . . My attempts to see these places, groovy or custodial, from the "right" perspectives, evaluative, future-oriented, "social," felt off from the very start: remote, once more, from the core of feeling. And one day at a Presbyterian church basement operation run for married university students in Laramie, Wyoming, I caught some light.

I arrived just at the hour when the majority of the children were being dropped off, 7:00 A.M. or so, and noticing (coincidence, naturally) that in a succession of cars, about a half-dozen, the little boy or girl rode alone in the back seat. The car would stop, the driver would reach back and open the door and wait while the child descended and moved up the church walk, slowly or otherwise, no baggage; before he was inside, the car door was shut and the driver too moved on, no waves, no looking back.

What else? A minor episode of shoving, featuring a boy I'll call Brook sitting in a tree and a three-year-old I'll call Amy. Amy advanced to where Brook sat in the crook of the tree, mid-morning break, and told him he shouldn't do what he was doing. Brook climbed down from his perch, walked purposefully toward Amy, pushed her onto the ground with a wordless two-handed shove, and returned to his tree. Rising, Amy did not weep, did not comment, did not look for justice, expected no line to be thrown. She rose and stared at Brook, kept her distance.

Mid-morning break.

Jo Davis, the director, is a short, energetic woman in her forties, wearing a short red skirt and having the build and manner of a talented golfer. I had the standard tour. Ms. Davis identified one or another child as he hove up as "real feisty," "a learning disability," "a newcomer here for four days and already working into the group." My notes say that on my private comparative scale the Laramie center rated C-. "Basement spacious but dark, stale air. Semicircle of small chairs set in rows before huge TV. Ominous. Two-hour afternoon naptime! Too much talk from JD about money, keeping charges down to $3.50 a day, problems of being cook, staff director, accountant, general negotiator all at the same time. Depressing sights . . . dark unfurnished windowless 'isolation area' for sick or hurt kids incarcerated until parents pick up . . . weeping three-year-old girl, clutching father, begging him not to leave (JD: 'He has custody'). Numbers: one aide to about every ten kids, staff of six, six and a half. Half of all children who've attended this center over its four years are from divorced parents . . . Children who spend longest days at center, from 7 to 5 P.M., are the young ones, the three-year-olds . . ."

As I was leaving this place, walking past a group of kids playing in clayey mud in a culvert, I realized 1 hadn't spoken to any of them, the children. And that I had probably never spoken to any children on any similar visit to any other center in the past.

It meant—?

"They"—that large abstraction I've made for day-care kids—

"they" don't feel kidlike to me. They're lean, stripped down, unencumbered. They have their wits about them. Public people, living far beyond the pure moment of intimacy of parent and child, into SATs, into admissions interviews. They live by their wits, have objectives. No waywardness need apply. "They need a lot of one-on-one"—how many times I heard that from day-care people. But no matter how true it was, it didn't feel true. They didn't need a fooling-around grown-up. You heard about the "thinkers," as some called them, the isolated children who sit alone, not watching the others who gather in groups or circles, watching their toes. The forlorn—there were always the forlorn . . . like the girl who arrived weeping.

But what I felt was something within them that lay beyond teasing, a gathered quality. These were copers, objectives, dealers with the world on the world's terms. Their capital lay in the world and they'd learned how to manage, invest, buy, sell. Good timing. As for helplessness, luxurious helplessness, secret intimacies, dream of sleeping within, never moving, breathing her breath, his scrapy cheek—forget it. Plucked out, provided with Museum of Science challenges. A chenille rug and a doll and a coat peg . . . Making do. Making out. Making it. Grouped by ability . . . professional staff . . . seat work with numbers . . . rates $20/18 . . . comings and goings.

They were new to me, and at length I defined the newness, felt how firmly it edged me back. I'm willing—says my tone of address to a child (or so I imagine it)—I'm willing to let you lean on me a while. Go ahead, lean. But there were no leaners in the crowd. Here was the newness: the straight-up, no-leaning, I-cope kid.

Revelation, it turned out, was a conference in a university campus building in Madison, Wisconsin. Mid-morning, sunny skies. Outside a file of summer-session kids, tanned and glowing in T's and cutoffs, sloped away down tree-shaded walks to a beach picnic and Frisbee by the lake. Inside the campus building a hearing was in progress, a heartland consultation of the kind that's always taking place somewhere in somebody's city, on somebody's issues.

Today the citizens' panel in residence in Wisconsin was called the Presidential Advisory Council on Women's Educational Programs—I belonged to it myself a while ago, for a year—and it was inquiring into "educational needs of rural girls and women."

Like many another meeting of the sort, this was one was intended to become a pressure point, a means of "raising consciousness." Certain that exploitation and oppression were worse in rural areas than elsewhere, council members had come to the boonies to drive for faster, surer progress toward "women's equity." They'd mau-maued vulnerable male witnesses. (One poor brother had observed that he knew a little about women's problems because "I have four of them in my house." "You have four of 'them,' " snapped a scornful young militant. "Okay . . . I date one of *you*. I don't like the way you talk.")

What's more, the councillors had been skeptical of presentations made by the farm women themselves, even by those like Jo Anne Vogel of Cato, Wisconsin, who had been active in seeking changes in IRS rules, inheritance law, and other matters of special rural concern. It was the directness of the pressure that produced the talk that brought the revelation. During the first hour there were out-and-out scraps between the militants and the farm women. Asked how she felt about "assertiveness training" and "women's lib," Betsy Thronson of Blue Mounds, Wisconsin, struck out wildly.

"Farm wives were liberated long ago," she said. "A farm wife is so liberated she can't hardly stand it. The minute you put them on a tractor, they're liberated."

"I resent the term 'feminist,'" Betsy went on strongly. "It sounds like you're some real radical. We want just to speak out and express our opinion . . . That doesn't mean you're a weirdo."

Cries of protest.

"I take exception—"

"I'm a militant activist feminist and—"

"If you describe liberation as the opportunity to do real hard work that men have always done, then all right, rural women are 'so liberated they can't hardly stand it.' But that's not what liberation is. Rural women are very *un*liberated. Put these words aside."

Three farm wives sitting together like stone, rock-stern expressions of solidarity on their faces. Abrasion. The gap. Impactment.

But soon enough things changed. Several local guests experienced in counseling farm wives were in the room and they spoke up firmly, building a bridge back to communication, reaching beyond resentment and defensiveness, retuning the atmosphere, soothingly strengthening the wives' belief that, if they did utter their true minds, they might be understood. ("You see," said a 4-H person from Grand Forks, North Dakota, "you see rural women think that what urban women are saying is that it's not right to be 'just a houseperson.' When that really is a very creditable thing to be doing . . .")

And a rural historian and extension professor named Robert Card introduced a historical theme—the greatness of the Wisconsin pioneer women—that did wonders in easing the wives toward their words. Card had barely launched upon talk of the Old Generation—"theirs was the true greatness"—than the farm women were contributing details of their own. Pleased, stimulated, he spread out a bit concerning his research into the early years of struggle—the time when survival was "related to physical strength and human idealism—the hope of having

something better later on, better opportunities for the children
. . ." In those days you hadn't a chance if you couldn't clear one
to five acres a year, so everything depended, Card explained,
on the strength of the men and the women. "And the women
took the beating," he said, pushing out his bottom lip as though
he'd seen the suffering himself. He'd gone through the old ceme-
teries, he told the group, in Dodge County and thereabouts,
looking at the headstones, the ones you could read, and how
many women were dead before fifty—overburdened, over-
worked, bearing six, twelve, seventeen children because a big
family was an asset. A man would wear out two or three women,
they would literally work themselves to death. "And somehow,
out of all this," he went on, with the farm wives nodding,
everyone listening hard, out of "this whole crucible of struggle
we've come all this whole way to here. And now you're talking
about better ways of living . . . rights and tenure . . . it could not
have happened if it hadn't been for this vast other thing . . . what
happened in the past." So, he told the group, the right action is
to honor these sacrifices, make them known. Because they were
the source of the good to come.

It seemed to set off a new current in the room, producing talk
remote from the gut issues of the movement, a spontaneous celebration, a fêting of farm women as persons continuous with a
noble past, winning their way forward out of deprivation.

Comforted, the witnesses found fresh speech. They found,
that is, a way of declaring that if living according to the new
vision required a refusal to honor sacrifices made under the
old, then they would hold back. If being in tune with, endor-
sive of, or hopeful about the new nurture, the new freedom
and variousness, required an absolute repudiation of the past,
if a downward re-evaluation of the worth of the strongest
cooperative and loving relationship they had known was
required, then they would hold back.

"Our husbands are exceptional men," said Jo Anne, going on to explain to the group how her family's supportiveness made it possible for her to do her chores as a working farm woman, in the barn at 5 A.M., at 11 A.M., in the evening again, and also to be a political activist on behalf of farm women's interests. "My husband," said Nancy Smidle, "never feels above me. If we're going to buy something . . . or go to the church picnic, we decide together."

Each of the wives seemed to be saying, My past holds me, lifts me—my luck in my husband's goodness and generosity, in his noticing my need, in his willingness to share house-personship, to *help* . . . I go to a university and a conference or a hearing and I meet and talk to people—strangers—and learn to care about them. Once when we watched the weather on TV and there was frost in New York, I'd think, Oh good, now we'll get a price. But then at a meeting I got to know a new friend, apple growers in New York, and we became like sisters, and there was a closeness, a knitting together of all the commodities, and now I don't want to profit from her bad luck or anybody's."

But they "sacrifice for me," Jo Anne Vogel explains. "My sons, my husband. A woman can't do it by herself. Our whole family discusses my experiences when I come home if I go away—like to here, this hearing. My daughter will be able to do better things. Our sons will have the past, the background, to let their wives do this and more. Our husbands are exceptional men."

2.5 percent of the population live on farms: can a principle of universal application, good in cities and suburbs, good for the alienated and the divorced, the adman and the ghetto kid, be derived from the domestic faith of a few rural women? Yes: the principle for which the farm people spoke, memory as virtue, is nowhere inapplicable.

The women's movement is the freshest, most energizing

phenomenon of our time: if somebody finds an answer to interior needs in words that only hesitantly salute liberation, hasn't the cause been denigrated? No, because the hesitation in this instance belonged to the surface, not to the core. In the end the farm wives were speaking simultaneously for liberation and for the other sources of their own best selves—complex affirmation.

Much that was said could have come from Ross or Alice or Ellen or a dozen others whose stories lie well off this page, also from many who play it hip. Blithe divorcers, TV stars who tease paternal obligation by treating their own as "a bit," Bel Air cosmopolitans who pretend that squares alone are distraught at the sight of breakdown in their children's lives, liberationists who affect to despise the sacrifices of the unliberated—as often as not these types are only hung up on another version of shock-the-bourgeois. Inwardly they know that the proper human work goes beyond framing jokes or forging special identities, that it involves learning the imperatives of care—growing out of illusions of invulnerability and into full understanding that others elsewhere, foreign, unknown, unborn, dead, those who came before and pushed the process forward, people under the hill whose minds and eyes made my mind and eyes, and made more extended vision possible, all make claims and must be remembered.

What was unique in the hearing room was a feeling, a conviction about how people learn. Half words, half tone, never fully articulated . . . a belief in the family as the essential classroom.

It's crazy. One minute I talk about the care and kindness of my own children for me. The next I'm talking about my own children's care and kindness for their mates once they're old enough to have them. The next I'm talking about my sisterly feeling for somebody who was a total stranger to me a week ago—but it's really not a puzzle. I know how you get from one feeling to the next. I understand the flow.

It goes from feeling for the nearest to feeling for the farthest. When my child was weak and I was strong, at the sign of his hurt I was with him at once, longing to ease his hurt because it was painful to me as to him. That's my past, my moral capital. I've hardly ever seen myself as "good" except in my responsiveness, whenever I've been responsive, to my children's needs. It's parent and child together. Parent and parent and child and child together—that's the beginning. The force of steadiness of concern for another as deserving of emulation comes across to the young. Grownups observe and foster the progress of the young in this . . . imitating the good.

I realized that I too knew the words and could say them aloud unembarrassed. Tell me about the broader family to come, the glory of more encompassing commitments ahead, and I'll listen and may one day believe.

But I'd expect also to go on believing that true morality is remembering—Malraux said this once—making visible the tradition that gives you your form. That couldn't change. Because the good of the imagined future can only have grown from the good of the shared past, the experience accumulated in the narrower family, experience of kindness, control of selfishness, authority denying itself dominion, conjoining power with remorse . . . The narrow dream nourishes the wider dream. It's as simple as this: whatever is good in the new nurture will be made of the same principles as the good of the past; therefore don't patronize the past, don't mock. Let it breathe.

On toward dusk Fridays and Saturdays at the Pier Park Recreational Center, ninth and Ocean Drive in Miami Beach, a fairsized crowd begins gathering, moving up the walkways toward benches set in rows at the edge of the beach in front of a platform and hutch. The people are locals, old folks mostly, guests at the Sorrento, the Ocean Garden, the Balfour, a dozen tiny hotels along the Drive and Washington Avenue, unposh places with wide porches and interiors that Hopper might have lighted, lobbies where card games, played at big round tables with glary tops, last to midnight and beyond. Here and there a familiar Miami style stands out—white-on-white patterned shorts, white and gold-tasseled moccasins, the *New York Times* folded under an arm. But plainness is the norm. More than a few of the women are in heavy black knit cardigans and peasant kerchiefs, and the men's clothes are nondescript, shiny serge trousers, straw hats, faded canvas shoes. The accents and sometimes the spoken languages belong to the Old World.

The magnet for the crowd is "the singing," a concert of folk tunes, lullabies, and love songs performed in Yiddish and other tongues by self-selected soloists. At about eight the walkway lights come on and a beach cop named Harry Rivetz, a sober, good-looking man in his mid-twenties, steps forward from the shadows with a clipboard, rousing anticipatory jostle and laughter along the benches. He tests the mike, welcomes the group, and asks whether there's anybody here who wants to sing and hasn't signed up. People are still arriving; traffic sounds mix with the washing of surf and the shouts of kids fooling around somewhere in the distance on the darkened beach. The first singer is announced and he leads the group through "The Star-Spangled Banner"; then, one by one as Harry Rivetz calls off his list, the other performers rise and do their numbers. Occasionally a singer opens with greetings to the crowd or offers a comment on the tune he's selected; occasionally quips are traded with the front rows. If your German is as weak as mine and you have no Yiddish, you can get help for the whole evening by asking one question of your neighbors early on. A mike failure or a drunk or junkie hovering on the fringes, mumbling to himself, can be a problem, but real interruptions are rare. When Officer Rivetz's flashlight picks out the last name on the list, he lets this be known and at the end there's protracted applause. The light goes off in the hutch behind the platform and the mike is unplugged and the cord rolled up, and the crowd makes its way back to the street, dispersing onto the hotel porches or into the lobbies, resuming the endless game.

Insiders attend "the singing" to refresh their memories and brighten old attachments. An inventory in words and music of vanished ways of cherishing and being cherished. An old lady chants in memory of a temple destroyed 2000 years ago. Mr. Edelman, strong-faced, tanned, with a forceful tenor, sings "*A Chazzandl Oif Shabbes*," a folk tune about the different ways in which a gifted cantor is prized by a tailor, blacksmith, and drover. (The refrain has eight oys—*Oy, how he did sing!*—and, guided by Edelman's authoritative spacing, the crowd joins in with a will.) Max Greenberg, affable, a star in worn blue canvas shoes and battered boater, invites the audience to relish the modesty of its shared longings and desires, singing "Just a Little Bit of Luck" in several languages, leading the assemblage with graceful hands:

> *It's only a children's game*
> *Who wants so much?*
> *(Unison) Not so much . . . Not so much*
> *Just a little bit of living*
> *Just a little, bit of luck*

The dominant themes of "the singing" are, predictably, familial and generational. There's a song about a mother blessing her daughter's new mother-in-law, begging the latter—*Dear relative, sweet relative*—not to wake the child too early, not to mourn if she sees that her son loves the girl . . . ("If she displeases you, please just forget it as I've always done.") Another mother in another tune pleads and teases for a letter from a loved one—*shribe geshvind. leebes kind,* write quickly, give consolation to your mother. There are musical toasts to the solidarity of the generations: "Toast the young and toast the old,/ Toast ourselves both young and old":

> *Far di kinder, far di z'keynim'*
> *Ay-ay, ay-ay, ay!*

Family roll calls ring out in holiday celebration songs:

> *Where is Berl? Where is Dvosye?*
> *Get Aunt Susie and Uncle Josie*
> *Let's everybody have some fun!*

There's a fine number about a poor relation arriving at a wedding with nothing but a lively heart and a threepenny gift who's instantly swept up into the dancing:

> *Though she be poor, an aunt's still an aunt!*

Mrs. Waxman sings "Oh, Papa!," a child's ecstasy at her father's playful teasing, and I notice, across the aisle from where I'm sitting, a tiny huddled woman in a black shawl beating perfect time, open hands slapping her knees, eyes bright, lips apart.

Toward the end a performer introduced by Officer Rivetz simply as "Helen" announces that her song is a son's farewell. *"Zayt gezunterheyt, mayne libe eltern."* goodbye, my dear parents, goodbye, she recites, then pauses. The surf behind her seems louder. Helen is dressed in a pink woolen sweater and black kerchief. All at once a single minor note comes from lips, held, shaped as a long lament in itself. Helen's voice is delicate at some moments, eerily powerful at others. Her audience is motionless, passionately attentive, sustaining her, lifting her like the sea a strong swimmer. Helen sings as though she hadn't a mike in her hand, as though the volume came from the darkness behind her. No vibrato yet an affection beyond measure. When she finishes, the memory of the held note floats, and a voice near me murmurs into the stillness: *Ooooh, gut.* Loud applause.

"These are gentle people," says Harry Rivetz, talking to me later about his job as emcee, and it seems a fair judgment. The poorer singers are applauded as well as the best. The audience calls out helpfully when words are forgotten, joins good-naturedly in the refrains of the comic songs, allows itself to be caught up, transfixed, when, as with Helen's song, an old favorite is stunningly done. But kindness isn't the point. What matters is the inventory, the re-animation of the tones and idioms of the traditional languages of nurture, reminders of the range and variousness of the older modes of human caring—within, as we say, the "family context." The idea of "the singing" is that of sustained relation, the sound is that of people who don't know how to let go. The trick, I thought, is to learn to speak from this sound as though it were present when it's vanished, to learn how to carry it in mind when there's nothing like it for ears to hear. It is the tuning sound, the pitch worth holding: a clarity about whence the best in us came.

PART THREE

Beyond the Politics of "Heart"

I have been arguing that the interrelated factors pivotal in sustaining junk politics are: self-inflation, unrelenting presentmindedness, fantasies of the USA as faction-and-difference free, and the marketing of consumer/celebrity culture as utopia. All these forces have positive aspects. Present-mindedness opens up paths forward from repression and racism, sexism and classism. Cultural material teaching that America is faction-free promotes fellow feeling, moderates hatred. In separate ways fame-obsession and delight in purchasable goods counter secular-society despair; they energize democratic faith that in this country careers are open to talents and they buoy hope that happiness (available to all) can be bought in stores. For these and other reasons, addiction to junk politics is impossible to kick; twelve-step formulas, hyped withdrawal strategies, quick fixes—none is functional.

Preventive measures, though, do exist—behavior that stiffens resistance to junk political temptation, viz:

1. Study of the past for guidance regarding progressive political effectiveness and ineffectiveness.

2. *Faithfulness to the imperative that democratic leaders clarify and dramatize public needs (not simply advertise their good hearts).*

3. *Rejection of the sentimentality that mistakes sympathy for the oppressed with action that improves their situation and the prospects for human kind.*

About history as a counter to temptation little new can be said here. The periods in the last century and a half wherein thought and action on domestic problems and policy (as opposed to military accomplishment) achieved remarkable distinction and promise were precisely those uncluttered by miniaturizing delusions. They were times when problems of large, national scope were understood to demand large, national solutions. I have in mind, of course, a half decade of the New Deal and seven years or so of Reconstruction. Both the expansively imaginative realism visible in these intervals and the daily, down to earth struggles it waged against miniaturizing sleaze can function as bracing resources for junk politics resisters. (Two striking studies of those struggles are W.E.B. DuBois's classic Black Reconstruction *(1935) and David M. Kennedy's* Freedom From Fear *(2000).*

As for the other helpful behaviors that I mentioned besides the study of history: their amplification is the business of this final section of Junk Politics.

1. The Weight of Self-Scorn

As this book's preface observes, the politics of personal testimony has little behind it except bonhomie. It's over-gratified by its kindness—distracted by its own presumed moral notability, and underinformed about human lives outside its circle. It doesn't know enough, speaking bluntly, to arrive at authentic identification with the unlucky. As a result, its efforts to communicate the urgency of social needs display the warmth and decency of the speaker but not the nature—the true interiors—of problems.

"After the Sexual Revolution," the essay that ended Part Two of this work, explicitly contrasted a self-involved world with a world of traditional attachments and nurture. The mixed dissatisfaction and admiration in the piece were grounded in a sense of the moral and political costs of sealing off the present from the past. They weren't grounded—the piece has this in common with junk politics itself—they weren't grounded in intimacy with the texture of lives in which self-expression and nurture are luxuries beyond reach. In numbers beyond counting such lives exist, obviously, and the pursuit of justice for them—the point can't be made too often—is a core mission of genuine politics.

But belief in that mission can't survive without telling evocation of the stuff of the lives—speech that reaches beyond the speaker to the realities known by those for whom compassion is expressed. The pressure of objective fact, freshly perceived, has to be felt. If the subject is family hardship, then the dailiness of the hardship needs animation. How the terms of the lives as lived affect "family feeling." How joblessness and poverty and the absence of a future—even floor space per adult and child in a household—can pulverize confidence, weaken belief in experiential knowledge and murder self-respect.

Political aspirants may or may not know at firsthand the grain of defeat and frustration—but they are not dependent on firsthand knowledge. Their obligation is to seek out lives and life stories— matter that can develop their own capacity to build compelling awareness both of public needs and of the possibility of public solutions. There's no dearth of films, books, poems comparable in effect to that of the movie—Killer of Sheep, by Charles Burnett—that I write about in the next piece. The latter movie spoke clearly to my ignorance when I saw it—moved me momentarily at least beyond ritual "concern" to something closer to informed identification. Work at this level is a resource for resisters.

Moral Exhaustion in Charles Burnett's "Killer of Sheep"

Charles Burnett's *Killer of Sheep* (1977) opens with parents and children—a moment of would-be preceptorship. A face appears from darkness—a scared-looking, black male adolescent. A grownup is talking threateningly offscreen.

> You let anyone jump on your brother again, Boy, and you just stand there and watch, I'll beat you to death.

The last words come in a stammering jumbled rush; the stammerer has to start over:

> I don't care who started what, if he was winning or losing, you get a stick or-or-or-or a goddamn brick and you knock the kid down whoever is fighting and if the son of a bitch is too big for you, you come get me. This off the wall bullshit about Henry started it—

The speaker breaks off again, this time in a coughing fit, and as the shot widens we see a heavyset man—the father—doubled over with coughing . . . a pregnant woman, the boy's mother . . .

The boy's younger brother presses his face into his mother's apron and skirt.

The father resumes, in a stagey tone—a voice of paternal, reasonableness and persuasion.

> If anything was to happen to me or your mother, you ain't got nobody but your brother, and that goes for your brother and he knows it. You are not a child. Son, you'll be a goddamn man soon. Start learning what life is about.

Abruptly as he pauses the boy's mother flings forth an arm—strikes her son across the face.

Thus Burnett begins. Set in the environs of the Watts section of Los Angeles, it's a movie about teaching right conduct to the young—or, rather, about trying and failing at that effort, trying again, ultimately giving up. The theme is the loss of that which practically defines the human essence, namely the saving right to reprove.

The father in Burnett's opening scene means to call up a world wherein choices count and elders give helpful guidance. Stand by each other. Respect experience. Life is hard. But there's static in the message. Mature reasonableness à la Judge Hardy ("You are not a child, son") clashes in the scene with bravado ("you come get me"), overdone profanity, and threats. The man chokes, seemingly, on the claim that he knows something worth knowing; his stammer and cough and fulminating—like the blow that the mother strikes—suggest bodily revulsion at the claim.

The movie digs deeper as it goes, probing comparable moments of frustration—comparable failures to speak up effectively for felt understandings of right and wrong. The filmmaker lives into his elders' doubt that lessons can be taught or paths chosen. His characters strike out blindly at each other; they regularly engage in defensive, mocking commentary on the delusion that, in the bottom-caste world, better and worse, right and wrong, exist. (The mockery is carried in variations on a single dominant refrain: "Shit on you, nigger. Nothing you do matters a good goddamn.")

The film's focus is the work and family life, in a black neighborhood, of the youngster who's chastised in the opening scene: Stan, now grown up—a husband and father in his thirties. Like every black adult he's ever known, Stan inhabits a world where the only jobs are befouling and the only living space is jammed, where nothing works—cars, appliances, whatever—for longer than a few days at a time, and where investments of aspiration seem programmed to prove senseless.

Stan's job is in a meat-processing plan (he slaughters and guts sheep); the pipes leak in his tiny cube of a house. When opportunity knocks, it's an invitation to disaster—a chance to earn money by serving as lookout for acquaintances bent on murder. When he attempts to speak of general life–forebodings to a friend, the friend asks matter of factly why he doesn't kill himself.

In "problem plays" mounded-up detail in this vein seems over-indicative; it leaves the impression that ideology, not observed life circumstance, is driving the dehumanization. In *Killer of Sheep* the impression left is that fantasts alone could avoid the truth that, hereabouts, bad news is the only news.

Pursuing his probe of lesson-giving and nurture, Burnett shows us that in these quarters indulgence of a child's truancy or other misconduct ("parental irresponsibility") functions as self-charity for grownups. It's their only affordable gesture of affection. Aberrant sexual behavior ("child molestation") arises from a cluster of closely related factors none of which is easily criminated. The factors include tight living space that incites sexual precocity in the young, the reasoned doubt that the young have a future, which undermines rationales for adult self-denial. People time and again imagine upholding the good as they conceive the good, and time and again, as in the opening scene, are balked.

Stan's daughter, a first-grader regularly exposed (in her family's tiny house) to her parents' sexplay, steps between her father's knees, caressing him; the child's mother, Stan's wife, watches her husband and daughter slip into a barely perceptible, quasi-sexual rocking movement; the parents' eyes meet, and inside the mother—in the involuntary movement of her jaw muscles—we feel an impulse of protest. But complicity shadows the moment, checks the response. What's the child doing but mimicking her elders? The grownup who wants to reprimand child or father would have to possess moral dignity and moral distance. Who can claim either?

Nobody speaks.

Stan's young teenaged son cruelly teases his sister, leers knowingly at his mother, calling her "my dear"—ducks and runs insolently from Stan's blows. Discipline is what's wanted, but reality tells the elders that discipline is unavailing; the misconduct needing correction lies vastly beyond anyone's reckoning. And as it goes in this house so it goes in the next. Grownups trying to act in accord with an obscurely intimated obligation to state rules or bear true witness lose momentum in mid-course—shed the obligation as though exhausted. A black adult bystander sees young black thieves stealing a TV from his neighbor and dares, briefly, to stare warningly at them. They stop in their tracks: "What you looking at, punk? I'll kick your heart out." The bystander turns away.

Once in the movie, once only, a voice of confident probity is heard—someone speaking as though it were conceivable for a black human being to point the better way efficaciously to another. It's a child's voice, naturally, one first grader scolding another: "How come you not in school any more? You gawn fall behind." The sound, which seems to come from a remote planet, defines the freakish direction of the ripening process in the castelike world: youngsters grow not into the authority of preceptorship but out of it—into the realization, as they "mature," that only frauds imagine they can teach.

Stan's wife tries to interfere when the would-be murderers come to enlist her husband as an accomplice, but they tell her her man is lucky to be offered a job. ("Nigger worked all his life and ain't got a decent pair of pants.") In the movie's most unbearable scene, Stan watches as a cripple lying helpless is kicked without reason—and he manages to cry out against what's happening. "I don't give a good goddamn about him," says a voice in response; others near at hand tell Stan to forget it, and their shared inertia fixes the horror.

Shit on you, nigger.

Charles Burnett, a son of Watts who's been a MacArthur Fellow, doesn't deal in gang warfare, drive-by shootings or black-white buddy sentiment. He seeks simply to do justice to the ordinary events that suck the most marginalized of his people into will-lessness and contempt for the fairy tale of "personal identity." In *Killer of Sheep* he quickens his themes through workplace images of faceless meat processors repeating the physical actions of herding, killing and gutting undifferentiated, unchoosing animal life.

Here, says his movie's manner, here is one basic level of black American life; consider the physical facts and the facts of feeling. Where there's work, it's miserably paid and ugly. Space allotments in the home and workplace cramp body and mind. Positive expectation withers in infancy. Minds fall into mockery of aspiration as though at the bidding of physical law. Obstacles at every hand prevent mates and children from loving and being loved in decent ways, prevent children from believing their parents can know what's what, prevent parents from believing they themselves know anything worth knowing. The only feasible acts of kindness the old perform for the young seem as likely to harm as to help them; men and women standing up for what is proper and good appear to themselves and others to be stupidly oblivious of their own impotence; one's only true self is the figure huddled under a sink in the cruddy damp (shit on you, nigger), swearing as a wrench slips again, wrecking the seal.

"Affliction," writes Simone Weil, "stamps the soul to its very depths with the scorn, the disgust and even the self-hatred and sense of guilt that crime logically should produce but actually does not." *Killer of Sheep* offers access to the terrible daily weight of such self-scorn. Burnett's art releases audiences from the abstraction that curses the standard language of compassion ("black despair," "absence of values," and the like); it offers direct access to experience in its wholeness and complication.

2. Sympathetic Horror v. Political Action

Time and again this book has stressed that junk politics measures itself by standards soaked in sentimentality—that it hungers for performances of concern *and demands frequent, coarsening public shows of sympathy. Among the responders to the demand: Bill Clinton, lower-lip licker; Joe Lieberman, solemn utterer of difficult truth ("I was wrong and I apologize"); twiceborn Dennis Kucinich ("I was lost, now am found"); George W. Bush, celebrant of secular saints who wash the feet of the heaven-bound. But what needs saying, here at the end, is that the politics that gives rise to these demands and the politicos who meet them are hardly independent, self-propelling agents; they reflect no less than shape feeling and opinion in the audiences to which they speak.*

The case is that the confusion in those audiences—ourselves— often closely tracks that of the aspirants for votes. And the source of the confusion is an exaggerated estimate of the value of sympathy itself as a stand-alone force both for the amelioration of immediate injustice and for the broad restructuring of beliefs and attitudes within individuals—restructuring that issues, over time, in significant human change. Putting the pertinent points bluntly: intense emotional response and effective political action aren't the same thing. The spread of tolerance does not, in and of itself, bring on genuine progress, political or moral. Experiences of shock and horror—sympathetic shock and horror—may awaken consciences and thereby open paths to social reform and to fresh conceptions of the good society and the good human being. But absent a seriously considered political thrust, they may as easily function as adjuncts to self-flattering complacency.

These general truths are embodied in dozens of first-rate studies of the country's civil rights struggles, whether focussed on non-violent Freedom Rides and marches, or on maneuvers on behalf of rights legislation in the Congress, or on the development and honing, for court action, of petitions and lawsuits. But the truths figure far less often in accounts of progress and setbacks involving sexual minorities—and they are, as the final essay of this inquiry into junk politics attempts to show, as powerfully relevant on that front as elsewhere.

The Sad Tale of Newton Arvin

Trust popular culture and you would believe—despite continuing outbreaks of murderous gay-baiting savagery—that enlightenment about sexual identity has been advancing. Movies about gay best friends flourish. Prizes and big box-office success go to a film in which a hero-lawyer, fired for being homosexual and contracting AIDS, sues his firm. The president's men in *The West Wing* want a strong, explicit stand against a "defense of marriage" bill just arrived from the Hill, not an evasive pocket veto. Ratings of sitcoms hint at the existence, in millions of fans of *Will and Grace, Frazier, et al.*, of broad affection for homosexuals. And, beyond show biz, elected officials on both the right and left seem discreetly responsive. One of the vice-president's children is widely reported to be out; Dick Cheney indicated during last year's campaign that he wasn't hostile to civil partnership legislation in defense of same-sex unions.

A recent biography—*The Scarlet Professor–Newton Arvin: A Literary Life Shattered by Scandal* (2001) by Barry Werth—tells the life story of a man who, together with his sex partners and colleagues, endured fearful persecution for homosexuality four decades ago; the book movingly evokes the victims' terror and self-disgust. It also suggests—indirectly—a question about current "advances."

As well as shaping changes in thought and feeling, aren't those advances also matter for excessive self-congratulation? The particulars of Newton Arvin's life and work, together with the remarkable subsequent transformation of the place he lived, are highly relevant to educated opinion now. Within the last quarter-century, moreover, intellectuals abroad and social historians here—most notably George Chauncey, author of *Gay New York* (1994)—have supplied a detailed background for interpreting that opinion and how it has changed. Barry Werth has drawn on materials such as these in an attempt, through a single life story, to define what "progress" toward acceptance of homosexuality has and hasn't meant. The attempt only partly succeeds, because here as elsewhere the grip of myths of progress is hard to break, and also, perhaps, because vicarious suffering is more marketable than careful historical analysis. But *The Scarlet Professor* has interest nevertheless: it freshens our memory of yesterday's superstition and casts valuable if veiled light on today's evasions.

Frederick Newton Arvin (1900–1963) was well known in the American literary and academic world a half-century ago. His critical study *Herman Melville* (1950) won the first National Book Award for nonfiction, and the penetrating books about Hawthorne and Whitman that preceded it were trailbreaking in their time and remain readable today. Edmund Wilson placed him with Van Wyck Brooks as one of the only two students of American literature "who can themselves be called first-rate writers." He was mentor to Truman Capote in the late Forties, taught American literature at Smith College for decades, and, until he backed away from Harvard's overtures, seemed certain to be chosen successor to F.O. Matthiessen, the outstanding scholar of American literature of his time, following Matthiessen's suicide.

On September 2, 1960, three Massachusetts state troopers

(two members of a state police antipornography unit and a plainclothes detective), accompanied by a town policeman and a U.S. postal inspector, hammered on the door of Arvin's Northampton, Massachusetts, apartment. Arvin admitted them, and allowed them to conduct a search that yielded "obscene pictures" and twenty daily diaries in which he recorded intimate details of his life. He gave them the names of those to whom he had shown the pictures, and was booked at the local district courthouse, charged with the felony of possessing obscene material and with being "a lewd and lascivious person in speech and behavior."

Arvin had come to the notice of the troopers through a postal investigation. According to Werth, "Either federal authorities had got his name from a mailing list seized from a magazine supply house in St. Louis, they said, or else a package addressed to him had 'broken open' in the Springfield post office, revealing obscene pictures." The postal investigation was the outgrowth of a crusade led in the mid-1950s by the U.S. postmaster general, Arthur Ellsworth Summerfield, a former car dealer. The postmaster general, self-appointed scourge of "pornographical filth in the family mailbox," had in several cases invoked the authority of the eighty-year-old Comstock Act, which authorized the postmaster "to ban any book, pamphlet, letter, or other material he found to be 'obscene, lewd, lascivious or filthy.'" But he had lately suffered some setbacks. The threat of a federal injunction thwarted his attempt to destroy a copy of *Lysistrata* impounded by a Los Angeles postal inspector, and a U.S. Court of Appeals decision reversed the ban he had personally set on *Lady Chatterley's Lover*.

In 1960, however, "six years after inheriting the puritanical zeal of a spent McCarthyism," he and Kathryn Granahan, chair of the House Subcommittee on Postal Operations, intensified their legislative campaign for stronger legislation against smut and won a victory—passage of the Granahan bill, which allowed the Post Office "to seize and detail the mail of anyone suspected of trafficking in obscenity." Eisenhower signed the bill, police censors were let loose, and in western Massachusetts a postal inspector who had seized copies of three magazines addressed to Arvin showing seminude men asked the state police to arrest him.

Pleading guilty, Arvin was given a one-year suspended sentence, fined $1,000 on the obscenity charge and $200 for being a "lewd and lascivious" person, and placed on probation for two years. The friends Arvin named when he was asked to whom he had shown "hard core" photographs—Edward Spofford and Joel Dorius—were untenured members of the Smith classics and English departments; they received suspended sentences and fines of $500 each. At the court proceedings a state trooper was allowed to read a signed confession, by a local car mechanic charged with "lewdness," that he had "committed homosexual acts" with both Spofford and Arvin "during the past two and a half years." The confession was fully reported in the press. The settlement Arvin reached with Smith College called for him to "retire" on one-half salary ($5,300 a year) until his scheduled retirement in 1968. Over faculty protest the college trustees fired Spofford and Dorius.

Almost immediately the courts began to reconsider the law. The Supreme Court in a related case (*Mapp* v. *Ohio*) ruled within a year, 5–4, that "the Constitution forbids the use of illegally seized material as evidence in state criminal trials," and shortly afterward it invalidated the last legal basis for the persecution, by "giving constitutional protection to photographs of seminude men in posing straps." The younger faculty members won reversals of their convictions on appeal. (Spofford taught for a time at Cornell and was a visiting lecturer at Stanford, retiring in 1988; Dorius taught at San Francisco State from the early Sixties until his retirement.) Deeply depressed, Arvin nevertheless managed to finish a book he had started on Longfellow; three years after the episode he died of pancreatic cancer, at age sixty-three.

The Scarlet Professor opens with a prologue describing the arrival of the police at Arvin's apartment, and reserves the story of what happened next (Arvin's betrayal of his friends, trials, recriminations, appeals, and settlements) for the final third of the book. The reader waits suspended while the biographer provides a dutiful account of the life of a talented English professor at a liberal arts college in New England.

Born in Valparaiso, Indiana, the fourth of six children, Arvin was the son of a "parched Midwestern housewife" and her stern, demanding businessman husband; he remembered himself as "certainly a girlish small boy, not a virile one, even in promise." He and his only friend, David Lilienthal (who became a labor lawyer, TVA head, and chairman of the Atomic Energy Commission), kept political scrapbooks, and "formed a political club and magazine of their own in a clubhouse they built from packing crates in the Lilienthals' barn." An English major at Harvard, Arvin read Van Wyck Brooks's *Letters and Leadership*, and was stirred by "Brooks's call to arms for a new American literature that defied puritan commercialism while rising triumphantly out of native soil." He conceived the ambition of being a "standard-bearer, conscience, and champion of American literature, a neophyte in Brooks's priesthood," and, as an undergraduate, began writing reviews for Brooks's magazine *The Freeman*. After graduation he took a job at a boy's school in Detroit but found that "the strain of working with boys just a few years younger than he while concealing his ambiguous sexual longings unnerved him." Quitting the place, he took another academic job, at Smith, the following year, aged twenty-two, and stayed on.

Werth's survey of the subsequent decades of teaching and writing describes the collapse of Arvin's dismally unhappy marriage to a Smith undergraduate (the marriage lasted six years), his aborted psychoanalysis (barely begun before broken off), and his extended periods of self-accusing gloom and illness. A few bright moments occur. In his late forties Arvin was swept up in a two-year love affair with Truman Capote—the "most productive period of Arvin's life." Earlier, we encounter Arvin in his twenties, president of the local La Follette Club in Coolidge's home town, happily exhorting the small membership to "lay the basis for a Progressive Party with a kick in it, and put the fear of God in the hearts of the politicians." Arvin and Granville Hicks provoke "a near riot" at a citywide meeting in a high school auditorium with a resolution urging the state governor to stay the executions of Sacco and Vanzetti.

Werth doesn't always resist the impulse to overwrite ("As the weather turned sultry, there emerged from within Arvin's concave breast the murderous heart of a full-blooded misanthrope"). And his touch with literary history seems insecure. Some "cultural circles" alluded to in this book are easier to connect with comedy skits than with real life. (Leo Lerman, of Condé Nast, for example, is described as the "center of a New York cultural circle that included William Faulkner, Evelyn Waugh, and Marlene Dietrich.") Other aspects of *The Scarlet Professor* deserve respect, not least because of Werth's avoidance of reflexive contempt for Twenties and Thirties leftism. About Granville Hicks's estimation of Arvin he writes: "Hicks thought Arvin exemplified what an intellectual ought to be, a scholar, but one who viewed knowledge and learning not as the property of a privileged elite but as 'the foundation of a decent life for all the people.' " And he describes as a "compelling statement of conscience" Arvin's response in 1930 to a later attack, by Hicks himself, on Communists as crude and "single-minded":

> It is a bad world in which we live [Arvin wrote], and so even the revolutionary movement is anything but what (poetically and even philosophically speaking) it "ought" to be: God knows, I realize this, as you do, and God knows it makes my heart sick at times: from one angle it seems nothing but grime and stink and sweat and obscene noises and the language of beasts. But surely this is what *history* is. It is not just made by gentlemen and scholars. . . . Lenin must have been . . . a dreadful man; so must John Brown, and Cromwell, and Stenka Razin, and Mahomet, and all the others who have destroyed and built up. So will our contemporaries in the American movement be. . . . I believe we can spare ourselves a great deal of pain and disappointment and even worse (treachery to ourselves) if we discipline ourselves to accept proletarian and revolutionary leaders and even theorists for what they are and must be: grim fighters in about the most dreadful and desperate struggle (perhaps) in history— not reasonable and "critically minded" and forbearing and infinitely far-seeing men.

Much of Werth's book, though, isn't about political commitments but about physical and mental distress, "crackups and breakdowns . . . physical weakness and cowardice . . . neuroses, hypochondria, and hysterical self-absorption." And if the dominant feelings Werth describes—fearfulness, shame, and self-hatred—lack Proustian texture, they become, for the reader, harrowing. In regular communication throughout an entire lifetime with Lilienthal, Arvin never dared to broach the subject of homosexuality with him. Incapable of raising the issue directly with Mary Garrison, his bride-to-be, he urged Whitman's "Calamus" poems on her, and when she seemed undisturbed by them (in fact she didn't read them) he responded to her "ecstatically" (Werth's word):

> Darling Child, thank God for you—thank God for you—thank God for you—and thank *you* for your sweet note and your miraculous inexplicable acceptance of everything, even of the things I thought I should never have the courage to speak of—such as my almost unconquerable inhibitions. I was sorry to strike the discordant note of melodrama, but, if I was to "come clean" at all, it had to be that way, and now it is over once and for all.

In his diaries Arvin carefully encoded every reference to sexual encounters. When Capote took him to a Harlem drag dance and cops appeared at the place (they claimed to be checking fire codes), Arvin cried, "My reputation, my reputation," and "went to hide, terrified, in a phone booth." There was more terror and mortification when photos of Arvin and Capote were juxtaposed in a *Life* spread about Yaddo, the writers' colony. Capote's flamboyance carried with it the message that shame was needless and that Arvin had the option of "accept[ing] and enjoy[ing] his homosexuality. . . ." In his fifties Arvin tried cruising "the Springfield [Massachusetts] demimonde" and he visited the famous Everard Baths in New York. Werth writes that he found more excitement, more *life*, in five minutes of groping a stranger at a highway rest stop than in a year of faculty meetings. At least in Springfield, when buying a drink . . . for a man he never saw before and would never see again, he didn't have to pretend. The other person would see him as he was, a small, sallow, well-dressed older man in glasses, bursting with sexual needs. And so he continued his pilgrimages, momentarily ecstatic when he found a taker. . . .

But there was immensely more misery than ecstasy—stays in mental hospitals, suicide attempts, X-ray treatments, electroshocks, spinal taps. We find barely a trace, in *The Scarlet Professor*, of the defiance and glee or the nutty turned-on "spiritual" hilarity of the gay worlds of the Sixties that are brought alive in Jane Kramer's *Allen Ginsberg in America* and in *Joe Orton's Diaries*, among other works.

At the climax terror is palpable. Taken prisoner, Arvin listens to troopers guffawing and sneering as they go through his photographs. He later tries to utter words of self-justification to the young professor he betrayed ("I couldn't go through this alone"). The atrocity is worsened by the behavior of the institutional guardians at Smith who pronounced their own separate sentence, out of court, on the three "criminal" teachers. Several of Arvin's colleagues showed admirably sustained forbearance and generosity toward his longstanding disabilities as well as toward the scandal itself; they were people, for the most part, of straitened means with complex careers of their own. His exceptionally staunch friends, Daniel Aaron and his wife, Janet, functioned for years as Arvin's counselors, nurses, rescuers. Helen Bacon, the classicist, cashed in her war bonds to pay the fines of her junior colleagues ("She had never written such a large check"). When the college trustees fired them, Bacon launched a full-scale campaign on their behalf, appealing to various lawyers and the ACLU to explore any legal recourse—and to

> distinguished friends and allies at Harvard, Yale, and other campuses to write letters of support; to the American Association of University Professors to push for some kind of public sanction against Smith; to sympathetic alumnae, who, she hoped, would restrict their donations in protest; and—an extraordinary breach of Smith decorum—to undergraduates.

The Smith College faculty managed to hold together long enough to unanimously request the college trustees to reverse their stand on the firings. Sixteen undergraduate students dared to sign a broadside protesting the trustees' decision.

But the performance of the trustees themselves was, throughout, lamebrained and cold. The college president, Thomas Mendenhall, argued for the reinstatement of the young faculty members, but most of the trustees wouldn't hear of it. After their eve-of-Good Friday vote refusing to reconsider, the president's wife, Nelly, was "appalled by the [majority's] easy conviviality, as if nothing had happened," at the president's house. "As they parted in the front hall," Nelly Mendenhall recalled, "I remember one of them saying, 'I'll see you at Vespers this afternoon.' They had just crucified two guys and were going off to celebrate the crucifixion of another one." The celebrants were mainly bankers and investment house partners separated by relative riches from Northampton townsfolk but akin to many of the latter in sexual politics. Werth's scorn of that politics is palpable; his invitation to readers to share the scorn and suffer with the victims of the politics is irresistible.*

Just here, however, lies the problem with *The Scarlet Professor*: it puts forward experiences of vicarious pain and (at the end) of the subsequent "victory" of sexual tolerance since the 1960s as answers to the politics that made life miserable for Arvin. In different circumstances such answers might be less objectionable. If they assume a simplistic conflict, between good guys and bad guys, they at least encourage concern for the persecuted. Yet for a book about Newton Arvin the answers Werth suggests are downright dim. Despite his illusions and failings, Arvin was not a facile moralist, and he was adept at the kind of critical thought that challenges readers rather than flatters them; in his work he asked readers to shed platitudes and examine their worlds and themselves freshly.

He dealt boldly and wisely with the subject of sexual inclination, recognizing both the narrow social "constructions" of traditional male and female identity (to use the language of later generations) and the possibilities of transcending them. In his *Whitman* (1938) he wrote that "what really interests us in Whitman is not that he was homosexual but that . . . he chose to translate and sublimate his strange, anomalous emotional experience in a

---

*To his considerable credit, Werth has led an effort in Northampton to persuade the college trustees not only to apologize to Spofford and Dorius but to offer monetary compensation for the damage done to their lives. On October 27, 2001, the Smith Board issued the following statement:

> The Board of Trustees of Smith College has been asked by the faculty to work with it on a suitable College response to the renewed attention being given to the cases of Newton Arvin, Joel Dorius and Edward Spofford, former members of the faculty whose employment at the college ended in 1960–61 after their convictions for distribution and exhibition of pornography.
>
> The members of the Board are sympathetic to the concerns that motivate this request. Accordingly, we will work with Faculty Council and the administration to explore appropriate responses by the College.

political, a constructive, a democratic program." He observed, further, that in Whitman's "Calamus" poems (the texts that he had
pressed on his fiance) the poet gave utterance to "that 'intense and
loving comradeship,' that 'adhesive love,' that 'beautiful and sane
affection of man for man' which he maintained to be as strong and
normal an emotion in men as love between the sexes." Using a
figure of speech that was brave in 1938 if unacceptable in 2001, he
insisted that "a harmless, wholesome, sane 'homosexuality' . . .
pervades normal humanity as the mostly powerless bacilli of
tuberculosis appear in the healthiest of lungs."

Two hundred pages before his book reaches Arvin's crisis, Barry
Werth quotes these passages from Arvin's *Whitman* (printing the
first of them in italics). He quotes pertinent passages from Oscar
Wilde as well. And his bibliography cites works not only by George
Chauncey but by Martin Duberman, Kim Townsend, and several
others (no Foucault, no Barthes)—books that have contributed
significantly to contemporary thought on issues of sexual identity.

But that thought, strong in provoking self-examination and
in challenging "settled sexuality," is sealed off from the story of
Arvin's life. Did Arvin develop further the reflections on "normal
emotion" and "normal humanity" we find in his Whitman
book, in his twenty journals, his letters, his half-finished autobiography? Did the friends with whom Arvin was open about
his sexuality ever hear him discuss—or discuss with him—
myths and delusions of straightness? Whatever the facts, Werth
might have explored such questions, but they don't seem to
interest him. Indeed, no reflective thought defaces the pure
melodrama that drives the narrative of *The Scarlet Professor* to its
climax. People of invincible meanness, crudity, and brutality are
pitted against a wretched, helpless victim, rousing intense pity
for the maltreated scholar. How could anyone be so heartless?
This question is ceaselessly, implicitly pressed on the reader.

Cop A, a thug, waves a confiscated "pencil drawing of 'a guy masturbating' " at one of the victims. "Who drew this, Professor?" he demands. Cop B, another thug, asks him, "Do you ever do the other thing?"—meaning sodomy. Cop C, a liar, tells the *Boston Herald* that everybody arrested was at an "orgy" at Professor Arvin's house. A Northampton city official, a fool, tells local reporters: "It makes me ashamed, ashamed to be a man." Several Smith College trustees, persecutors, express the view that "homosexuals were ultimately weak, abominable, predatory creatures." Some people stop using their phones, "on the chance that they were tapped." Others abruptly leave town, "hoping the hysteria would end before the term began." Friends of Arvin burn in their fireplaces letters, photos, and works of art or throw them in the river.

The reader is meant, as I say, to be harrowed and appalled—overwhelmed by sympathy with the persecuted. But beyond these appropriate responses stands another that is less attractive, namely self-elevation on the cheap. It's the same compensation available in many *60 Minutes* segments or Sunday-magazine stories that grieve for abused homeless children or wrongly convicted prisoners. By enduring torment vicariously with its victims, one rises—at no personal expense—high above thuggish cops, stupid Wall Streeters, selfless inflicters of torment whoever and wherever they are. The gift offered is the wish-fulfilling sense of oneself as engaged, simply by virtue of sympathetic horror, in significant self-scrutiny and pointed political action.

At the end of *The Scarlet Professor* there's an intensification of this sort of fulfillment when Werth tells of an ironic victory over darkness—the routing of puritanical bigotry by understanding and goodwill. Mercifully he avoids reminding us that the tabloids currently speak of Northampton, Massachusetts, as a gay capital of the Northeast. But he can't deny himself the satisfaction of noting that, although the place remains divided between natives and newcomers, its politics have shifted in ways Arvin wouldn't have imagined. In November 1999, . . . Northampton elected its first openly homosexual mayor, an Irish Catholic woman and the longtime administrator of a publicly funded day-care center. The city council president, a popular male high school guidance counselor in Amherst, is also openly gay.

That is the end of Werth's story.

The division between "natives and newcomers" slickly masks (and celebrates) the fact that primitive, stereotypical concepts of sexual identity—gays here, straights there—may not change all that much when this or that locale becomes a "gay capital." The book as a whole evades the entire issue of what kind of change has genuine consequences. For Wilde, Whitman, Arvin as Whitman's explicator and critic, not to mention a generation of intellectuals, novelists, and historians, significant change leads toward a broadened grasp of human variousness and a richer imagination of the human creature.*

The Scarlet Professor, by contrast, tells a tale analogous to numberless others about a self-perfecting America that is largely raceless and classless (except for villainous grandees on boards of trustees). Such tales cloud our national consciousness, nowhere exposing the general vapidity of the culture they discuss, everywhere flattering what they take to be a general shared compassion. A well-conceived life of Newton Arvin might have illuminated the conventions that underlie such stories; Barry Werth's shallow although heart-rending *Scarlet Professor* endorses them.

*Thoughtful journalists as well as scholars think along these lines: see, for example, the discussion of "fluid rather than regimented" sexuality in the epilogue of David Ehrenstein's shrewd and well-informed *Open Secret: Gay Hollywood 1928–1998* (Morrow, 1998).

INDEX

ACKNOWLEDGMENTS

For generous assistance of many kinds I'm grateful to Donald N. Bigelow, Benj, Peggy and Tom DeMott, Margaret Groesbeck, Michael Kaspar, Michael Kinsley, Jeff Kreines, Judith Nagata, Daniel Okrent, Marie Prestonari, David and Megan Quigley, Robert B. Silvers, Richard Todd, and Katrina vanden Heuvel. I owe my largest debt, as far beyond words here as it's often been in the past, to a nonpareil editor and researcher: Joel DeMott.